BLESSED ARE THE PEACEMAKERS

BLESSED ARE THE PEACEMAKERS

A Christian Spirituality of Nonviolence

Michael Battle

Mercer University Press
Macon, Georgia

ISBN 0-86554-871-4
MUP/P251

First Edition.

Library of Congress Cataloging-in-Publication Data

Battle, Michael, 1963-

Blessed are the peacemakers : a Christian spirituality of nonviolence /
Michael Battle.
    p. cm.
Includes bibliographical references and index.
ISBN 0-86554-871-4 (pbk. : alk. paper)
1. Nonviolence—Religious aspects—Christianity. 2. Spirituality. I. Title.
BT736.6.B38 2004
261.8'73—dc22
                                                        2004002837

To Sadie Juliet Battle, my mother

Thank you for teaching me not to kill,
even the pesky insects in our house.

CONTENTS

FOREWORD

As I write this foreword, the United States has concluded its war on Iraq with what consequences the world will not know for several more months. Yet there is a sense of jubilation among those who supported the war because the evil Satan, Saddam Hussein, has finally been eliminated and the world is saved from devastation. What we don't seem to be asking ourselves is which of the two is the greater evil—Saddam Hussein or violence? We assume that the Saddams of the world are born as Satans and once we eliminate them the world becomes that much safer. The truth is that the Saddams, the Hitlers, and all the others that we dehumanize as Satan and proceed to eliminate are the products of the "culture of violence" that we humans have deliberately created and allowed to pervade human society.

Toward the end of his life, Russian philosopher Count Leo Tolstoy wrote a lengthy poignant letter to my grandfather, Mohandas K. Gandhi, in which he confessed the urgent need to share his thoughts on "passive resistance"[1] with the world to save it from self-destruction. Tolstoy says that passive resistance (civil disobedience, nonviolence, or the many other names by which Gandhi's philosophy has come to be known) is "nothing else than the teaching of love uncorrupted by false interpretations."

Tolstoy and my grandfather had long since come to the conclusion that the "philosophy of nonviolence" is the "philosophy of love" and *not* simply nonviolence or the absence of violence or war. It is only through love that we can bring about a "union of human souls" and create a

---

[1] C. F. Andrews, *Mahatma Gandhi's Ideas*(George Allen and Unwin Ltd, London) 195-96.

climate where conflict would be reduced, if not eliminated altogether. I know you are going to ask, "How can anyone love people like Hitler and Saddam?" We may view them as tyrants, but we must respect them as human beings. We don't like the bad things that people do, so we need to concentrate on eliminating those bad things rather than eliminating the person. One may think: We fought World War II and sacrificed almost 60 million human lives to stop Hitler's hateful madness. We got rid of Hitler, but the hate that he spouted continues to plague human society everywhere. To apply the law of love in this case, one would focus on the problem rather than the person and discover ways to eradicate hate and prejudice rather than the person.

Tolstoy quotes Christ: "In love alone is all the law and the prophets." But we humans who have opted for a materialistic way of life find it more convenient to do this through the law of force rather than the law of love. It is this pervasive attitude that compels us to build weapons of mass destruction and threaten each other because this is quicker and gives one the sense of power and dominance. The law of love, on the other hand, evokes in human beings compassion and commitment to share our resources and help the unfortunate in attaining a better standard of living. Love requires sacrifice and commitment, which, because of our greed to amass wealth, we are unwilling to make. Tolstoy argues it is because we need to justify the all-pervasive culture of violence that we deliberately corrupt the divine law of love, replacing it with the law of force. This corruption of the divine law has taken place in every faith tradition; therefore, we find it necessary to discuss and debate theories of "just wars" and "necessary violence" so that we can justify the pursuit of a lifestyle that by no stretch of anyone's imagination can be regarded as civilized.

Tolstoy continues, "As soon as violence is permitted, in which ever case it may be, the insufficiency of the law of love is acknowledged, and by this the very law of love is denied. The whole Christian civilization, so brilliant outwardly, grew up on this self-evident and strange misunderstanding and contradiction, sometimes conscious but mostly unconscious."

Tolstoy then raises a very significant question for the Christian world to ponder: "Either to admit that we do not recognize any Christian teaching at all, arranging our lives only by power of the stronger, or that all our compulsory taxes, court and police establishments, but mainly our armies, must be abolished."

If humanity is willing to face the truth posed by Gandhi and Tolstoy, then we find ourselves standing at the crossroads. To turn right would mean accepting the law of love and proceeding to work toward creating a compassionate and committed world. To veer left would mean consolidating the culture of violence and the brutal lifestyle that never ceases to amaze us.

It is against this background that I appreciate and value the scholarship of the Reverend Michael Battle. When I first met Reverend Battle he was neither a scholar nor a reverend. He was a student at Princeton Theological Seminary. Ours is a relationship that can withstand a little criticism, and I know Michael will take it in the spirit in which it is made. I have read so many books on nonviolence that I can understand now why Dr. Martin Luther King Jr. was moved to say that we suffer from the "paralysis of analysis." We have analyzed the philosophy from every conceivable angle but only to justify our narrow, preconceived notions. In the process, we skip the truth: Do we accept or reject the law of love?

In the late 1990s, while Michael was a professor at the University of the South in Sewanee, Tennessee, I talked him into joining the board of directors of the M. K. Gandhi Institute for Nonviolence in Memphis. Before Michael went to Duke University to take up his present assignment, he served as the vice chair of the board of directors of the Gandhi Institute for Nonviolence.

Over the many years of friendship we often have discussed the philosophy of nonviolence, not always conclusively. It is because of this close relationship and the confidence that I have in Michael's scholarship that I would dare write a foreword to this book. I have scanned thoroughly the contents page and skimmed through the rest of the book and was impressed with Michael's scholarly analysis. My question to Michael and the many other scholars who have written books on nonviolence is this: If we have rejected the law of love as a way of civilized life, does it matter at all what the spirituality or spiritual context of the philosophy is? I believe the acceptance and the practice of the law of love is spiritual in itself.

Scholars and laypeople alike have tried to compartmentalize nonviolence and peace. Can there be any difference between Christian nonviolence and peace and Hindu or Muslim nonviolence or peace? When love itself is universal, how can the law of love be any different? Does it help the practice of nonviolence or the understanding of the philosophy by putting sectarian labels on it?

Grandfather's lifelong effort to replace the culture of violence with the culture of nonviolence was to teach people to remove these constricting labels and to build relationships based on respect, understanding, acceptance, and appreciation. A friendly study of all the Scriptures, he said, is the sacred duty of every individual. His prayer services every morning and evening consisted of hymns from all the major religions of the world. This humble effort on his part was his way of telling the world that no single religion "possesses" the whole truth, but that all religions have a tiny bit of the truth. Believers, therefore, must have the humility to accept that we can only "pursue" the truth with honesty and diligence.

Grandfather often used the analogy of the six blind people who were asked to describe an elephant by feeling it. Each one felt a different part of the elephant and came up with different perceptions. None was wholly wrong, nor was anyone entirely accurate. Each had just a fragment of the truth and could come close to the whole truth only through sharing and interacting. In many ways modern society is like the six blind people, holding on steadfastly to their fragment of truth and thereby perpetuating the culture of violence.

This book will certainly add to scholarship and will provide one more perspective, but I hope it will also help readers understand the urgency of the need to replace the law of force with the law of love.

Arun Gandhi
Memphis, Tennessee
May 2003

ACKNOWLEDGMENTS

This book attempts to invite the reader into a different vision of Christian spirituality than the one typically portrayed in the Western world, in which nonviolent practices are often unintelligible. If anyone ever studied my life, it would be evident that my worldview was born from my mother, Sadie Juliet Battle, who taught me a lifestyle of prayer and nonviolence instead of the mere words and concepts of nonviolence. From such birth, I traveled the world, seeking out nonviolent masters like Mahatma Gandhi, Mother Teresa, and Archbishop Desmond Tutu. I met two of these saints, befriended the grandson of the other, and I have come to realize that one need not shy away from the difficult character of remaining nonviolent. Especially, as I became discipled by Archbishop Tutu, I realize even more that the Christian church is obligated to learn how to be nonviolent.

I am obligated to thank many people, but I am unable to acknowledge everyone in these introductory pages. I must, however, acknowledge my wife, Raquel, whose work with children in special education to find healthy solutions in violent realities has become a great inspiration to me. I also want to thank her for giving me the space and time to do such a work as this. Raquel and I both pray that our children, Sage and Bliss (and any other children born to us), will grow up in the prowess of nonviolence and so lead the world. To my aunt, Lois Williams, I will always admire your preemptive spirituality, which never tolerates a faithless world. My sisters, Dr. Constance Battle and Attorney Carmen Battle Mumford, have also been a great inspiration for me. I would like to acknowledge my father, Dr. Lorenzo Battle III, for his unrelenting pursuit of education. I would like to thank Deans Greg Jones and Willie Jennings and Professor Reinhard Huetter for their support of me at Duke University. Of course, I am greatly indebted to my colleague, mentor, and former PhD supervisor, Stanley Hauerwas. A special thanks also to Alex Semilof, my research assistant, who wonderfully engaged my work from the perspectives of Buddhism. I would like to thank the St. Ambrose Episcopal Church for allowing me to break the mold and preach nonviolence even when it seemed more appropriate to proclaim revenge. I also owe a great deal to others in the Episcopal Church, such as Bishop Frank Griswold, Bishop Herbert Thompson, Bishop Michael Curry, Bishop Gary Gloster, and Mr. Ethan Flad.

Lastly, I am in great debt to Marc Jolley at Mercer University Press. I will always be grateful for Marc's encouragement of this book as he approached me about it at the American Academy of Religion in November 2001.

I hope this book will be of service to many contexts, not just the Christian church. As I argue in this book, this world will have to cross the threshold to decide at a pivotal stage whether community or destructive self-interest is the goal. If it is the latter, God help us all.

Michael Battle
Duke University
June 2003

INTRODUCTION

We must be the change we wish to see in the world.[1]

According to the three-year effort to gather information from about 150 countries, the World Health Organization (WHO) concluded that about 1.6 million people die violently each year, accounting for about 3 percent of all deaths. As one might expect, most of the victims are men, half are suicides, and 90 percent are poor. Implied in the 346 pages of data given through the WHO report is the grim news of how violence is specific to countries, regions, age, culture, and availability of resources to do harm. For example, Colombia leads the world in homicide, with 9 times as many murders per capita as the United States, and 88 times as many as France. China may be the only country where more women than men kill themselves. One in every 236 Cambodians has lost a limb to a landmine. In Alexandria, Egypt, nearly half of all female murder victims are women who have been raped and killed by family members as an act of "cleansing." One third of rapes in Johannesburg, South Africa, are gang rapes, with boyfriends participating. About 500 elderly women are killed each year in Tanzania as suspected witches. Etienne Krug, a Belgian physician at WHO, concludes, "This is not only an emotional issue. It also has to be treated as any other public health problem. We need to

---

[1] M.K. Gandhi quoted in *Truthseeker*, M.K. Gandhi Institute of Nonviolence, Vol. 9, no. 1, February/March 2002, 7.

study the data, the risk factors, and the interventions."[2] One such intervention is Christian spirituality.

Christian spirituality is the mystical process of losing and finding identity in the Triune God, who demands continuous submission to a nonviolent lifestyle. Individuals are incapable of living outside the covenants of community. Central to this thesis is that Christian spirituality should show no contradiction between individual and communal fulfillment, especially since the goal of Christian desire is the Triune God, in whose communal image is perfect peace. Therefore, spirituality as a seemingly impossible lifestyle of Christians is crucial for nonviolent practices in which there is acknowledgment that despite the reality of death, the Triune God is constantly facilitating a new reality in the world. The reality of God as Trinity spawns my definition of Christian spirituality as nonviolent lifestyle. Jesus' Great Commission to his disciples was "to make disciples of all nations, baptizing them in the name of the Father and of the Son and of the Holy Spirit" (Matt. 28:19). The implication is that the making of disciples was indeed a Trinitarian process of conjoining individual and communal fulfillment.

This Trinitarian work is also established in the Johannine narrative since the Spirit "proceeds from the Father" (John 15:26) at the prayer of the Son (14:16). The Spirit calls to remembrance (14:26) and declares the things of Christ (16:14), which Jesus also described as being the things of the Father since "all that the Father has is mine; therefore I said that he [the Spirit] will take what is mine and declare it to you" (16:15). Just as Jesus spoke the words of "the Father who sent me," so also the Holy Spirit, "whom the Father will send in my name...will teach you all things, and bring to your remembrance all things that I have said to you" (14:24–26). St. Augustine, commenting on this same passage, noted, "The whole Trinity, therefore, both speaketh and teacheth; but were it not also brought before us in its individual personality, it would certainly

---

[2] See the report, "World Study shows how people die," *The Washington Post*, October 3, 2002.

altogether surpass the power of human weakness to comprehend it."[3]
Because of this Trinitarian connection between individual and
communal, St. Bernard of Clairvaux found all three persons of the
Holy Trinity involved in the process of creating the state of
flourishing in which the clarity of truth is revealed:

> Those whom the Son first humbles by word and example,
> and upon whom the Spirit afterward pours out love, these the
> Father receives at length in glory. The Son makes us disciples.
> The Paraclete comforts us as friends. The Father raises us up
> as sons. And because not only the Son but also the Father and
> the Holy Spirit are truly called Truth, it is agreed that one and
> the same truth...works in these three steps. The first teaches
> us like a master. The second comforts us like a friend or
> brother. The third embraces us as a father does his son.[4]

My discussion of the Trinity here lays the foundation for my
argument to come—namely, Christian spirituality is derived from the
image of God's interpersonality, in which peacemaking naturally
defines Christian spirituality.

St. Augustine's exploration of the Trinity suggests analogical
connections between the nature of the Triune God and the Christian
understanding of human nature as being created in the image of the
Triune God. In *De Trinitate*, Augustine uses the doctrine of the
Trinity to discover and explain human nature. Employing the
concept of "triads" (groups of three elements), Augustine developed a
sort of "Trinity of the mind" that was to be understood as "a real
image of the Trinity."[5] In the mind's self-knowledge and self-love,
Augustine found a reflection of the image of the Triune God: "In
these three, when the mind knows itself and loves itself, there remains
a trinity: mind, love, knowledge; and this trinity is not confounded

---

[3] Augustine, *The Works of St. Augustine*, "Homilies on the Gospel of John,"
Homily LXXVII, in NPNF, Series One, Vol. II, 338.

[4] Bernard of Clairvaux, "On Humility and Pride."

[5] Andrew Louth, "Augustine," in Jones, Wainwright, and Yarnold, eds., *Study of
Spirituality*, 141-45.

together by any combining: although they are each severally in themselves and mutually all in all."[6]

That God is three persons in one nature suggests the irony of the individual's fulfillment through reliance on others—not through the destruction of others. In turn, Christian spirituality, practiced in the midst of a solipsistic and violent world, participates in the birth of divine reality that bids the human heart toward shalom (the fullness of reliance). In my understanding of a Christian spirituality of nonviolence in which reliance becomes a virtue, individuals are perfect when they know what they lack. This paradox of perfection through awareness of dependence reiterates the thesis of this book—namely, Christian spirituality seen through the image of God's Trinity addresses personal spirituality only to the extent that it enables communal practices of nonviolence. In order for the reader to understand the impetus for this thesis, it is important to understand my primary assumptions: (1) an individualistic Western Christian cosmology hinders full expression of Christian spirituality, and (2) the *imago dei* is community.

The Claustrophobia of Western Spirituality

I assume that many of the current forms of Western Christian life tend toward individualism, in which one's spirituality is self-contained. In such a static, self-contained spiritual worldview, solipsistic expressions predominate Western Christianity as a religion, with minimal practice and understanding for a nonviolent lifestyle. If life is seen ultimately from the first person, then there is little escape to any worldview other than the protection of self, and therefore the just use of violence. Much of Western Christianity focuses upon "my personal relationship with Jesus" or "Have you asked Jesus into your heart to be your personal Lord and Savior?" In such a cosmology,

---

[6] Augustine, *On the Trinity*, in NPNF, First Series One, Vol. III, 128, bk. IX, ch. 5, para. 8.

spirituality is relativized to mean what is in the best interest of the individual.

In this Western worldview there is little impetus for relating spirituality and nonviolence because spirituality is seen as self-contained and atomistic. Instead of the typical discourse of popular spiritualities that privilege individualistic or personal fulfillment, Christian spirituality begins with the recognition that God's triune image among the church points to the mystery that can be fulfilled only in the discovery of *shalom*, which is the goal, or *telos*, of creation. For example, the Gospel of Matthew uses the word *teleios*, or perfection, to describe the end of the Christian journey.[7] This end is not simply about an individual's salvation. For Matthew, *teleios* is a communal goal of the spiritual life, which reflects the breaking into history of a new age and lifestyle. In other words, God is just as concerned about our personal salvation as God is for our communal salvation.

A scientific example of the discovery of shalom comes from the very air that we breathe. Well-known Harvard astronomer Harlow Shapley helps us see that air is a matrix that joins all life together, pointing out that while 99 percent of the air we breathe is highly active oxygen, about 1 percent is made of argon, an inert gas. Since it is inert, it is breathed in and out without becoming part of the human body. Shapley calculated that each breath contains about 30,000,000,000,000,000,000 atoms of argon, plus quintillions of molecules of carbon dioxide. If one exhales a single breath and follows those argon atoms, within minutes they will diffuse through the air far beyond the spot where they were released. After a year, those argons have been mixed up in the atmosphere and spread around the planet so that each breath a person takes includes fifteen atoms of argon released in that one breath a year earlier. What this means is that all people over the age of twenty have taken at least 100 million breaths

[7] Matthew 5:48. Scriptural texts (NRSV) hereafter cited in text. Journey or pilgrimage is a dominant image in Western Christian spiritual writings. See Bonaventure, *The Soul's Journey into God* (c. 1259); John of the Cross, *Ascent of Mt. Carmel* (1587); Robert Bellarmine (1542-1621), *The Soul's Ascension to God*; John Bunyan, *The Pilgrim's Progress* (1675).

and have inhaled argon atoms that were emitted in the first breath of every child born in the world a year before. A person's breath now can contain more than 400,000 of the argon atoms that Ghandi breathed in his long life. Argon atoms are here from the conversations of Jesus and his disciples. The longer each of us lives, the greater the likelihood we will breathe part of Christ. In this scientific worldview, every breath becomes a sacrament, an affirmation of how all life is interconnected.[8]

The question "Do you have a personal relationship with Jesus?" is intelligible only to the extent that one can see how the personal is inextricably linked to the communal. In other words, Jesus said, "If you know me, you will know my Father also" (John 14:6). A personal relationship with Jesus means a communal relationship. Without such an interdependent cosmology for Christian spirituality, Western Christians will have both little interest and little practice in nonviolence. God's goal (*teleios*) for the world is not destruction, nor is it a commitment of words to individuals. The claim made in this book is that our *teleios*, our goal, through the Trinity, is through mystery of individuals losing and finding identity through behavioral and relational change. This relational change toward true community becomes the *imago dei* as active nonviolence.

Teleios relates to the completion of such a goal. Such a journey to the ultimate state of flourishing, however, is arduous and difficult to complete because Christian spirituality as defined through the nonviolent life in God is so demanding that some have dismissed it as being completely unrealistic or have projected its fulfillment to some kind of future kingdom. There is no doubt, however, that Jesus displays and teaches a nonviolent spirituality for all Christians, realizing that the demands of such spirituality cannot be met in an individual's power. This leads to the question of what I mean by the increasingly ambiguous phrase of "Christian spirituality." What I mean by Christian spirituality is the spiritual consciousness of dependence on the Triune God, who informs the church as to the

[8] "On Air, the Unusual Glue," from David Suzaki, *The Sacred Balance, Rediscovering Our Place in Nature*, (Greystone Books, 1997).

appropriate lifestyle by which creation is being redeemed. In other words, Christian spirituality is the reversal of the effects of violence through the practice of a lifestyle that does not depend upon the Christian disciple's own survival but upon the flourishing of creation. The disciple's life is relativized by the life of her neighbor. Life becomes so interconnected that one's survival is dependent on the other's survival. As I have lectured and taught this notion that at the heart of Christian spirituality is nonviolent community made in the image of God, inevitably detractors argue that I have either neglected individual agency or have failed to address Jesus' injunction to go into your closet alone to pray. They usually quote the King James translation to me:

> But thou, when thou prayest, enter into thy closet, and when thou hast shut thy door, pray to thy Father which is in secret; and thy Father which seeth in secret shall reward thee openly. (Matt. 6:6)
>
> Therefore whatsoever ye have spoken in darkness shall be heard in the light; and that which ye have spoken in the ear in closets shall be proclaimed upon the housetops. (Luke 12:3)

What these exegetical challenges seem to forget, however, is that when Jesus went alone to pray, several things usually happened. First, when Jesus engaged in prayer alone, he was usually struggling with others—whether with the devil in the wilderness (Matt. 4:1–11) or with the Father in Gethsemane (Matt. 26:36–46). Second, whenever Jesus went alone, he always seemed to take at least Peter and two others (Mark 14:32). Lastly, when Jesus prayed alone, all of sudden there would appear Moses and Elijah (Matthew 17:1–13; Mark 9:2–13; Luke 9:28–36; 2 Pet. 1:16–18). Matthew 17:8 reads, "And when they looked up, they saw no one except Jesus himself alone." Of course, they saw Jesus alone because the disciples could not bear to see the full glory of the transfiguration (Matt. 17:6). This means that a person's character shapes what and how they see.

An example of this may be seen in the December 2002 release of the movie *The Lord of the Rings: The Two Towers*. Many Americans used the movie to endorse the invasion of Iraq, to rally the troops, and to lead them into battle against the forces of darkness. "I don't think that *The Two Towers* or Tolkien's writing or our work has anything to do with the United States' foreign ventures," Viggo Mortensen, who plays the protagonist Aragorn, said.[9] Mortensen was upset by the comparisons between the war for Middle-earth and the war on terrorism.

J. R. R. Tolkien, the author of *The Lord of the Rings*, would agree. Published in 1954 and 1955, the trilogy appeared in the shadow of World War II and in the increasing tensions of the Cold War. Some readers saw Hitler as the evil wizard Saruman or read nuclear Armageddon into the dark Lord Sauron's war to wipe out all the people of Middle-earth. Tolkien wrote a preface in 1965 to set the record straight, insisting that his "prime motive was the desire of a tale teller." Although Tolkien, a veteran of World War I, was a Christian and a medievalist, he concluded that the trilogy "is neither allegorical nor topical" and pointed out that its composition developed long before "the disaster foreshadowed in 1939." In "Tolkien, Hitler and Nordic Heroism," R. J. Smirak quotes Tolkien's 1938 denunciation of the Nazis' "pernicious and unscientific race-doctrine."[10]

The spiritual demands of fully seeing the need for nonviolence instead of our propensity for justifications of violence can only be met in the fulfillment of Christian community. My thesis stands that Christian spirituality seen through the image of God's Trinity addresses personal spirituality only to the extent that it enables communal practices of nonviolence. Herein, a crucial problem for my thesis presents itself—namely, does one have to confess God as Trinity to be an expert on nonviolence? Or, as several readers of this book in its unpublished form asked me, "Do you have to be a

---

[9] See Karen Durbin, "Some interpret Tolkien's trilogy as war propaganda," *New York Times* News Service, Wednesday, December 18, 2002 in the News & Observer, December 18, 2002, 14E.

[10] See Karen Durbin, "Some interpret Tolkien's trilogy as war propaganda," *New York Times* News Service, Wednesday, December 18, 2002 in *The News & Observer*, December 18, 2002, 14E.

Christian to be an expert on nonviolence?" Obviously, the answer to these questions is no. In fact, many could argue that what has come to be known as Christianity pales in comparison to other faith traditions when it comes to the practice and articulation of nonviolence. My thesis is not exclusive of other faith traditions in naming the relationship between spirituality and nonviolence; rather, my thesis is explanatory for the need for Christians to cease the contradictions between person and community that prevent the natural relationship between spirituality and nonviolence. Plato said that to be is to be in relation. Similarly, Aristotle defined the human being as a political animal, *zoe politike*. In more contemporary terminology that I previously have researched extensively, to be human assumes the African quality of Ubuntu, in which personhood is intelligible only in community.[11] For us to be, we must exist in a community, in which our identity does not stop with our skin or self-interests, but extends into the corporate reality of nonviolence. Indeed, as I will argue later, Western Christians need those outside of our formal, cognitive systems to see where we fall short in living up to what we say we believe. Examples like Mahatma Ghandi, a Hindu, and Desmond Tutu, a Christian, certainly display lives that model to the world a better understanding of Jesus and nonviolence than many self-professed Western Christians who are comfortable being Christian by themselves in private.

The goal of this book is not to be negative and pessimistic about Western Christianity, however. My incentive is to recover the discourse of spirituality and nonviolence together so that the church does not find herself complicit with systemic violence. If spirituality is only about individual salvation, there is little hope that we will envision how God seeks to save us all through practices of nonviolence. Because the Christian spiritual life is both personal and communal, Christians should develop habits of peacemaking, enabling a future for violent societies to practice nonviolence. Without the practices of nonviolence, we learn that a future cannot be practiced.

---

[11] See Michael Battle, *Reconciliation: The Ubuntu Theology of Desmond Tutu* (Cleveland: The Pilgrim Press, 1997).

Herein is the genius of the spiritual life, namely, that as communal persons we are able to see and practice a future through nonviolent lifestyle. In his book *A Place Called Community*, Quaker Parker Palmer makes this point:

> Most of us fear community because we think it will call us away from ourselves. We are afraid that in community our sense of self will be overpowered by the identity of the group. We pit individuality and community against one another, as if a choice had to be made, and increasingly we choose the former.
>
> But what a curious conception of self we have! We have forgotten that the self is a moving intersection of many other selves. We are formed by the lives which intersect with ours. The larger and richer our community, the larger and richer is the content of the self. There is no individuality without community; thus, the surprising finding that an affluent suburb with all its options, but without community may nurture individuality less than a provincial village with few choices but a rich community life.[12]

The cosmology that Palmer assumes here is one in which the principalities of this Western world favor self-determination over and against the communal, dependent spirituality of Christians. Largely, as a result of living in this Western milieu, I seek in my book to determine how habits and disciplines within the Christian life constantly make Christians look nonviolent. In order to narrate this vision for how Christian spirituality is inherently nonviolent, I assume a doctrine of God and theological anthropology in which the communal image of God (*imago dei*) is Trinitarian nonviolence. While there are many theories as to the meaning of this *imago dei*, the organizing idea that makes sense of this concept of God always leads back to how human personality harmoniously and symbiotically

---

[12] Parker Palmer, *A Place Called Community* (Wallingford, PA: Pndle Hill Publications, 1977), no. 212, 5.

reflects divine personality. This means that human beings and the persons of God are deeply intertwined in fellowship. This looks and is nonviolent. This interwoven character of divine and human persons led to the expressions in what Augustine and John Calvin described as "double knowledge" (*duplex cognitio*).[13] Such double knowledge means two things. First, one cannot look upon self without immediately turning such thoughts to the contemplation of God. Secondly, and conversely, one may never gain a true knowledge of self unless one has first looked upon the face of God.[14]

The Imago Dei

The theological concept of double knowledge allows for my thesis of the *imago dei* being that of nonviolent community. Persons are made in God's image of community in which the central dynamic of shalom or flourishing life becomes the basis for Christian lifestyle. In other words, the particular description of Christian spirituality as communal lifestyle is seen through the individual's reverence of the other, which creates a new reality outside of self (*exstasis*). Those who are most exstatic in Christian spirituality are those who become selfless, journeying to truly love the other outside of self. And by doing so, self is discovered more completely. Double knowledge is important to understand and correct against self-centered notions of spirituality in which the chief focus is upon the individual's salvation or wholeness. Such misunderstandings of spirituality are common in the Western world in which the individual's priorities take precedent over more

---

[13] Not to be confused with "double-minded" (Grk, dipsuchos, lit. "two souls") in which Paul describes such people as conflicted persons. Paul states, "I can will what is right, but I cannot do it. For I do not do the good I want, but the evil I do not want is what I do. Now if I do what I do not want, it is no longer I that do it, but sin which dwells within me" (Rom 7:19-21). James (1:8) describes such a person as "double-minded," they are a walking civil war.

[14] See R.S. Pine-Coffin, trans., *Saint Augustine: Confessions* (London: Penguin Books, 1961) Bk. I, ch. 1-2,6, 21-25. Also, John Calvin, *Institutes of the Christian Religion*, edited by John T. McNeill, 2 vols. (Philadelphia: Westminster Press, 1977) Vol. I. 35, 40, 37.

communal understandings. Self-understanding takes on a whole new meaning if one now understands the concept of being made in the image of God, who is community. Individualism, however, will be one of the obstacles to overcome in light of how I present spirituality in this book. We can see that individualism affects even the meaning of prayer.

What Is Prayer?

As discussed above, one of the challenges to my notion of Christian spirituality as nonviolence is how prayer is seen individualistically. Before proceeding further into the book, there should be some explicit discussion of prayer per se. More germane to Christian spirituality is this question: If God already knows what I need before I ask, then why pray? The following question leads me to some resolution for the above question: Is the purpose of prayer merely to inform God of our needs? Thomas Aquinas is helpful here:

> 1. We do not have to present our prayers to God in order to disclose to Him our needs and desires, but in order to make ourselves realize that we need to have recourse to His help in these matters.
> 2. As we have already said, our prayer is not designed to change what God has already planned.
> 3. God gives us many things out of sheer generosity, without being asked. The reason why He wants to give us some things in response to our petitions is that it is profitable for us to acquire a certain coincidence in running to Him and to recognize that He is the source of all that is good for us. So Chrysostom says, "Consider what a joy is granted you, what glory is bestowed upon you, that you can speak with God in

your prayers, that you can engage in conversation with Christ, and plead for whatever you want, whatever you desire."[15]

It seems as though a typical Western dichotomy forms in order to answer the question of prayer. If God already knows what I need before I ask, then the dichotomy forms between answering that one prays in practice but not in theory. In other words, one may answer yes to prayer—that we must constantly practice remembering that there is God. One illustration of this side of the dichotomy is my experience at a conservative, evangelical, Presbyterian church in which the associate pastor asked for prayer requests as he proceeded to write them down on his clipboard. After everyone informed him of the prayer requests, the pastor asked everyone to bow their heads and then "to ask God for His help." The pastor began to pray on behalf of the congregation as if he were a CNN news correspondent informing God of the needs of the church. God was being informed as if God did not know what was going on in the life of the church. "Please come to the aid of Larry Johnson, who has back pain" or "deliver Eastern Europe from the constant political conflicts that exist over there." To inform God of the events of people's lives still accepts a cosmology in which God is transcendent and detached from created beings. Such a view seldom finds cohesion between communal and personal forms of prayer because the worldview of God's transcendence never makes sense of how God is fully here with us. A more helpful answer to how prayer is practice comes from Hans von Balthasar, who defines prayer as a beholding and hearing without really distinguishing the two.[16] Von Balthasar states,

> Most Christians are convinced that prayer is more than the outward performance of an obligation, in which we tell God things he already knows. It is more than a kind of daily

---

[15] Thomas Aquinas, *Summa Theologica*, II,II, Question 83, *Albert and Thomas: Selected Writings*. Simon Tugwell, trans. (New York: Paulist Press, 1988) 476-489.
[16] Hans Urs von Balthasar, *Prayer*, trans., Graham Harrison, (San Francisco: Ignatius Press, 1986) 24ff.

waiting attendance on the exalted Sovereign who receives his subjects' homage morning and evening. And although many Christians experience in pain and regret that their prayer gets no further than this lowly stage, they are sure, nonetheless, that there should be more to it.[17]

The second part of the dichotomy between the practice and theory of prayer is in how we think we know God—or have heard from God. In other words, how do we know God in theory? The notion that God listens in theory does not hold up to careful thinking about God, who does not necessarily share such creaturely qualities like ears and sound waves. We only understand in theory that God listens if we understand prayer as tacit knowing. Such a distinction of prayer as tacit knowing is given to us by Richard of St. Victor when he states that listening prayer "is the penetrating and free gaze of the soul extended everywhere in perceiving things."[18] That is to say, prayer is contemplation. Prayer is simply the request of the Spirit already praying in us, a request that does not portend to inform God about anything; rather, such a request of Spirit informs an understanding of prayer as our increasing mutuality with God, a seemingly impossible existence since the creature can never reciprocate mutuality with the Creator. Where the impossible becomes possible is in the understanding of prayer, at least in theory, that God is not only transcendent, but also imminent. God's incarnation in Christ has made it possible for the creature to call the Creator "friend" and thereby participate in a mutual relationship without enmity. Von Balthasar states, "Prayer is a conversation between God and the soul, and secondly, a particular language is spoken: God's language. Prayer is dialogue, not man's monologue before God. Ultimately, in any case, there is no such thing as solitary speech; speech implies reciprocity, the exchange of thoughts and of

---

[17] von Balthasar, *Prayer*, 13
[18] Richard of St. Victor, *The Mystical Ark*, trans. Grover A. Zinn, I, 4.

souls, unity in a common spirit, in a common possession and sharing of the truth."[19]

There is often paralysis when we pray in this cognitive manner, knowing that God is omniscient, and yet we seek to only inform God about our dire needs. Why should I pray for Larry Johnson when Jesus says that God even knows the number of hairs on Johnson's head? Or why should I pray for Eastern Europe when God aims to heal all the nations? Does a person pray to inform God about something? I answer that prayer is more than information and monologue; it is primarily the relational practice of remembering the presence of God already in our midst. Prayer is a digging—an unearthing—of God's presence. However, in the church's liturgical prayer, "Please add your prayers and intercessions," some people proceed to pray as if to inform God about current events. This traps us into Western Christianity's problem of individualism in enclosed spaces.

The task of this book is to help spiritual people understand this deeper form of prayer in which the mind and heart, person and community, are so inextricably linked that prayer becomes the nonviolent habits and lifestyles of persons and communities. My goal is to get many to see that when they pray to God as a Santa Claus figure—informing God about a wish list of healings and intercessions—what may really be happening is the need to inform the person and community about how to proceed peacefully together. For examples—that there is a violent crisis in the Middle East, that George is in the hospital or that it is not good to have cancer, and that Jane needs help with her marriage—these are all means of informing persons and communities about who it is we should be persons and community for, namely, God in three persons and one nature. Prayer is the habit of knowing for whom we are to be persons.

There are, of course, many approaches to prayer. In Scripture we meet examples of praying according to a set form, such as the Lord's Prayer (Matt. 6:9–13; Luke 11:2–4), as well as praying spontaneously as need arises (Luke 22:39–44). Thus, there needs to be room in the Christian tradition for the Anglican Book of Common Prayer and the

---

[19] Von Balthasar, *Prayer*, 14

Roman Catholic Missal as well as for the extemporaneous prayers preferred by many Protestants. Jesus taught extensively on prayer (Luke 11:5–10; 18:1–14, for Jesus' parables on prayer; Matthew 6:5–7; 11:24; 15:22–28). He also modeled an active prayer life (Luke, in particular, is interested in reporting that Jesus prayed regularly: Luke 3:21; 5:16; 6:12; 9:18, 28; 11:1; 22:41–44). Many Christians interpret the Lord's words "When you pray...pray then like this" (Matt. 6:5–9) as a holy injunction that should be followed. Prayer, as Karl Rahner notes, is a dialogue in which our creatureliness is brought before God in an act of utter self-surrender.[20] Christians are enjoined to pray with unquestioning faith (Mark 11:24) and to pray in the name and spirit of Jesus (1 John 5:14).

Intercessory prayer, or prayer on behalf of others, is another important part of the New Testament teaching on prayer (Luke 6:28; John 17:9–26; Rom. 15:30; 2 Thess. 3:1). We are also reminded that as we pray, Christ intercedes for us "at the right hand of the Father" (Rom. 8:34), and the Holy Spirit "helps us in our weakness" and "intercedes for us with sighs too deep for words" (Rom. 8:26–27). Monks in many religious traditions advocate for such a kind of wordless prayer. Besides more contemplative forms of prayers, such monks often participate in active prayers using begging bowls as the spiritual discipline of asking and giving in the continuum of seeking God.

Prayer as Meditation

Classical Christian commentators like Origen of Alexandria and Abba Isaac of the desert fathers distinguished four resources in prayer: supplication, prayer, pleading, and thanksgiving. What is interesting about current discussions on prayer is in how current spiritual writers often distinguish only between prayer and meditation. In the most basic sense, prayer is talking to God, whereas meditation is listening for God. In listening, the contemplative hears God speaking, as

---

[20] Rahner, *Practice of Faith*, 88-94.

Thomas Merton described it: "in the depths of our being: for we ourselves are words of His."[21] Thus for Merton, "Contemplation is this echo. It is a deep resonance in the inmost center of our spirit in which our very life loses its separate voice and resounds with the majesty and the mercy of the Hidden and Living One. God answers God's self in us and this answer is new life, divine creativity, making all things new."[22] Divine creativity spawns the practice of meditation to employ mental or physical images as focal points. Such a practice assumed the need for the creativity of many kinds of people and even the need for all animals and creatures to know God more meditatively. Meditation understood in this way means that Merton could not focus on individual or personal salvation in prayer, but on the salvation of creation. This means that prayer becomes equally an individual and communal practice. For example, Merton thought that African Americans gave the greatest example of Christian faith because of their communal way of being Christian. Merton joined a pacifist group because he thought that the best way to pray was through a life dedicated to nonviolence. On 10 December 1968, Merton was electrocuted in Bangkok. Ironically, Merton's body was transferred to the United States through the air force with dead bodies of American soldiers from the Vietnam War.[23]

In classical Christian spirituality, particularly in the Roman Catholic tradition, meditation was often approached by the method of prayer known as *lectio divina*. The first step in this process is *lectio*, or "reading" the Scriptures. This is not a pedantic sort of reading; it is a meditative reading. It is reading with a listening attitude, and with willingness to personalize the words so that they are read as though God is speaking directly to the reader. The second step, *meditatio*, uses the imagination to expand and draw upon what was read. This

---

[21] Thomas Merton, *New Seeds of Contemplation* (New York: New Directions, 1961) 3.

[22] Merton, *New Seeds of Contemplation*, 3.

[23] Christobal Serran-Pagan y Fuentes, Boston University, "A Contemplative in action: Thomas Merton and the Civil rights Movement in the South." paper given at the Christian Spirituality Group of the American Academy of Religion, Spirituality and the Civil Rights Movement, Nashville, November 21, 2000.

process may combine mental visualization with meditative listening
to gain illumination. The third stage, *oratio*, or "prayer of the heart,"
makes emotion—rather than thought—the vehicle for illumination
and transformation. The heart pours itself out in longing after God
and is filled with love for God. The fourth step, *contemplatio*, or
"contemplation," is entered through a sense of inward darkness
(divine absence). Out of this darkness comes a piercing awareness of
God's presence that is so powerful that it overwhelms our natural
faculties and leaves us only with a loving, awed awareness of God's
presence. This presence is so awesome that it causes the
contemplative to long for union with God.[24]

Prayer as dialogical speech implies that the word "pray" is an
intransitive verb: "Sarah prays for the baby." Transitive uses of
"pray" are also used. "Pray" is a transitive verb in that "Sarah prays
the rosary" or "Sarah prays the office." What becomes more
complicated is when one uses the word pray with God. God prays. The
understanding that God prays seems to lack coherence in
contemporary understandings of prayer, and yet Pauline prayer
explicitly states that "when we cry, 'Abba! Father!' it is that very
Spirit bearing witness with our spirit that we are children of God, and
if children, then heirs, heirs of god and joint heirs with Christ—if, in
fact, we suffer with him so that we may also be glorified with him"
(Rom. 8:15b–17). Paul goes on to say that God prays in us as "the
Spirit groans inwardly while we wait for adoption, the redemption of
our bodies" (Rom. 8:23).

Most explicit to how God prays is Paul's thought concerning how
God helps us—namely, "the Spirit helps us in our weakness; for we do
not know how to pray as we ought, but that very Spirit intercedes
with sighs too deep for words. And God, who searches the heart,
knows what is the mind of the Spirit, because the Spirit intercedes for
the saints according to the will of God" (Rom. 8:26–28). In this

---

[24]This summary of lectio divina is based on Thelma Hall's work, *Too Deep for
Words: Rediscovering Lectio Divina* (New York: Paulist Press, 1988). A similar,
sthree-step process is utilized in the eastern Orthodox tradition. Kallistos T. Ware,
Praying with Orthodox Tradition (Nashville: Abingdon Press), 1990.

Pauline light, it is easier to understand Van Balthasar's advice about prayer: "The better a man learns to pray, the more deeply he finds that all his stammering is only an answer to God's speaking to him; this in turn implies that any understanding between God and man must be on the basis of God's language."[25]

Overcoming Obstacles

Beyond the search for the meaning of prayer in nonviolence, the thesis of this book has several obstacles to overcome within the Christian tradition. First, the obvious obstacle of "just war" raises its ugly head. Second, any spirituality of nonviolence must confront anew the inescapable struggle for survival within this world; and third, to what extent (as mentioned above) does my understanding of Christian spirituality lend itself to other spiritual traditions? The way that I address these obstacles is by getting the reader to see that spirituality is our participation in the divine bending toward grace, the suffering participation in disorder, and the redemptive power of forgiveness. Participatory spiritualities that articulate redemptive suffering reverberate across spiritual traditions. This divine bending relieves us from being homeless souls, separated from God and unable to know and love ourselves apart from our knowledge and love for God. Bernard of Clairvaux is helpful here as he teaches that love of God and neighbor require an appropriate love of self, but only love of God could provide genuine love for one's neighbor and oneself. [26] Bernard described these as four degrees of loving God, in which one matures through the four degrees, eventually healed of alienation with God, our neighbor, and ourselves. Bernard states, "O holy and chaste love! O sweet and tender affection! O pure and sinless intention of the will—the more pure and sinless in that there is no mixture of self-will in it, the more sweet and tender in that everything it feels is

---

[25] Von Balthasar, *Prayer*, 15.

[26] *Bernard of Clairvaux: Selected Works* G.R. Evans, trans. (New York: Paulist Press 1987), "On Loving God," 192-95. Also printed as "Four Degrees of love," on 148-53.

divine. To love in this way is to become like God [deification]."[27]
Such a call to deification is foreign to Western ears, yet such a
concept of full participation in God through the transforming power
of divine love (1 John 3) is a central theme in Christian spirituality in
which Christians become partakers of God's divine nature (2 Pet.
1:40).

Through an understanding of prayer as participation in God, self-
understanding is now understood as *duplex cognitio*. In other words,
one's understanding of self deepens through the understanding of the
other. In this book I argue that Western Christians have little
experience or practice of this kind of exstatic spirituality[28] in which
human personality deepens through its reverence of the other.
Instead, Western Christianity often produces the kind of Christian life
that fails to understand why anyone would refrain from killing insects.
Much less, such Western persons want to give up anything of their
individual power in the pursuit of other realities (whether such
realities be insects or other persons). In other words, Western society
has socialized persons to forget how innately violent we are. Here,
James Cone is extremely helpful: "I contend, therefore, that the
problem of violence is not the problem of a few black revolutionaries
but the problem of a whole social structure which outwardly appears
to be ordered and respectable but inwardly is 'ridden by psychopathic
obsessions and delusions'—racism and hatred. Violence is embedded in
American law, and it is blessed by the keepers of moral sanctity."[29]
Cone helps us see that violence is part of the fabric of Western life
and the critical insight is to determine whose violence is winning.

If Christians are to reach the goal God has set for us—eternal
life—then we must participate in the mystery of transfiguration—
losing life to save it. In heaven, Gabriel Fackre explains, selflessness
evokes selflessness and its fruit is mutuality.[30] Such selflessness is a

---

[27] *Bernard of Clairvaux*, 196.

[28] I define ex-static as the notion of being capable to move beyond self to the
other.

[29] James Cone, *Black Theology and Black Power* (New York: Seabury Press,
1969) 218.

[30] Gabriel Fackre, 213.

foreign concept among many popular Christian spiritualities in which Christian sentiment follows the privilege of Western individuals. In this world the need to understand spiritual fulfillment as inextricably linked to the other's fulfillment is unintelligible. For example, in Dante's *Divine Comedy*, Dante tries to understand this mutuality of interest between personal and communal as he asks those in heaven: "Do you envy the happiness of others? Do you desire, you who are here, to be higher, to see more, to be more loved."[31] In the end, Western Christians use Christian spirituality like Dante, asking inappropriate questions while having a difficult time learning authentic existence. Dante learns from the hosts of heaven that God transforms disparate individuals into a symbiotic chorus of heaven. If we wish to be more than God's perfection for us, then our desire is the residual effect of a world that can only accept the authority of individualistic caprice.

My Methodology

In the end, what I argue through a spirituality of nonviolence is that the goal of the *imago dei* makes us look more like a being for others. This being for others is what I imagine heaven to be like. A Christian spirituality of nonviolence or shalom disallows the concept of heaven as one's contentment that others are in hell. How could there ever truly be heaven if others are in hell? Being for others means that heaven can only be intelligible in consciousness of the fullness of the other—not the other's suffering. For in shalom, our creaturely form (both corporal and spiritual) will be held in composite unity within the divine will in which there is longing that the other's well-being takes into account my well-being. In other words, Christian spirituality should be practiced in such a way that each day we look more and more like the nonviolence of God. This deification process, articulated best in the Eastern Church, suggests that we grow more like God as the church becomes more authentic in her display of shalom.

---

[31] Par. III.64–66.

There is also the Buddhist concept of imagining an afterlife in which the fullness of joy is interdependent. This concept is called Bodhisattva. The breakdown of this word displays the interdependence of joy in life to come. "Bodhi" means enlightenment, the state devoid of all defects and endowed with all good qualities. "Sattva" refers to someone who has courage and confidence and who strives to attain enlightenment for the sake of all beings. Those who have this spontaneous, sincere wish to attain enlightenment for the ultimate benefit of all beings are called Bodhisattvas.[32] Eastern Christians are more in touch with a worldview in which the concept of joy and heaven in life to come cannot be imagined only in a self-interested way. Personal salvation is less the goal; rather, communal salvation becomes the norm.

In order to illustrate the thesis of this book, that Christian spirituality in the image of the Triune God addresses personal spirituality only to the extent it enables communal practices of nonviolence, it is important that Christian communities reflect upon nonviolence to see where they measure up and where they fall short in relationship to the perfecting goal of creation as shalom. Unfortunately, the assumed violence in many Christian communities (that is, the legitimate use of violence) reminds us that nonviolence may not be normative behavior for some Christians. A spirituality of nonviolence, however, invites Christian communities to develop a spirituality that would set them apart from violent societies (Matt. 5:46–47). Jesus said, "In a word, you must be made perfect [*teleioi*] as your heavenly Father is perfect [*teleios*]" (Matt. 5:48). In the Beatitudes, Jesus reminds Christians that such perfection requires the norm of nonviolence. The church's understanding of nonviolence demonstrates that her share in the perfection of God is both possibility and process. As Christians, and as the church, we consciously declare submission to God's ways of bringing us to the

---

[32] This definition of Bodhisattva comes from: *A Flash of Lightening in the Dark of Night, A Guide to the Bodhisattva's Way of Life by H.H. The Dalai Lama* (Boston: Shambahala Publications, Inc. 1994) 12. I am indebted to Alex Semilof for bringing this definition to my attention.

fullness of life by practicing nonviolence through confession, forgiveness, and repentance. And although this pattern of behavior requires submission, such submission is neither passive nor oppressive. The letter to the Hebrews says that Jesus was perfected through his submission to God's plan, though without sin, becoming the power of eternal salvation to those who identify with his pattern of submission (Heb. 9:8–9). So whoever lives under (submits to) this authority of God's nonviolence is also "made perfect" in the nonviolent way in which Jesus revealed perfection.

The crucial problem in naming a methodology of Christian nonviolence is that submission to God's nonviolence carries the irony of being passive and yet really being extremely active and disciplined. Because of the rigor of many nonviolent lifestyles and the idealistic connotations that are often associated with nonviolence, spiritualities of nonviolence are often interpreted for the select few, who themselves could never achieve such a reality. Or nonviolence is so idealistic that some have dismissed it as being completely unrealistic or have projected its fulfillment to the *parousia*, or a future divine kingdom. A more common interpretation is that nonviolence is an impossible ideal designed to drive believers first to desperation so that they might realize their only hope is trusting in God's mercy. Instead of these interpretations of nonviolence as passive, idealistic, and impossible, I am more convinced by Martin Luther King Jr.'s understanding of how pragmatic a spirituality of nonviolence may be: "We had to make it clear that nonviolent resistance is not a method of cowardice. It does resist. It is not a method of stagnant passivity and deadening complacency. The nonviolent resister is just as opposed to the evil that he is standing against as the violent resister but he resists without violence. This method is nonaggressive physically but strongly aggressive spiritually."[33] This pragmatic understanding was illustrated to me when Tony Campolo, a sociologist and progressive evangelical thinker, told me that he knew the Civil

---

[33] Martin Luther King, Jr., "The Power of Nonviolence," in *I Have a Dream: Writings and Speeches that Changed the World*, ed., James M. Washington, (Harper SanFrancisco, 1992) 30.

Rights movement and Martin Luther King Jr. had "won" when Campolo saw white police officers brutalizing black Christian nonviolent resisters.[34]

In short, my methodology discussed below seeks to address the problem of how nonviolence is seen as passivity. Howard Thurman is helpful in terms of understanding the practical side of nonviolence when he suggests that historical Christianity has misunderstood the teaching of Jesus concerning reverence for life, as Jesus insisted that God cares for the sparrow that falls by the wayside, the grass of the field, the birds of the air, and even the numbering of the hairs of the head. Thurman notes that Western, historical Christianity has wrongly limited the concept of reverence for life to human personality. Such limitation produces the kind of logic in which to deny personality to human beings, one may no longer reverence such a life. When such a definition of subhumanity has social sanction and approval, all kinds of brutality take place as a matter of course and there is no sense of ill-doing.[35] This means that nonviolent resistance is extremely active, not passive, in the pursuit of the *imago dei* among creation.

Because of Western Christianity's seeming acceptance of some forms of legitimate violence and the stereotype of nonviolence as passivity, the onus of my book is in showing how interpretations of nonviolence often interiorize the Christian life in such a way that directly contradict personal and communal goals of shalom. In other words, Western individualism paralyzes any consensus by which one may discern God's presence in both personal and communal realms. As President Dwight D. Eisenhower, himself a general and veteran of World War II, observed, "Every gun that is made, every warship launched, every rocket fired signifies, in the final sense, a theft from those who hunger and are not fed, those who are cold and are not

---

[34] In seminary at Princeton Theological Seminary, Tony Campolo was my field education supervisor over my work with an inner-city ministry in Philadelphia. I met Tony every Monday during my 1989 spring semester.

[35] See Howard Thurman's insights in Walter Earl Fluker, et.al., eds., *A Strange Freedom: The Best of Howard Thurman on Religious Experience and Public Life* (Boston: Beacon Press, 1998) 38.

clothed."[36] This is all exacerbated by the fact that the United States spends over \$2 billion a month fighting in Afghanistan and has proposed to double the budget for domestic security from \$19.5 billion in 2002 to \$37.7 billion. How does such spending promote security for the world's 1.2 billion poor people who live on less than a dollar a day? Pamela Brubaker provides this serious warning: "Those of us in the North need to take seriously the claim of people from the South that structural adjustment programs and the larger neoliberal agenda are forms of recolonization."[37]

This is why the discourse of Christian spirituality becomes important. A Christian spirituality of nonviolence is a lens by which Christians realize that God's call to perfection cannot be met through personal power alone. In other words, we are to learn to be awake to God's presence in each other, and such presence can be seen in the most unexpected places—in the poorest and the least of all people and even in our enemies. Those of us called American Christians must be especially discerning of a spirituality that is often co-opted by insular political policies. Many Americans believe that the United States is the most generous government in the world—sending food and monetary aid around the world. But we must educate those who live in the United States and the rest of the world that the reality is in how the United States spends a smaller portion of its gross national product on official development aid than do Japan and the European Union. Even less known is the impact of U.S. policies in cooperation with the International Monetary Fund (IMF) and the World Bank on the poor. These structural adjustment polices function as structures of economic violence on thousands of people who die needlessly from malnutrition, lack of clean drinking water, HIV/AIDS, and other basic medical care. These are people required by the IMF to cut back on social spending, shift from subsistence agriculture to export production, and privatize or deregulate their economies. Of course,

---

[36] Quoted in Pamela Brubaker, "What Price Security," *Echoes: Justice, Peace and Creation News*, an occasional publication of the World Council of Churches, 21/2002, 4.

[37] Brubaker, "What Price Security," 5

many Americans are totally oblivious to these harsh realities and policies, having little interest outside of the U.S. purview. And yet the United States is selectively called a Christian nation.[38] As Brubaker concludes, "Those of us seeking economic justice must sharpen our analysis of the failures of neoliberalism and clarify our alternative vision. Churches and other groups in civil society must take the lead in asking what really contributes to human security."[39]

Instead of an interior Christian spirituality that blesses the interests of a nation-state's isolation, this book argues for the recovery of nonviolent traditions within Christian spirituality. Christian spirituality is but the form of Christ's nonviolent life; his life, death, and resurrection comprise the prism through which Christians interpret their existence. This understanding of Christian spirituality was taught to my by Stanley Hauerwas, professor of Christian ethics at Duke University, years ago when I wrestled with making sense of a discourse called spirituality. In short, Christian spirituality does not appear impossible, passive, or idealistic to a people who have been called to a life of discipleship which requires them to contemplate their death in the light of the cross of Christ.[40]

The impossibility of Christian spirituality reminds me of the true account told by Madeline L'Engle of a woman who one day took her children to an animal park. Upon leaving the park she found that her red Volkswagen bug had been smashed in the front. Needless to say she was startled and upset. After a frantic period, she found out from the park ranger that her car was sat upon by an elephant trained to sit on

---

[38] Only Denmark, Luxembourg, the Netherlands, Norway, and Sweden meet or exceed the 0.7% of GNP target for economical development aid set by the United Nations. On average, 0.22% of the GNP of economically developed nations is given. In 2000 this was $56 billion. Compare this to $400 billion spent on advertising, $700 billion on military. Pamela Brubaker quotes this data from Kjell Magne Bondevik, et. al, "Official Development Aid: The rich countries will have to do better," *International Herald Tribune*, March 21, 2002. Also see the website: www.realityofaid.org for insightful analysis.

[39] Brubaker, "What Price Security," 6.

[40] I owe this insight to Stanley Hauerwas, "The Sermon on the Mount, Just War and the Quest for Peace," in *A Council for Peace*, eds., Hans Küng and Jürgen Moltmann, (Edinburgh: T&T Clark, 1988) 38.

red buckets. Thankful for her insurance, she drove off. On the way
home, she was held up by horrendous traffic. Up ahead she could see
that a minor accident had just occurred. She maneuvered around the
site but as soon as she was in the clear, wild, flashing lights pulled her
over. From the midst of the spectacular light a police officer
appeared: "Lady, do you know that it is a crime to leave the scene of
an accident?" The woman replied, "But officer, I'm merely trying to
get out of the way." The officer observed the damage to the woman's
smashed VW Bug and asked, "And ma'am, could you tell me about the
damage to your car—how did this happen?" The woman responded,
"An elephant sat on it." The policeman then asked her to get out of
the car for a breathalizer test. This story speaks to the truth that that
which is plausible and impossible is better than that which is possible
and implausible. For, you see, even though the story of the woman
with the red VW is true, it is an impossible story.[41]

The impossibility of a Christian spirituality of nonviolence turns
into possibility when, instead of a Westernized individualistic
spirituality, persons learn how to advocate a Christian spirituality
seen through the lens of God's life among us—communal spirituality.
In order to clarify such a definition of communal spirituality, I have
chosen Mahatma Gandhi's life and thought as a critique of
pathological forms of Christianity that often lead to the vapid
spiritualities that many of us still believe in today.[42] This vapid
pattern of individualistic spirituality is evident in the interiorization
of experience that is at the core of Western spirituality. Instead of
continuing to look toward the other in biblical, historical, and
contemporary exemplars of Christian spiritual experience, Western
Christianity has shifted epistemological attention to the inner
illumination of the self. Because of this Western trend to define
spirituality as a self-contained enterprise, it is important to have an

---

[41] Madeline L'Engle told this story while I was on a writing retreat with her at
Holy Cross Monastery, New York, 1988.

[42] Figures who claim to be outside of the church like Gandhi and Simone Weil,
whose lives seem to model the Christian life more than those who proclaim
Christianity, provide a rich resource for my book as I inductively try to convince the
reader of my thesis.

external viewpoint outside of Christianity, such as Gandhi. With the aid of Gandhi, therefore, my definition of Christian spirituality relies more on the exstatic lifestyle of individuals who move beyond their own personal realms into the participatory life of God. For example, Jesus instructed his disciples to constantly give their lives away in order to find life: "The one who finds life will lose it, and the one who loses life for my sake will find it" (Matt. 10:39).[43] This process of losing and finding identity is akin to Howard Thurman's insight into how an individual matures or becomes more of a person, that "instead of its spreading him out so that all the margins of the self fade and vanish away, it deepens and intensifies his essential sense of uniqueness without the devastation of a sense of being different."[44] Thurman states further,

> The individual must have a sense of kinship to life that transcends and goes beyond the immediate kinship of family or the organic kinship that binds him ethnically or "racially" or nationally. He has to feel that he belongs to his total environment. He has a sense of being an essential part of the structural relationship that exists between him and all other[s], and the total environment. As a human being, then, he belongs to life and the whole kingdom of life that includes all that lives and perhaps, also, all that has ever lived. In other words, he sees himself as a part of a continuing, breathing, living existence. To be a human being, then, is to be essentially alive in a living world.[45]

---

[43] I find this Scriptural passage especially interesting in that the context of the text is Jesus' instructions for his disciples to move beyond biological family ties.

[44] Fluker, *A Strange Freedom*, 246.

[45] Fluker, *A Strange Freedom*, 245. Thurman provides this major theme of the need of the individual to "extend life that belongs to him and to which he belongs," Ibid., 246. Also see Anthony Appiah's *In My Father's House: Africa in the Philosophy of Culture* (New York: Oxford University Press, 1992) for insight on the need to move beyond biological kinship in order create stronger communities.

Thurman helps us see that my book is a description of Christian spirituality as exstatic lifestyle in the context of the Christian practices of peacemaking. Perhaps there is no more impossible lifestyle than that of peacemaking or nonviolence. To understand this lifestyle as practiced in the church, one has to understand that human reality is acted upon at least as much as acting. Christian spirituality, again as mentioned above, is the spiritual consciousness of dependence on the Triune God, who informs the church as to the appropriate lifestyle by which creation is being redeemed. In other words, Christian spirituality is the reversal of the effects of violence through the practice of a lifestyle that does not depend upon the Christian disciple's own survival but upon the flourishing of creation. The disciple's life is relativized by the life of her neighbor. Life becomes so interconnected that one's survival depends upon the other's survival. Therefore, Jesus gave his disciples the insight of nonviolence that human reality is acted upon at least as much as acting itself, in which one's actions are always in relation to being acted upon by the other. With this insight, violence can never be condoned as a Christian lifestyle, unless the goal of the Christian universe is to end in anarchy. Instead, Christian spirituality allows for how the impossible lifestyle of nonviolence is made possible in a violent world.

I must conclude this introduction with two further difficulties—namely, defining spirituality in relationship to flourishing Christian communal contexts, and defining an intelligible pneumatology that accentuates nonviolent strategies. The former difficulty inspires my methodology in which I begin with the problem of defining Christian spirituality, especially as Christian spirituality relates to the practice of peacemaking. Terry Holmes helps me with this problem of defining spirituality:

> "Spirituality" has too little intellectual substance. It has to be more than a name for warm feelings, which in our search for assurance we attribute to God. These feelings may very well be an intimation of our awareness of God's presence, but until we can distinguish spirituality from what it is not—an initial criterion for any definition—then we do not know what

it is. It cannot be everything and have any meaning. The word
needs to point to a discrete, identifiable something before we
can talk about it intelligently.[46]

Unfortunately, few attempts have been made to articulate how
peacemaking is this "identifiable something" that defines Christian
spirituality. This book is such an attempt.

Unlike the concepts of piety and sanctification, the term
"spirituality" allows me the opportunity to define the Christian life as
more of a communal effort. To reiterate, my thesis is that Christian
spirituality is nonviolent or exstatic lifestyle in which persons
consciously depend on the Triune God to know true identity. My
conclusion is that there can be no relevant Christian spirituality
without the vital practices of peacemaking or nonviolence.
Otherwise, a discourse of Christian spirituality without a hermeneutic
of peacemaking becomes a Western contraption by which to exalt
solipsism, a philosophy of self-preservation. Christian spirituality
depends upon the practices of peacemaking in order for such
spirituality to be made intelligible in a public realm.

Spirituality is one of those things everyone appears to know
about until they have to define it.[47] For example, spirituality is a way
of believing, for Alan Jones defined as the art of making connections,
connections not only between individuals, but also between
communities and nations.[48] The difficulty in giving a definition for
Christian spirituality comes from the breadth of experiences involved
in the process of becoming a Christian. Thus, the concept of

---

[46] Urban T. Holmes, *Spirituality for Ministry* (San Francisco: Harper & Row,
1982) 11. The unfortunate methodology of this book is that Holmes does that which
he criticizes, namely, he defines spirituality in his book as "generic and
experiential" (ibid.); however, he does devote two pages to peacemaking, 91-93.

[47] See Cheslyn Jones, Geoffrey Wainwright, and Edward Yarnold, *The Study of
Spirituality* (New York: Oxford University Press, 1986). They write that spirituality
"is a vague word, often used with no clear meaning, or with a wide and vague
significance, but we can think of no better single word to describe the subject" (p.
xxii). Also see their extensive "Note" (pp. xxiv-vi).

[48] See Alan Jones, *Soul Making: The Desert Way of Spirituality* (San Francisco:
Harper & Row, 1985).

spirituality often is found with various descriptions, such as "African-American spirituality," "Franciscan spirituality," "Anglican spirituality," "Wesleyan spirituality," which point to various historical patterns of the church. Such descriptions of spirituality are often the celebration of unity in unimaginable diversity, of a transcending meaning that holds all things together through divine coherence. In other words, some believe that we are meant to have a difficult time defining spirituality in light of the multifaceted way that God creates. If this is what spirituality is, then it has no content unto itself as a discourse. It is only method. Defining spirituality without such a context or name is like a Garrison Keillor joke: A grasshopper hops into a bar and sits down to wait for a drink. The bartender says, "We haven't had many grasshoppers come into this bar, but despite what people may think, that's surprising because we have a drink named after you." The grasshopper responds, "Well, that is unusual because I have never heard of a drink named Bob."[49] The gist of this joke points to the problem of forgetting that a grasshopper may have particularity beyond the name of the species. Can Christian spirituality have such particularity? I argue in this book that it can through the understanding and practice of nonviolence.

Howard Thurman provides another example as to the difficult process of defining spirituality in light of the tendency to forget the particularity of personhood:

In a conversation with three Indian chiefs in one of the Canadian provinces, I was deeply impressed particularly by the reply of one of them to the query, "Are you a Canadian and then an Indian, or are you an Indian and then a Canadian?" His reply, as it came through the interpreter, was essentially this: "I come from some miles near the Arctic circle in the north country. I live with the snow, the ice, the sharp wind in the winter; with the streams, the flowing waters, the sun and the blossoms in summer. These flow into me and I flow into

---

[49] Garrison Keillor, "A Prairie Home Companion Radio Broadcast," National Public Radio.

them. They keep me and I keep them. I am a part of them
and they are a part of me. I am not sure what you mean when
you say Indian or Canadian."[50]

Both Thurman's example and Keillor's grasshopper joke give us
insight to see that Christian spirituality as an area of study must be
capable of particularity if we are going to attempt to study it
together; therefore, the particularity of Christian spirituality implies
maturation, a constancy of newer and deeper life both for individuals
and communities. Such maturation looks like nonviolent lifestyle
practiced both as individual persons and whole communities. As the
personal realm opens up to the possibility of the other, new life is no
longer a possession. It is, simply, new life—that is to say, a new world
of possibilities, a new future, which is to be constructed day by day.
The personal expands to include the communal, and this, in a
nutshell, is the process of peacemaking—the personal giving birth to
the communal self. And perhaps this rather banal and obvious point is
an indicator of what must be central for any adequate understanding of
Christian spirituality because if personal realms include other realms,
there become fewer unskilled persons in peacemaking. For the self to
mature is for the self to grow in awareness of the other.

As I mentioned before, I am without illusion that my
hermeneutical privilege of peacemaking for Christian spirituality does
not go unchallenged. Perhaps many would find it surprising that the
crucial identity of Christian spirituality is peacemaking since church
history demonstrates the alleged legitimacy of just war. In light of this
history, I do not assume realized eschatology when I speak of the
church. In other words, what I assume as Christian community in this
book is a community still in the adventure of the discovery of truth.
The church is *in medias res* as she tries to see through a mirror dimly
as to who she truly is. Despite her imperfections, the church is
responsible to follow her calling in the world to bring the new reality
of God. There is no excuse for the church to join in the dehumanizing
frenzy of the world to remove God. Howard Thurman provides a good

[50] Fluker, *A Strange Freedom,* 245-246.

example of how the church remains imperfect and yet obligated to her potential of God: "With reference to the Negro, the church has promulgated a doctrine that makes the Negro the object of its salvation while at the same time it denies him the status of a human being, thereby enhancing the difficulties he must face in his effort to experience himself as a human being. Time after weary time, the church has dishonored its Lord. When I asked Mr. Gandhi, 'What is the greatest handicap that Jesus has in India?' instantly he replied, 'Christianity.'"[51] Thurman laments why the church has been such a tragic witness to its own gospel.

Thurman is fond of saying that the church is not sufficiently religious. By this he means that the church does not always stay conscious or awake to the spirit of the living God. For Thurman, the church's genius as an institution is to be sectarian in character. In other words, there can be no such thing as a generic church. It is the nature of institutionalism to be adjectival; some qualifying word must always precede the word "church." It has to be some kind of church, and this gives it its unique character and position. This fact creates a terrible dilemma. How important is limiting and defining the character of the church? It may be that the church as such is an abstraction that only becomes concrete when a peculiar pattern or style of worship, etiquette, or doctrine emerges to define the character and give context to the abstraction. Nothing is ultimately admissible that may threaten the institutional structure that gives to the church its form and substance. But suppose as a part of the form and substance of the church, all believers must commit themselves to nonviolence, as children of God and therefore members one of another. Then the tremendous resources of such a church would be at the disposal of the performing ethic of nonviolence in which persons constantly seek a future through nonviolence. Under such a circumstance, the whole missionary-conversion process would be reversed—persons would knock at the door of the church to find out what they need to do to become what, in evidence, the Christian is.

---

[51] Fluker, *A Strange Freedom,* 252.

The life that the church lives in the world would "bring the world to Christ."[52] A Christian spirituality of nonviolence offers the break of the double standard of belief and quietism. It is from the double standards of Christian thinkers on the issue of peacemaking, however, that I claim spirituality ends up in vapid state of individualism. Philip Sheldrake is helpful when he states, "In recent years the criticism has sometimes been leveled at spirituality that it is an artificial entity that relies for its existence on a variety of other disciplines without having anything that it can call its own, or that it 'enjoys an unlimited wealth of resources but possesses no tools for getting those resources organized.'"[53] A Christian spirituality of peacemaking is the means or methodology by which the church, although maturing in her particularity, may become more intelligible and useful to the world.

In summary, the methodology of this book attempts to recover the premise of peacemaking in Christian spirituality, more particularly, peacemaking as defined through the flourishing of God's triune image of community in the world. The lack of association between spirituality and peacemaking creates a picture of individualistic Christian spiritualities—namely, many methods of Christian spirituality simply cater toward "personal growth" or some kind of individual journey in which one learns prayer techniques or psychoanalytical skills by which one feels more in control of self-reality. My critique against Western spirituality is not necessarily unique or external to Western Christianity because the Protestant Reformation also displays criticism of self-contained Christian spirituality. In the Protestant Reformation, the concept of personal pilgrimage or personal journey to God was attacked because such spiritual conceptualization seemingly approved of a kind of works righteousness instead of a proper understanding of God's grace given to the whole community. Someone who undergoes a personal journey is not witnessing to saving faith.[54] Spirituality as personal pilgrimage

---

[52] Fluker, *A Strange Freedom,* 254.

[53] Philip Sheldrake, *Spirituality & History: Questions of Interpretation and Method* (New York: Crossroad, 1992) 32.

[54] Cross and Livingston, s.v. "Pilgrimages" in *Oxford Dictionary of the Christian Church*, 1288.

only is a particularly Western Christian spirituality that lacks the ability of peacemaking. This Western picture of the spiritual life is different from what is given to us by the Holy Spirit, who teaches us through Pentecost that there is no reality we can truly control. Christian spirituality, displayed to the church by the Holy Spirit, displays to the world that to be a peacemaker requires the ability to love your enemy—to do that which does not come naturally to our current instincts. In a sense, the life, death, and resurrection of Jesus have always given the church the means of critique against self-contained spirituality.

Given this introduction, my first chapter continues this attention to the divorce between Western Christian spirituality and peace-making, which cannot help but produce the kinds discussion in which Western Christians often lack the ability to move beyond self-interested piety. In order to make this divorce more tangible, I discuss the problem of Western Christian spirituality as being self-contained without recourse to relational practices. In order to do this, I offer a brief history of the term "spirituality," informed greatly by Philip Sheldrake's work. Perhaps a surprise to some but to others standard knowledge, we are shown to be deeply influenced by a self-contained understanding of spirituality that lacks social commitments to one's neighbor. Through this discussion of the Western definition of spirituality, I intend to show how Westernized Christian spirituality lacks a conceptual framework for understanding how spirituality is essentially a relational concept in which peace or nonviolence is an assumed characteristic of such relationality.

The Western church's problem of a lack of relational spirituality leads me, more particularly in the third chapter, to select Mahatma Gandhi as a figure of critique against Western Christianity in which there are claims to relational spirituality, for example, with Benedictine communities. Gandhi, however, shows how Western spirituality often results only in a civil religion whose sole purpose is to endorse the British Empire. Gandhi becomes a continuously critiquing voice throughout the book, pricking the conscious of Western spirituality to be a spirituality capable of relationality. This leads to the subsequent chapters of the book, which illustrate how

Western spirituality would understand Gandhi's critique and who from Western spirituality would be able to offer a response to Gandhi's critique of the lack of a relational spirituality within the Western Christian tradition.

In the second chapter, I lay out the need to define spirituality alongside pneumatology in order to articulate a framework that supports my thesis for how Christian spirituality is not self-contained but in essence an *imago dei* concept of relationality. Through a more careful understanding of the Spirit of God, Western Christians come to understand how the Holy Spirit's manifestation is most clearly seen through flourishing community or shalom. Through pneumatology, I argue that the primary aim of Christian spirituality is shalom, a flourishing community. Based upon this reasoning, the goal of Christian spirituality is to produce a reality in which peace always exists, not in some static function, but exstatic, in the manner of shalom or proactive peace. How shalom relates to pneumatology is difficult because there are inevitable problems with how the Spirit of God makes persons flourish. In other words, God's Spirit often leads persons first into the desert, a place that seems antithetical to shalom. In the desert tradition of Christian spirituality, such a leading of the Spirit was common before the reality of peace could be fully understood. This problematic of the Spirit deepens my analysis of the Western Christian's response to peacemaking as pneumatology accentuates the fact that Western churches lack a consistent framework from which to articulate how God's Spirit makes peace.

The articulation of how God's Spirit makes us flourish proceeds to the third chapter—namely, a particular focus on Mahatma Gandhi's ascetical spirituality and peacemaking. A Gandhian understanding of Spirit, in conversation with Christian pneumatology, appropriates the amorphous nature of spirituality away from Western individualistic pursuits of creating only therapeutic selves. Instead, Gandhi provides Christians the creative referent in which students of Jesus learn how to make sense of flourishing and suffering, without allowing the latter to destroy Christian faith. Gandhi demonstrates how the images of the ocean and the desert are complementary and need not lead one to despair. In other words, Gandhian spirituality allows the space for Christian students to synthesize Christian ideals with the harsh realities of a violent world. Gandhi's asceticism then raises the question of seeking the perfection of the nonviolent life. Of course, the greatest ideal for a Christian is to become perfect. Jesus stated, "For if you love those who love you, what reward do you have? Do not even the tax collectors do the same? And if you greet only your brothers and sisters, what more are you doing than others? Do not even the Gentiles do the same? Be perfect, therefore, as your heavenly Father is perfect" (Matt. 5:46–48). It is difficult for the Western mind to hear and understand Jesus' words, especially as the Western mind finds the ascetical goal of perfection incongruent with Western cultures. Gandhi becomes extremely helpful here in providing a non-Christian perspective of perfection. With Gandhi, I argue that spirituality is the kind of sensibility in which Christian students learn how to appropriate the interruptions of God.[55]

For a Westernized Christian to engage the thought and practices of Gandhi is to disallow a provincial worldview in which God's Spirit fits into a neatly constructed taxonomy that justifies violence according to the caprice of Western individualism. Because Gandhi so effectively articulated how British people did not practice what they preached, he became a crucial, analyzing voice for how Western Christianity grew to be self-contained, without recourse to helpful understandings of nonviolence. Because of Gandhi's challenges to Western Christianity, my closing chapter of the book is a constructive display of what a Christian spirituality of nonviolence looks like in the ongoing practices of the church. My controlling idea for this constructive display is in how nonviolence becomes the spiritual logic of community. In such community, the practices of this spirituality of nonviolence would be confession, repentance, forgiveness, and reconciliation.

Inherent in my definition of Christian spirituality is the realization of the seemingly impossible lifestyle of nonviolence that Christian spirituality implies. In my fourth chapter, I lay out a

---

[55] Here I am indebted to Dietrich Bonhoeffer's insight that Christians must prepare to accept the interruptions of God..

teleology of the Christian lifestyle that points to how peacemaking is enacted in present practices of becoming a saint. Herein, the tradition of spiritual direction, articulated by the desert tradition, provides discernment for individuals and communities by which to practice nonviolence. Spiritual direction privileges Christian practices of peacemaking as the best form of sainthood; therefore, inherent in the lifestyle of saints is the kind of shalom that displays what the Christian vision of God's heaven looks like. In the end, this book offers a vision of a Christian spirituality of nonviolence that roots out that which hinders a progressive lifestyle of peacemaking in the Spirit. To continue a violent world concedes to the overwhelming understanding that enslavement to sin is our only reality. Such a pessimistic view remains a threat that could easily deluge the desire to be for others.

The lack of association between spirituality and peacemaking creates a picture of individualistic Christian spiritualities—namely, many methods of Christian spirituality simply cater toward "personal growth" or some kind of individual journey in which one learns prayer techniques or psychoanalytical skills by which one feels more in control of reality. This is a particularly Western Christian spirituality that lacks the ability of peacemaking. Again, I argue in my second chapter that the Western picture of the Western spiritual life is different from what is given by the Holy Spirit, who teaches through Pentecost that there is no reality that creatures can truly control. Christian spirituality, displayed to the church by the Holy Spirit, displays to the world that to be a peacemaker requires the ability to love your enemy—a reality that is certainly beyond individual control. Such ability places Christians in the most precarious of circumstances, many of which require suffering and lack of control. Desmond Tutu helps me explain:

> The last mark of the operation of the Spirit seems to be that those who are chosen to be special instruments are destined for suffering.... Those who are God's friends are distinguished by the fact that they suffer.... There is an unbroken link in the mystery of service and suffering, witness

and persecution, stretching from the Old Testament to the
New Testament.... A church that does not suffer cannot be
the Church of Jesus Christ, the suffering servant of the
Lord.[56]

The need not to control the concept of a suffering God becomes
a Christian spirituality of nonviolence in which exemplars like Tutu
and Gandhi have much to teach a postcolonial world. Having learned
from such exemplars, especially through dialogue with Gandhi in
chapter three and the wisdom of desert fathers and mothers in chapter
four, I see the marriage between spirituality and peacemaking in my
concluding chapter occurring particularly in the church. The goal of
my concluding chapter is to offer a relevant spirituality of the church,
as opposed to typical personal spiritualities, which have defined
current Christian spiritualities as irrelevant to peacemaking. The
demanding task of peacemaking combined with the pursuits of the
spirit produces an extraordinary form of the Christian life that can
indeed be practiced by the church, and the pessimism against such
practice of nonviolence can be overcome. Although this is my
concluding chapter, I do not imply in this methodology that
peacemaking as a supererogated form of the Christian life need be
relegated to the *eschaton*, or the last days. It seems clear, however,
that Jesus teaches the church that the Christian life is not relegated to
some future existence. Jesus even said to the one who desired his
nonviolent lifestyle, "Truly I tell you, today you will be with me in
Paradise" (Luke 23:43). Jesus teaches us that the church's current
attitudes and practices create particular futures. Christian practices of
loving enemies demonstrate the potential creation of peaceful
realities, unlike the violent ones so many of us believe in, which
assume no future at all—that is, they assume no future beyond the
survival of the self.

---

[56] Tutu, "The Holy Spirit and South Africa."

1

WESTERN SPIRITUALITY AND VIOLENCE

Christian spirituality and nonviolence should form a natural symbiosis. Unfortunately, there is little study of this relationship between Christian spirituality and nonviolence in Western Christianity. Some discussion is to follow as to how some have come to disembody spirituality from its relational practices of nonviolence. In short, one can attribute this division to Western interpretations that juxtapose the spiritual against material existence in such a way that one can be spiritual and, at the same time, justify the destruction of God's creation. I will attempt to recover the symbiosis between the spiritual and nonviolent reality through a brief historical display of Christian spirituality, beginning with the mystery of the church's deepest experience—a mystery because the church's origin is deeper than our minds can take us.

By the time the church became conscious of her experience of being the church, God had already become an experience of an experience; therefore, the church constructs an image of a reality that in itself is occurring before her normal, historical awareness can become operational to describe it. In other words, what we know at the deepest place of the church, we know not with the clarity of our cognitive minds but through what is often seen as the obscure hermeneutics of particular communities calling themselves the church. I name this knowing through obscurity because the church, since her beginning, has had to seek God in unknowing.[1] Only a few in the church have claimed an immediacy of contemplative intuition.

For even as we attempt this description of something sensed, spirituality, even more particularly, Christian spirituality, we find ourselves bringing our cognitive, categorizing faculty of knowing into operation, as opposed to affective ways of knowing by heart, the heart as defined by the core of one's being where one is most truly oneself. In order to recover the symbiosis between spirituality and nonviolence, Christian spirituality must be seen as more than the practice of individuals seeking explanation of their sole existence, or of their experiences, because to do so would be like the dog who thinks itself born to turn in circles to chase its own tail or even tale. Herein, in this chase to define Christian spirituality in light of nonviolence, I argue that a discourse in Christian spirituality carries with it the daily need of habits and skills given to Christian individuals through the church.

There can be no experience of God solely as an individual's experience per se, as if God's presence resides only in the personal realm. For example, it is common to hear many preach that one must have a personal relationship with Jesus as Lord and Savior. Many times I have heard someone preach to me "that if you were the only one alive, God would still come and die for you." This homiletic way of articulating relationship with God, however, is individualistic and unintelligible to the way that Jesus taught us how to pray. Jesus taught his disciples to pray in this way: "Our Father in heaven" (Matt. 6:9). It is with this communal connection between spiritual formation and daily life that Rowan Williams helps us understand that no such individualistic understanding works outside of a communal understanding of spirituality. Williams writes in *The Wound of Knowledge*:[2]

---

[1] See the work of one of the first articulators of Christian mysticism, Pseudo Dionysius, *Mystical Theology* in the Western Classics of Christian Spirituality.

[2] Rowan Williams, *The Wound of Knowledge: Christian Spirituality from the New Testament to St. John of the Cross* (Cambridge, MA: Cowley 1991) 2.

Once we have stopped drawing a distinction between "compromising" activities and spheres (the family, the state, the individual body or psyche) and "pure" realities (the soul the intelligible world), the spiritual life becomes a much more complex, demanding and far-reaching matter. "Spirituality" becomes far more than a science of interpreting exceptional private experiences; it must now touch every area of human experience...and the goal of a Christian life becomes not enlightenment but wholeness—an acceptance of this complicated and muddled bundle of experiences as a possible theater for God's creative work.

Williams helps us see the goal of the Christian life as full participation in God's creative work. This work becomes apparent in our image of God more than through words but through diverse persons in the unified nature of the church. The pursuit to be the church becomes the pursuit of the image of God. This must always imply communal spirituality rather than individualistic forms of Western spirituality. In this chapter, it is my goal that Western spirituality may learn from the following African proverb: The reason that two antelopes walk together is so that one might blow the dust from the other's eyes.

I seek to recover this communal sense of how spirituality and nonviolence assume each other in the Christian tradition. In a post-9/11 world, now is the opportune time to remarry spirituality and nonviolence because there has been a major shift in Western spirituality away from reflection on how persons pray in their communal particularity. The focus is usually upon personal salvation or personal piety. I argue in this chapter to move away from a self-contained approach to the Christian life, embodied in an analytical and abstract spiritual theology, toward a more dynamic and inclusive concept of spirituality in which personhood becomes normative in light of communal existence. I choose the term "spirituality" because it offers the bridge between those who are disillusioned with institutional religion and those who have remained faithful to such institutions. In addition, "spirituality" has gained ecumenical acceptance and now tends to be eclectic in its approach as it seeks to draw upon the riches of a shared Christian heritage rather than to limit itself to a narrow understanding of "life in the Spirit." Spirituality, in other words, is a far better expression of community than terms like "piety" or even "religion."

There are four characteristics of spirituality that enable its symbiosis with nonviolence. First, spirituality, as opposed to religion, is not exclusive—certainly not associated exclusively with any one Christian tradition, or even necessarily with Christianity as a whole. Second, spirituality is more, rather than less, associated with solid theology than in the recent past because it offers language in which to move beyond dogmatic principles that often stifle creative approaches to God. Third, spirituality does not so much concern itself with definitions as with surveying the mysteries of relating fully to God. Finally, spirituality is not limited to a concern with the interior life but seeks an integration of all aspects of human life and experience. These four characteristics of spirituality underline the importance for how nonviolence and Christian spirituality fit together.

Christian Spirituality Defined

Without specific characteristics, it is difficult to say precisely what spirituality is and what it is not, and what is appropriate or not to displaying its definition.[3] Criticisms of generic definitions of spirituality are undoubtedly valid because spirituality is unavoidably

---

[3] The word "spirituality" has a short history. A comparison of *The Catholic Encyclopedia*, published between 1912-15, and the revised *New Catholic Encyclopedia* of the 1970s reveals that there are no references to 'spirituality in the first text, while in the second there are numerous references. In both the Oxford Dictionary and in the Webster's International Dictionary of 1961, six meanings are given. Five definitons correspond to 'spirituality' as religion: three definitions refer to incorporeal beings, and two to the clergy as spiritual persons. The sixth definition perpetuates the dualism between the condition of being spiritual on one hand, and material on the other. See Philip Sheldrake, *Spirituality & History: Questions of Interpretation and Method* (New York: Crossroad, 1992) 34.

conditioned by historical and religious contexts. I argue here that Christian spirituality embodies a particular commitment to nonviolence as Christian spirituality's distinctive symbols of cross and resurrection emerge into reality. Certainly, when it comes to defining contemporary Christian spirituality, the emphasis on nonviolence does not in practice exclude specific reference to the tradition. While spirituality, in Christian terms, is not about some other kind of life but about the whole of human life at depth, our understanding of what this might mean cannot avoid questions posed specifically by the Christian tradition of revelation about the nature of God, human nature, and the relationship between the two. This becomes a dialogical form of spirituality in which spiritual theologians such as Philip Sheldrake are successful at outlining a history of Christian spirituality.[4]

Christian spirituality and nonviolence are understood together to include not merely the techniques of prayer and civil disobedience, but, more broadly, a conscious relationship with God, in Jesus Christ, through the indwelling of the Spirit and in the context of the community of believers. Spirituality is, therefore, concerned with the conjunction of active nonviolence, theology, prayer, and practical Christianity. Christian spirituality and nonviolence are symbiotic in that they derive their identity from the belief that human beings are capable of entering into relationship with God, who lives beyond violence and survival. This relationship with God is lived out not in isolation, but in a community of believers sustained by the active presence of the Spirit of God in each person and in the community as a whole. In Christian terms, nonviolence involves a reference to life as a gift of the Spirit of God, which establishes life-giving relationships. In other words, Christian spirituality is explicitly nonviolent, doctrinally and practically.

Doctrinally, for the church, the Latin root of the word "spirituality," *spiritualitas*, attempts to translate the Greek noun for spirit, *pneuma*, and its adjective, *pneumatikos*, as they appear in the

---

[4] I am greatly indebted to Philip Sheldrake's history as I display especially the form of spirituality that comes to us from the medieval era.

epistles of St. Paul. Thus, to be united to Christ is to enter into the sphere of the Spirit (1 Cor. 6:17), or faith in the Lord is from and in the Spirit (1 Cor. 2:10f.). In Pauline theology, "Spirit" and "spiritual" are not contrasted with "physical" or "material" (for which the Greek *soma*, Latin *corpus*, is the root) but rather with all that is opposed to the Spirit of God. The "spiritual person" (for example, 1 Cor. 2:14–15) is not someone who turns away from material reality but someone in whom the Spirit of God dwells. Gertrude Mueller Nelson is helpful as she speaks of material existence as *Mater*, or material as mother.[5] The contrast to spirituality that merges is between two ways of life. The "spiritual" is under the influence of, or is a manifestation of, the Spirit of God. A dualistic contrast between "spiritual" and "physical," or "body" and "soul," is not part of the Pauline understanding of the human person or of created reality in general. There is no justification for using the Pauline contrast as the basis for a denial of the flesh or a rejection of the material.

The abstract Latin noun *spiritualitas* (spirituality) as opposed to the adjective *spiritualis* (spiritual) was not used until the fifth century. A letter once described to St. Jerome exhorts the reader so to act as to advance in "spirituality" (*ut in spiritualitate proficias*). As the context is living within the power of the Holy Spirit this continues to reflect the basic theology of the Pauline letters. Herein is the problem of adjudicating what an advance in the spiritual life looks like. Later, I will display such a problematic through the thought of Gandhi, who also found it difficult to display criteria for how an individual and whole communities progress in the spiritual life. Such a notion is not foreign to Christian spirituality because at its heart has always been the notion and practice of community. It is to such a patristic display that we now turn.

---

[5] Gertrude Mueller Nelson, *To Dance with God: Family, Ritual, and Community Celebration*, (New York: Paulist Press, 1986).

Patristic Communal Spirituality

In the patristic period, the individual's movement toward union with God was viewed as all Christians baptized in Christ. [6] The unifying practice of baptism is the context within which the fathers and mothers understood the spiritual life.[7] This understanding of the spiritual life has changed in Western Christianity. Unlike Western discourse, study of the spiritual life was conceived as a unity to which later divisions (for example, ethics, systematic theology, pastoral care, etc.) were anachronistic.[8]

The patristic period provided a formative time for what has been called "mystical theology." Mystical theology was the attempt to provide a context for the direct apprehension of God, who is revealed in Christ and within us as the Spirit. For example, orthodox doctrines of the Trinity and Incarnation were worked out in the patristic period through what was known as "mystical doctrines," formulated through

---

[6] I assume the patristic period to be the limited sense of the early Christian centuries. There is disagreement about how long the patristic period lasted. Some would limit it to the earliest centuries of the Christian era, for example, the Protestant tradition has tended to accept the Council of Chalcedon 451 C.E. as an approximate end. The Eastern Orthodox would include such figures as Gregory Palamas who lived from 1296-1359. Others say it describes the whole period up to the development of the 'new theology' of scholasticism in the West in the twelfth century.

[7] Philip Sheldrake offers an important critique of how one appropriates patristic spirituality. Sheldrake states that the intellectual pattern of the patristic theologians was necessarily forged by their social origins and education. In fact, apart from Athanasius and Augustine, all the outstanding spiritual and theological leaders seem to have been born into elite classes and all were men. So their spirituality which was inherited and relied upon by succeeding generations for almost a thousand years needs to be relocated within its social milieu-that is, the estates of landowners or the sophisticated upper-class circles of the leading cities of the Roman Empire. In practice, this mean a grafting on to the biblical vision of Christianity of the humanistic values and traditional philosophical attitudes of the contemporary upper-class and male elites. Sheldrake, *Spirituality and History*, 40.

[8] The unifying feature was the Bible, and theology was generally biblical theology, exegetically-based interpretation of Scripture aimed at producing both a fuller understanding of Christian faith and a deepening of the Christian life in all its dimensions.

the consensus of the church. What Western minds interpret as doctrinal theology was the patristic attempt to understand the spiritual life in precise language, which in turn inspired a mystical understanding of God. It is important to realize, however, that mystical theology of the patristic period is not the same fascination in the West with subjective experience or with the development of a detailed itinerary for the spiritual journey. This brings us to the understanding that patristic "mysticism" is neither abstract nor systematic; instead, such mysticism refers to the spiritual life of the Christian who knows God as revealed in Christ belonging to the fellowship of the "mystery." In other words, patristic forms of prayer made little distinction between communal and personal ways of praying. In short, patristic spirituality displays how divine mystery begins with our incorporation into Christ in baptism and comes to fruition in us through the sacramental life and by growth in virtue.

This problem of spiritual maturity is illustrated through the debate about whether some virtues should be more prominent in certain stages of life than in others. For example, we almost think it unseemly for children to be wise, but we think it important for them to be obedient. Of course, one could object that such obedience is not a true virtue as children have not developed the capacity for virtue. But we do associate certain virtues with stages and functions in life, making it difficult for any one account of the virtues and their interrelation to be satisfactory. Thus, Alasdair MacIntyre argues that it is a mistake to try, as Aquinas did, to provide an exhaustive and consistent classification of the virtues.

The problem with the virtues is that they seem to invite a subjective arbitrariness into moral considerations that it has been the purpose of modern moral philosophy to avoid. Thus, the virtues have largely been treated as morally secondary to an ethics of obligation that emphasizes the centrality of rules and principles. The latter, it is assumed, are more likely candidates to ensure widespread agreement. Yet defenders of the stress on the virtues argue that rules and principles involve the same problems.

There is a renewed interest in the virtues in contemporary Christian ethics. Some claim that an emphasis on "what ought we to be" is more amenable to the display of how theological convictions work morally. Moreover, an emphasis on the virtues is said to offer a constructive alternative to the situation ethics debate, which seemed to require that we choose between situationalism and a rule-determined ethic. Virtues are communally recognizable they are expressions of respect and honor for other human beings as children of God, and for one's own physical and spiritual nature as the work of the creator, redeemed in Christ (cf. 1 Cor. 6:9–20); and may be violated by other forms of indulgence besides the overtly sexual. One may note that the Rule of Benedict, which assumes monastic chastity, has to guard against temptations to indulgence in food and drink and personal possessions. Hence, in the Sermon on the Mount, the commandment against adultery is applied to unlawful desires as well as the physical act of adultery (Matt. 5:27–28). Interestingly enough, Jesus seemingly creates a double standard: one standard of holiness and one standard of law. Monastic chastity has a similar double meaning. Externally, it means the preservation of the virgin (or widowed) state by the monk or nun; spiritually, it is the devotion of all powers of body and soul to the service of God. For this reason, perhaps, it does not appear as a special vow in the oldest monastic customs, but as a necessary aspect of the monastic state. Benedict, for instance, does not prescribe a separate promise of chastity but includes it in the general promise of monastic behavior (*conversatio*; or, in later texts, *conversio*; *Rule*, ch. 58 read ch. 58 of the *Rule*). In Italy the experience of two centuries of monasticism was brilliantly codified in the Rule of Benedict, which combines ascetic piety with the classic spirit of moderation and the Roman feeling for law and order. By the time of Charlemagne the Benedictine Rule had replaced all others in the Western church, except for some lingering Celtic survivals. But in the feudal age, Benedict's pattern of work, study, and worship was distorted by the abandonment of physical labor. For those not occupied in business or intellectual pursuits this left a gap that was only partially filled by the increase of devotional exercises. The result was to give medieval Benedictinism a certain abstraction that even its great reforms did not escape, such as those associated with the great center of Cluny, or the revival of the monastic life in England inspired by Dunstant.

New forms of the monastic life developed as medieval life became more complex. The Rule of Augustine (derived from two of his letters) was revived after the tenth century. Having the advantage of simplicity and flexibility, it was found useful by those who wished to combine the monastic life with active work for the church—missionary, educational, pastoral, even military. On the other hand, longings for a return to ancient austerity led to the appearance of settlements of hermits. Out of these grew several orders that combined the common and the solitary life. The most significant of these were the Carthusians (founded by Bruno, but organized by their third prior, Guigo, after 1110). Among Benedictines, the Cistercians (after 1098) aimed at a return to the primitive life of the *Rule*, while avoiding the dangers of isolation by a federal organization of their numerous monasteries.

Within these monastic movements, patristic spirituality was pastoral, a spirituality for the edification of the Christian community. Because patristic theology was primarily a way of interpreting the Bible, the most common written genre was scriptural commentary. The "fathers" did such spiritual study of Scripture within the limits of their time, but their interest was primarily pastoral. All study was placed in the context of the baptized Christian, resulting in a spirituality in which various patristic figures did not separate personal piety from the spiritual life of the church. Patristic theology encapsulates an idea of Christian knowledge accessible by the baptized in which biblical exegeses, speculative reasoning, and mystical contemplation are fused into a synthesis. In other words, spirituality was communal for the early fathers and mothers of the church. The communal setting for the spiritual life was a given for the patristic community as the baptized worked for consensus of the central features of Christian faith. Individual Christians could not understand the spiritual life apart from common baptism and communal worship. This was especially true of the African patristic figures. Howard Thurman provides an example of such a patristic worldview from a contemporary African setting. Thurman describes how spirituality is communally dependent if it is to be understood by individual persons. Thurman illustrates through the following story of when he was in Nigeria:

> At the close of a lecture before the Press Club, to which reference has been made, I was invited to a small room for refreshments. I asked for a kind of soft drink called ginger beer. My host opened the bottle, poured a little on the floor as he said, "For my ancestors," and then he filled my glass. In this concept of the extended family, as I saw it, there is a variation of the same theme. To experience oneself as a human being is to know a sense of kinship with one's total environment and to recognize that it is this structural relationship that makes it possible for one to experience himself as a human being. Being white or black becomes merely incidental and is of no basic significance. Does this seem far-fetched and speculative or unrealistic?[9]

Our contemporary answer must be yes, but to the church fathers and mothers, communal spirituality was the presupposition for knowing God.

The patristic period connoted a style of theology that chiefly contributed to the orthodox formulation of the church's faith. So, for example, Athanasius's victory over the Arian view of salvation assumed a communal medium through which he became a champion of the interpreters of what would be orthodox. Again, Augustine's rejection of Pelagian spirituality assumed the communal medium by which he claimed orthodoxy. This assumption of communal epistemology may be due to the fact that nearly all of the major patristic writers were bishops. Therefore, it was entirely natural that their theology should be involved in the life of the church. In addition to being mostly bishops, a large proportion of patristic writers were ascetics whose lifestyle had to model the pastoral lifestyle of Christ (for example, Antony, Pachomius, John Chrysostom, Basil, Jerome).

---

[9] Fluker, *A Strange Freedom,* 246.

As a result of aligning personal asceticism to Christ's asceticism, patristic thought carries the strong theme of the Christian life as participation in God's perfecting reality. It is through this perfecting reality that the Christian tradition is accused of disallowing any sustained methodology for nonviolence. To illustrate this troubling criticism of Christian spirituality, we now turn briefly to Origen.

Like the patristic period, there seems little evidence for any interest in mysticism as a subjective experience, or in the kind of spiritual-mystical states that privileged personal spirituality. The monastic style of theology, as it continued until overtaken by that of the schools from the twelfth century onward, drew its inspiration from the traditional meditative reading of Scripture, or *lectio divina*, and monastic liturgy. The fundamental insight of Origen flowed together with certain Neo-Platonic elements.[10] Origen offered a "mystical theology" that was not concerned with enumerating the means toward the technicalities of mystical union but rather explored the nature of the soul's return to God. Christians were called to pass beyond the obvious world to be fully grasped by the mystery of God and so be transformed into the community of God known as Trinity. Origen's spirituality is not caught up in the individual's subjective experience as we are wont to do in our Western context. This Western interest in subjective experience is not present for Origen, for "the mystery" is still the objective fact of God in Christ into which all are drawn through a life of prayer.

Origen's *On Prayer* provides a text of mystical theology, illustrating the spiritual movement of the persons passing beyond sign and concept to be fully grasped by the mystery of God. Knowledge is the operative word for Origen, but it is a knowledge that calls for intellectual understanding, including moral and spiritual practices. These practices cannot be divided; they are one. Through Origen's synthesizing sensibilities, his patristic understanding facilitates my argument that a compartmentalized, Western spirituality is not the original understanding of Christian spirituality. In short, Origen is

---

[10] See Rowan Greer, ed. *Origen* (New York: Paulist, 1979) for his insight on influences on Origen's thought.

most helpful in understanding Christian spirituality as communal spirituality. Such spirituality articulates prayer as the common pilgrimage of the baptized in which Christians move from creation to salvation.

Origen's narrative behind his understanding of spirituality as prayer begins with preexistence. Before there was anything, there was God. This is an important distinction from Neo-Platonism, which could not separate within preexistence God from God's creation. As God always creates, God is not contained by the created order; rather, God informs it with divine presence and power. For Origen, God is transcendent of everything created, meaning that God limits God's self if so desired. This theology is pertinent to mystical theology in that one should never confuse God with God's limitation. For example, when a person prays "Our Father in heaven," one should not think God is in a place or that God is corporeal.[11] Prayer, then, for Origen implies how diversity finds its fulfillment in unity, just as creation finds its fulfillment in God. In other words, prayer is the desire for union with God.

God's unity provides the cosmology in which there can be diverse beings who commune with God. Since corporeality carries with it the implication of diversity, God is the mystery of being corporeal and unitive. Herein, the Trinity complicates Origen's understanding of God. For example, the Second Person of the Trinity is in relation to God in the same way that no real difference can be made between a thought and its thinker. For Origen, the distinctions of Father, Son, and Holy Spirit are not meant to divide the Godhead. The Word of God mediates between God the Father and the rational creation. At one level the Word is identical with God, at another, with the souls who participate in God through him. The eternal generation of the Son by the Father is compared to the will proceeding from the mind or radiance issuing from light. All of this leads to the complication in which Origen teaches the church that one does not pray to the means, the Word, but to the end, God.[12]

---

[11] Greer, ed., *Origen,* 127.
[12] Greer, ed., *Origen,* 112-114.

Rowan Greer sums up the crucial impact of Origen's cosmology of the Word in that Origen was not so concerned about the ontological debate about God; his view insists that the Word acts as mediator, binding God and the creation together in unity.[13] God the Father is pure being, truth, life, goodness, and beauty. The Word as his image participates in all these aspects, thereby demonstrating love, wisdom, power, righteousness, and truth to Christians.[14] The Word is the image of God, and we are made after the image of God (Col. 1:15; 2 Cor. 4:4, Gen. 1:26).[15] Because of this *telos* in being created, the Christian mind or soul is constituted by nature to participate in the intelligible world.[16]

Origen's cosmology displays how God created Christian community perfectly as incorporeal being. In this community, we all paid attention to the ultimate meaning of life, known as the Word, who revealed the Father. To illustrate this original bliss containing complete attentiveness to God, Simone Weil's understanding of *attente* is helpful. In Simone Weil's "Reflections on the Right Use of School Studies," the key to a Christian conception of studies is the realization that prayer consists of attention. Weil believes that something in our souls has a far more violent repugnance for true attention than the flesh has for bodily fatigue. Every time we really concentrate our attention, we destroy the evil in ourselves.[17] Weil states, "If...we consider the occupations in themselves, studies are nearer to God because of the attention which is their soul. Whoever goes through years of study without developing this attention has lost a great treasure."[18]

Attention consists of suspending thought, leaving it detached, empty, and ready to be penetrated by the object; it means holding in our minds, within reach of this thought, but on a lower level and not in contact with it, the diverse knowledge we have acquired that we are

---

[13] Greer, ed., *Origen,* 10.

[14] Greer, ed., *Origen,* 226.

[15] Greer, ed., *Origen,* 125, 215

[16] Greer, ed., *Origen,* 76.

[17] Simone Weil, *Gravity and Grace* (New York: Putnam, 1952) 49.

[18] Weil, *Gravity and Grace,* 51.

forced to make use of. Above all, our thought should be empty, waiting, not seeking anything, but ready to receive in its naked truth the object that is to penetrate it. Not only does the love of God have attention for its substance; the love of our neighbor, which we know to be the same love, is made of this same substance. Those who are unhappy have no need for anything in this world but people capable of giving them their attention. The capacity to give one's attention to a sufferer is a very rare and difficult thing; it is almost a miracle; it is a miracle. Nearly all those who think they have this capacity do not possess it. Warmth of heart, impulsiveness, pity are not enough.

As long as we direct our attention toward God through his Word, the primordial unity is preserved. For Origen some of us let our attention wander in the back of the class that the Word was continually teaching on God the Father. All of us directed our attention away from God, except the soul of Jesus. The soul once fallen is on pilgrimage, and its destiny is to return to God. Origen doesn't explain why this happened other than through the insight: "The Beginning is unstable because it is innocent."[19] It is the experience acquired by souls during our pilgrimage back to God that furnishes our motive for being attentive to the divine teacher and in this way renders the end stable. In falling, the rational natures moved away from the "divine warmth" and became cool; hence, we became souls (although Origen uses *psychai*, or souls, interchangeably with mind or rational nature). But his notion here is that the soul is a "cooled-off" mind. In our cooled-off state we are given a body, partly as an outward symbol of the state of the soul and partly as a function of God's providence to catch us before we completely fall.[20] Furthermore, the kind of body given the soul is proportionate to the degree of the fall. Thus, there is constituted a hierarchy of embodied souls, ranging from angels at the top, through human beings, and, finally, to demons at the bottom of the scale. The souls, once unified, are now incorporated and unequal. They have the possibility of

---

[19] Greer, ed., *Origen,* 11.
[20] Greer, 186.

moving up or down the hierarchy established by the original fall. This is where Origen elaborates on even more esoteric speculations.[21]

Ultimately for Origen, the spiritual life encapsulates violence and struggle. The soul is capable of struggling back to God; therefore, the soul is not limited to being moved by another or moved as a simple reflex of its nature. Freedom is part of the definition of a rational being that makes choices. Origen's world is not deterministic despite his static view of temptation. Origen is a pivotal figure in distinguishing the purpose of temptation. The problem of temptation is either in the proclivity to sin or in the battlefield of testing or affliction. In both senses, temptation is meant to display whatever virtues lie in the Christian. Origen's distinguishing mark is found in his concern for the glory of God in the world, yet he is unwilling to see this as emerging, in Jesus or in ourselves, from trial or moral struggle.[22] Here, Rowan Williams's insight is helpful in seeing that temptations are permitted for Origen so that we may see more clearly what we already are (de orat. XXIX. 17–18); they have no very positive or constructive role. The passionless condition of the spiritual person makes a person invulnerable on this level. This is perhaps the most important area in which Hellenistic preconceptions have closed certain options to Origen. He is anything but a Gnostic, yet there is the same unwillingness, in the long run, to confront the contingencies of the human situation. The preoccupation with the illusory and precarious nature of the material clouds the perception of the precariousness of spirit and will, and so, again, leads to an emphasis on ignorance or distance rather than bondage and sin.[23]

Temptation not only tests what we are, but it is also a providential process by which we are fashioned into what we should be.[24] The soul's freedom of choice enabled the fall, and it is this same capacity that allows it to move toward God. The soul does not lose its freedom in the fall, even though it is more difficult to exercise

---

[21] Greer, 196f; Also see Origen's notion of successive world orders which seems akin to the Mormon obsession (pp. 144ff.).

[22] Origen, *On Prayer*, 160-161.

[23] Williams, *The Wound of Knowledge*, 48.

[24] Greer, ed., *Origen*, 21.

freedom in the conditions in which it falls. Origen's emphasis on freedom was retained by his successors and ultimately became the Pelagian theme—that a human being can still take the first steps toward God. But Origen always emphasized paradox. The progress of the soul is dependent upon God's providence. If God is providential, forseeing everything that is, how can we be said to have freedom? Freedom is the gift of providence.

God's providence is the divine and mysterious power that weaves the consequences of all human actions together into harmony. Origen believed that God foreknows even the activity of our freedom. Nevertheless, God does not foreordain our free choices, but only what "meets" them from providence. That is, the consequences of our choices inevitably depend upon the causal framework of God, who weaves life into a higher pattern of harmony through providence.[25] The person who makes a wrong choice by her use of freedom brings punishment upon herself. But God uses that punishment as a way of satiating the sinner with her vice and so driving her back to God. So providence is punitive and corrective. Origen concluded that ultimately God's providence will restore the whole creation again so that we may live in the paradox of beginning before the beginning. Through God's providential web of life we may exercise perfect freedom by continually choosing God. The best way to understand providence is through the view that God stands alone, both before and at the end of time, summoning us to the flourishing life.

The end of the story is *apocatastasis*, or restoration of broken communities. Origen believed that the end will involve not only a return to the perfection of the beginning, but the winning of a greater perfection from which we can never fall. Herein is Origen's most provocative thought—namely, the corporeality and inequality of the souls at the end stand for the experience they have had on their pilgrimage. It is that experience that enables them to address the Word with endless questions and to maintain their interest in God. Greer concludes that Origen's theological story as a whole is the same

---

[25]Greer, ed., *Origen,* 90-97; 156ff.

as the great patristic figures Irenaeus or Gregory of Nyssa—the fundamental pattern is a movement from innocence to experience.[26]

How does Origen inform our pursuit for a Christian spirituality of nonviolence? The conclusion behind the patristic narrative is that prayer implies maturation, a constancy of new life that is not a possession of the individual but of the Christian community wrought by God. Origen teaches us that Christian spirituality is, simply, new communal life—that is to say, a new world of possibilities, a new future that is to be constructed day by day. Communal life, after all, implies movement and growth. Given this patristic narrative of Origen, however, it is important to ask how the church appropriates its pilgrimage toward union with God in light of what Western Christian spirituality has become.

Western Christian Spirituality

The reference to Christian spirituality as communal in sensibility remained constant up to the twelfth century. At this time Western theologians invented the later interest in subjective experience not present for patristic figures like Origen, for "the mystery of *apocatastasis*" is still the observable fact of God in Christ into which all are drawn through the church. A combination of factors bore fruit in Western Christian writings, exercising subjective influence on subsequent directions in medieval spiritual theory. The influence of a new philosophical trend in theology, known as scholasticism, began in the twelfth century and led to a sharper distinction between spirit and matter. The word "spiritual" began to be applied to intelligent creatures (that is, humankind), as opposed to non-rational creation. Thus, it lost its Pauline holistic sense and took on a meaning more radically opposed to corporeality. However, the new meaning of "spirituality" did not completely replace the former Pauline emphasis. In the thirteenth century the two meanings stood side by

---

[26] Notes taken in Yale Divinity school course on Patristic Theology with Rowan Greer, 1989.

side. Thus, Thomas Aquinas used both the Pauline and the anti-material senses of spirituality. A third juridical sense, "spirituality" as the clerical state, also came into being at this time and, from the thirteenth to the sixteenth centuries, is the most frequent usage. This juridical sense of spirituality as only exemplified by priests and those in religious communities (that is, monks and nuns) created a moral theology in which there two primary levels of the Christian life: one for the "spiritual" clerics, the other for the normal laity.

It was only in the seventeenth century that the word became once again established in France in reference to the spiritual life. In a positive sense it was used to express deep relationship with God. However, this new meaning was also used pejoratively of enthusiastic or quietistic movements. Here, it was contrasted with words such as "devotion," which seemed to preserve a proper emphasis on human cooperation. For example, Voltaire used the word in his violent attacks on the "salon mysticism" of Madame Guyon and Fénelon because it appeared too refined, rarified, and separated from ordinary Christian life. In fact, a variety of words were used in the seventeenth and eighteenth centuries to express life in the Spirit: "devotion" in Francis de Sales or the Anglican mystic William Law; "perfection" in John Wesley and the early Methodists; "piety" among evangelicals.[27] The problem, however, is that for many of these Western Christians, the spiritual life is seen as separate from ordinary life. Urban Holmes explains:

> A Retreat master when I was a seminarian told us that if we were marooned on a desert island and could choose to have three books with us, we should choose the Bible, the Book of Common Prayer (an obvious choice for Episcopal seminarians), and Frederic P. Harton's *Elements of the Spiritual Life*. Harton's book is one of those products of Anglo-Catholic scholarship that flourished between the two world wars and consists of a totally nondiscriminating assimilation and regurgitation for unsuspecting Anglicans of

---

[27] Sheldrake, *Spirituality and History,* 35.

the worst in post-Vatican I Roman Catholic theology.... Probably every denomination has its own *Elements of the Spiritual Life*. I was also required to labor through parts of Adolphe Tanquerey's *The Spiritual Life*, which is a Roman Catholic version of Harton's book.[28]

Holmes goes on to say that both works bear no discernable relation to the life we live today. But the intentions of the authors cannot be completely dismissed. These so-called classical writers of spirituality wished for a life of prayer that expressed an awareness of God's presence in everyday life. The problem lay in the execution of that intention. Holmes believes that "on the one hand, [Harton] was closely tied to a tradition that appeared limited by time and geography. On the other hand, as far as we can tell he ignored what was happening in the world in which he lived and consequently wrote for a church people who lived largely in his fantasies. Far too much spiritual theology suffers from such limited insight, despite its very laudable intentions."[29] Holmes is helpful as he goes on to define spirituality as "(1) a human capacity for relationship (2) with that which transcends sense phenomena; this relationship (3) is perceived by the subject as an expanded or heightened consciousness independent of the subject's efforts, (4) given substance in the historical setting, and (5) exhibits itself in creative action in the world."[30]

The word "spirituality" virtually disappeared from the religious and theological vocabulary of Roman Catholic circles in the early eighteenth century. This undoubtedly had a great deal to do with a suspicion both of religious enthusiasm and quietism. In the nineteenth century the use of the world "spirituality" was confined mainly to free religious groupings outside the mainline churches. In the early decades of the present century, "spirituality" once again appeared among

---

[28] Urban T. Holmes, *Spirituality for Ministry* (San Francisco: Harper & Row, 1982) 1.
[29] Holmes, *Spirituality for Ministry*, 1-2.
[30] Holmes, *Spirituality for Ministry*, 12.

Roman Catholics in France and then passed into English through translations of French writings. The use of "spirituality" was closely tied to the debate concerning the nature of the spiritual life in itself. Those who saw a continuity between the "ordinary" and "extraordinary" (that is, mystical) dimensions of Christian living preferred the word "spirituality" because of its comprehensiveness. Its increased use was also associated with attempts to distinguish between dogma and the study of the spiritual life as well as with an increasing emphasis on religious consciousness and the experiential. The foundation of *Revue d'Ascetique et de Mystique* in 1920 and the beginning of the continuing *Dictionnaire de Spiritualité* in 1932 further established the respectability of the term. In the years after the Second Vatican Council, the theological dictionary *Sacramentum Mundi* and its one-volume popular edition included a comprehensive article on the subject. More recently, a dictionary and a general introduction to the subject have been published in English as the result of ecumenical collaboration.[31]

Precisely because the word "spirituality," in its present sense, has a relatively short history, we are faced with a problem of translation when we attempt to explore how spirituality was viewed in different periods of Christian history. What precisely should we look for, and how can we avoid an unhelpful imposition of contemporary assumptions on the evidence we find? If we look back merely over the last hundred years, it soon becomes apparent that "spirituality" is not simply congruent with the older concepts of "spiritual theology" or "ascetical-mystical theology." If we extend our exploration further into the past, we will soon realize that defined concepts of any kind with regard to "the spiritual life," let alone with reference to a distinct discipline, have a limited history. Translation, therefore, is not merely a question of looking for terminology equivalent to "spirituality" in different ages. Philip Sheldrake states,

---

[31] Sheldrake, *Spirituality and History*, 36. See Geoffrey Wainwright, et al., *The Study of Christian Spirituality*.

Our understanding of what the word broadly seeks to express (that is, the theory and practice of the Christian life) has evolved as individuals and historical or cultural environments change.... The approach of traditional ascetical-mystical theology, or spiritual theology, over the last hundred years or so implied an agreed theological language in reference to the Christian life which no longer applies. The universal categories of the old theology textbooks were based largely on an approach to the truths of the Christian faith that was framed within logical and rigorously constructed theses.[32]

Spirituality grew detached through an a priori approach to doctrine. This

gave birth to a similarly structured theory of the spiritual life which was separated from the core of human experience and consequently was largely alienated from, for example, nature, the body and the feminine. In recent decades, there has been a paradigm shift in the general approach to theology towards a greater reflection on human experience as an authentic source of divine revelation.... This has brought about substantial changes in the way that the study of the Christian life has been conducted and, in particular, has facilitated a movement from the static concept of "spiritual theology" to the more fluid "spirituality."[33]

Sheldrake articulates that spirituality is dialogic, meaning that spiritual theory and practice operate on the frontier between contemporary experience and the tradition and do not simplistically apply the latter as the measure of the former. In other words, the contemporary problem of defining "spirituality" lies in the fact that it is not a single, trans-cultural category but is rooted within the lived

---

[32] Sheldrake, *Spirituality and History*, 32.
[33] Sheldrake, *Spirituality and History*, 33.

experience of God's presence in history—a history that is always specific.[34] Therefore, it is impossible to define spirituality in abstract terms apart from historical questions and attention to changes in theological presuppositions. Such changes can be seen as women, African Americans, the poor, and a diverse range of contexts began to shape theological discourse.

In the West, from the seventh to the twelfth centuries, literary theology developed almost exclusively within the confines of male religious houses. A notable liberation of women's spiritual experience has been associated with the shift toward a more human-inclusive and experiential approach to spirituality. This is important not only for women, but for Christian spirituality as a whole. A disembodied spirituality, which had problems not only with the body and material reality but with the feminine in particular (that most potent symbol of embodiment, not say of sexuality), was firmly rooted in theological concepts. These were dogmatic and thus free from emotion, objective, rational, and logical in contrast to the muddy waters of personal experience. To say that women's religious experience was caged within a male theology is more than to note that theological teaching was for so long dominated by men. Although, theoretically, theology was a priori, in practice the categories and tone expressed a male mentality. The result was a spirituality whose values included the individual and separateness and the quest for achievement, self-determination associated with dominance, control, and conquest—of the self and of the world. Such values inevitably led to a hierarchical conception of the human and spiritual life.

Consequently, the language of traditional spiritual theology tended to prefer images of ladders of perfection, the language of "stages" and detachment achieved by rules and formulae. The end in view was undivided love of God, which in fact implied being divided from large parts of the self and separated from created reality. In contrast, the liberation of women's experience has meant the reinforcement of other values, such as subjectivity, feelings, the relational, nurture, reverence, compassion, and the sacredness of life

---

[34] Sheldrake, *Spirituality and History*, 33.

and the earth. Although the shift in contemporary spirituality is not simply the result of this liberation (it is, to a degree, a precondition of it), there is no doubt that the explicit contribution of women to the debate about spirituality has offered a great deal to the whole field. For example, Maggie Ross has discussed what she understands to be the vision at the heart of the gospel, a vision shared by early Semitic (Syrian) Christians; at one time it was the focus around which institutional Christianity began to develop. Ross's vocation is to Christ's priesthood, not to function as part of the ordained secular power structure that currently organizes the church and regards itself as the church. Her discernment suggests that while there are a few clergy of singular priestly holiness, there are many more who may be ordained but evidence in their behavior that the meaning of priest is unknown to them. Their dedication is rather to power and expediency.[35]

Ross thinks there is a fluctuating middle ground between so-called academic theology, on the one hand, and practical pastoral training, on the other. The two have always informed each other. The dualism is based on a questionable epistemology, one that admits only "reason," that is, discursive, logical, and propositional (therefore, ultimately hierarchical and reductionist). In her work she attempts to interrelate large areas of thought not only to expose the models of power that underlie the development of certain doctrines, but also, and more importantly, to show how that power cheapens, trivializes, and ultimately belittles the fathomless mystery of kenotic life that is true Christian spirituality.

For some, the emphasis on experience as the starting point for spirituality is associated with what is experienced as a tendency to define spirituality in generic terms, that is, "spirituality as such" or "in general." In practice, spiritualities are specific and have particular religious or doctrinal referents. Such practice makes it possible to sift the authentic from the inauthentic in spirituality. There must be tests for the authenticity of spiritual experience based not only on empirical considerations but also on the revelation or foundational

---

[35] Maggie Ross, *Pillars of Flame* (San Francisco: Harper SanFrancisco, 1986).

beliefs of the religious tradition. This testing criterion addresses many concerns about what spirituality has to do with "ordinary" people who claim their own spiritual experiences as from God. Otherwise, one has no recourse to answer. What does one do when someone claims, "God told me to give you the word that you should marry me," or "a word from the Lord was given to me that I should devote the rest of my life to the U.S. military."

The way Western spirituality tends to test these words from the Lord is based more in rational explanation, dating back to the twelfth century and even more strikingly to the thirteenth century, which witnessed the birth of a more "scientific" understanding of the theological enterprise. The new theologian of scholasticism criticized the old theological method, which was limited to reading, reflecting, and commenting on traditional sources. The new theologians wanted to develop a more systematic and precise method of research based upon the increasing availability of the Greek philosophy of antiquity. Until the twelfth century, therefore, what we might call "spiritual theology" or "mystical theology" had continued, in the main, to appear in the context of collections of homilies or scriptural and patristic commentaries, although there were some exceptions to this general rule.[36]

---

[36] "Firstly, some writings appeared that were associated specifically with religious life, particularly with the new monastic or canonical communities which arose in the eleventh and twelfth centuries. These promoted a series of reflections on the way to God appropriate to reformed religious life. For example, there were the Customs of Guigo I composed for the Grand Chartreuse during the years 1121-28 as well as his Reflections on the interior life of the solitary. There were also Cistercian texts, such as the Carta Caritatis of Citreaux in 1114 and Bernard's Apologia for the cistercian emphasis on detachment and spiritual simplicity. Secondly, there were a small number of treatises on specifically spiritual topics which, however, also came into existence predominantly within the context of monastic renewal. For example, Guigo III of Chartreuse produced the *Scale of Perfection* which was a fairly systematic approach to God. traditional monastic lectio divina. William of St Thierry, a Benedictine turned Cistercian, wrote his Letter to the Bretheren of Mont-Dieu (often known as the Golden Epistle) for the Carthusians but it also encapsulates a vision of mystical theology. Although St. Bernard wrote on prayer and asceticism, and saw his teaching as valid for all Christians, we need to remember two things; that his spiritual doctrine cannot be separated from his overall theology, which is all of a

Writing on the spiritual life began to take new directions from the twelfth century forward, as the result of several factors. First, the spiritual life became separated from theology, although this process took some time. This related to the fact that theology as a whole began to be organized into different components.[37] Second, Pseudo-Dionysius's mystical theology reemerged. In the late fifth century, Christian doctrine began to flow together with certain Neo-Platonic elements in the writings of a theologian known as Pseudo-Dionysius, who for many centuries was thought to be the Pauline convert Denis (or Dionysisus) the Areopagite. Pseudo-Dionysius's *Mystical Theology* was not concerned with enumerating the means toward spiritual maturity with the technicalities of mystical union but rather explored the nature of the soul's surrender to God as the person passed beyond sign and concept to be fully grasped by the mystery of love and so be completely transformed. This is the beginning of speculative spiritual discourse in the sense that spirituality is not caught up in the individual's subjective experience, as we are wont to do in our Western context, but in the individual's movement toward union with God. In short, originally Christian spirituality did not assume individualism.

The shift of emphasis in medieval mysticism away from communal participation in the objective mystery of Christ (as Origen envisioned) toward the experiences of individual mystics as an identifiable group was clearly, in part, a result of the interest in

---

piece; that he took for granted that the monastery was the best place to put his teaching into practice. He remains, as Jean Leclercq describes him, essentially a doctor monasticus." Sheldrake, *Spirituality and History*, 41.

[37] "For example, in the thirteenth century, St Thomas Aquinas (who tried to retain the unity between loving contemplation and theological speculation) divided his Summa theologiae into parts. The first dealt with God as first principle, the second with God as the 'end' of creation, the final part with the Incarnate Word as the way to that 'end.' In other words, he effectively established the classical scholastic divisions of theology into dogma and moral theology. Most of what he had to say about the Christian life appeared in the second part as an aspect of moral theology." Sheldrake, *Spirituality and History*, 41.

Pseudo-Dionysius.[38] As a result of these factors, growth of interest in a distinct body of knowledge associated with the spiritual life was born. What has come to be known as a distinct Western body of knowledge known as spiritual theology is shaped primarily through individualism, spiritual direction of the individual, romantic love, and personal prayer. Some discussion of each will help emphasize the point of the Western understanding of spirituality in the medieval period as the individual's experience of God.

The Development of Western Spiritual Individualism

Medievalists have concentrated their attention on an increasing interest in the individual and in the realm of subjective feelings where individuality was most apparent. However, this needs careful qualification. The individual, in the modern sense of a unique person in isolation from group membership, was not discovered at this time. Yet there does seem to have been a new sense of the self, or of the inner mystery and inner human landscape. This change of individualistic perspective in Christian spirituality is at the heart of the questions of defining Christian spirituality. The broader the perspective, the greater the issue of coherence and the danger of subsuming spirituality into an interest in religion in general. Many contemporary writers would explicitly reject the limitation of spirituality to interiority. Rather, '"the spiritual life is the life of the whole person directed towards God.' For example, Rowan Williams rejects the notion that spirituality is merely the science of interpreting exceptional private experiences and suggests that 'it must now touch every area of human experience, the public and social, the

---

[38] However, there seem to be other reasons for this development. Some medievalists have noted the emergence, from about the twelfth century onwards of a new religious sensitivity of which practical, experiential mysticism was merely the most marked expression. The major intellectual and cultural movement known as the "twelfth-century Renaissance," which divides the early from the High Middle Ages also involved a shift of feeling and sensitivity which was at least as important as its new intellectual content.

painful, negative, even pathological byways of the mind, the moral and relational world.'"[39]

Contemporary theorists accept that once we cease to drive a wedge between sacred activities and the secular, or between the spiritual dimension of human existence and materiality, the issues become more complex. However, whatever the problems, contemporary spirituality is characterized more by an attempt to integrate human and religious values than by an exclusive interest in the component parts of "spiritual" growth, such as stages of prayer.

Although chapter four will primarily develop the role of spiritual direction as a more communal concept, a word should be said here as to how and why spiritual direction became an individualistic endeavor. The development of spiritual guidance was another phenomenon associated both with the rise of affective mysticism and the proliferation of new forms of Christian life, eremitical or community-oriented. Several important texts on the mystical way, such as *The Cloud of Unknowing*, were written (or purported to be) as treatises by directors for those under their guidance. Much of the writing that is known as the Rhineland school of mysticism arose from the developing ministry of guidance by Dominican friars among communities of contemplative women.

One cannot overlook the influence of what has come to be known as erotic love in the increasing prominence of individualism. The twelfth century witnessed a striking increase in the cultivation of the theme of love, both in religious circles and in secular culture. The degree to which the latter influenced religious writing or developments in mysticism cannot be settled definitively. Whatever the case, a preoccupation with *eros* was encouraged by the poetry and songs of troubadours, by the Arthurian myths and other romances. At the same time, love became a central theme for religious writers, particularly in the new Cistercian order. Many, like St. Bernard, turned their attention to the Old Testament book the Song of Songs as a contemplative text that offered a ready expression for a spirituality

---

[39] Williams, *Wound of Knowledge*, 2.

of intimacy. The Song of Songs became a major source of imagery for mystics and writers of mystical theology.

A further factor in the development for how spirituality became associated with individualism can be seen in the gradual systematic appropriation of meditation and prayer. Although people such as John of Fécamp and St. Anselm, in the eleventh century, produced collections and meditations, these were still aimed at providing material for traditional monastic *lectio divina*, or free-flowing, ruminative, and prayerful reading of Scripture. There was no attempt to be methodical. It was really the canons of St. Victor, in the twelfth century, already noted for their promotion of the influence of Pseudo-Dionysius, which tried to describe and formalize meditation as one of the activities of prayer with much greater precision than the monastic tradition put to that date. This gradually led to several ways of classifying meditation, which became more and more systematic but did not include a method in the strict sense. However, it was a result of these distinctions and schemes that there later developed the interest in methods of prayer and meditation.

Writings on methods of prayer rapidly increased from the fourteenth century onwards in the context of the movement of spiritual renewal, known as the *devotio moderna*, in Germany and the Low Countries. Its leading figure, Gerard Groote, composed a systematic treatise on the kinds of things on which to meditate. Other representatives of this movement, such as Florent Radeqijns, Gerard of Zutphen, and Jan Mombaer, further developed the methodical prayer. This technique of prayer developed the "science" of meditation and structured prayer, arranging groups of exercises day by day, week by week, and month by month. This tradition of methodical prayer gave rise to a considerable literature over the next few centuries—not merely in the Roman Catholic Church but, after the Reformation, in some Reformed communities as well.

In summary, the period from the twelfth century onward in the West saw a process of development in the approach to the spiritual life, which may be characterized as one of separation and division. There was, first, a division of spirituality from theology, of affectivity from knowledge. Second, there was a gradual limitation of interest to interiority or subjective spiritual experience. In other words, spirituality became separated from social praxis and ethics. Finally, there was a separation of spirituality from liturgy, the personal from the communal, expressed most graphically by a new attention to the structures of personal prayer and meditation. The practical context, of course, for the late-medieval believer was not to face God in isolation, but through communal experience, for example in the numerous religious confraternities. Through these divisions and separations, an interest developed in specific experiences and activities: prayer, contemplation, and mysticism. This was increasingly linked to theories about spiritual progress and growth. And growth was conceived more and more in terms of ascent, whereby the active life was merely a preparation for the contemplative and was thus viewed as a "lower" way. By the end of the Middle Ages, the "spiritual life" had increasingly moved to a marginal position in relation to culture as a whole. A more internalized, personal religious practice assumed an existence of its own and therefore demanded a new, specialized language.

To some extent the division between a "science" of the spiritual life and doctrine or ethics, begun in the later Middle Ages, was already well entrenched by the sixteenth and seventeenth centuries. We only have to contrast the approaches of Thomas Aquinas and Bonaventure, on the one hand, and the Carmelites Teresa of Avila and John of the Cross, Ignatius of Loyola, and Francis de Sales, on the other, to realize that, while the latter did not use the precise terms "ascetical" or "mystical" theology, they certainly showed clear signs of subscribing to a new discipline, separated from academic theology. The word "ascetical" is derived from the Greek *askesis*, which means how an athlete trains and practices.

It was the intense interest in the life of Christian perfection that developed in the course of the seventeenth century, especially in France, that led to this becoming an object of detailed study in the eighteenth and nineteenth centuries. It appears that the Jesuit Giovanni Battista Scaramelli, with his *Direttorio ascetico* and *Direttorio mistico*, was the first to establish the titles of "ascetical" and "mystical" theology in a way that subsequently became firmly established in Roman Catholic circles. During the following 150 years or so, the vocabulary of "Christian perfection" stabilized and a field defined as "spiritual theology" became well established. This was classically divided into ascetical theology, which dealt with the form and progress of the Christian life up to the beginnings of passive contemplation, and mystical theology, which analyzed further stages up to mystical union. The word "mystical" comes from the Greek *musterion*, by Pseudo-Dionysius, who named the ascent of the soul to union with God.

The approach of the manuals of ascetical and mystical theology was to seek to reduce the study of the Christian life to manageable categories, precise distinctions, and reliable definitions. This kind of precision turned into the static approach to theology, in general, lasting through the period up to the Second Vatican Council. The theological method used was primarily deductive because divine revelation and rational knowledge were assumed to be its principal sources. Unless universal principles governed the study of the spiritual life, it could not claim to be scientific within a scientific theology. The classical works of these genres tended to be divided between "principles" and "applications." Although defended as a distinct branch of theology, spiritual theology was subordinate to dogmatic theology, from which it derived its principles, and was frequently thought of as a subdivision of moral theology. The latter was primarily concerned with what was "of obligation" for all Christians, and the subdivision of spiritual theology went on to discuss what was "additional."

There were numerous written sources for spiritual theology in this period. Perhaps the most familiar were those written by A. A. Tanquerey (the most common textbook in Roman Catholic seminaries in the period before Vatican II), J. de Guibert, and R. Garrigou-Lagrange. There was a difference of opinion with regard to whether the spiritual life was fundamentally a unity or not. In the debate about the distinction or continuity between the "ordinary" (ascetical) way of Christian living and the "extraordinary" (mystical) way, Tanquerey and Garrigou-Lagrange may be taken as representatives of the two contrasting views.

For Tanquerey there was a fundamental division between ordinary growth in the moral life and the extraordinary gifts of mystical prayer. Ordinary life passed through stages, in a gradual progression toward the fulfillment of the counsels of perfection, by means of observing the commandments and ascetical practices. The mystical state was reserved for a very few, and the study of it focused on special experiences and extraordinary phenomena. In contrast, Garrigou-Lagrange emphasized the unity and continuity of the Christian life in all its aspects. Mystical prayer was a goal to which all were called and for which they were offered God's grace. He agreed that mystical phenomena were extraordinary but was not happy with the limitation of mysticism merely to these.

The phrase "spiritual theology" came into vogue with de Guibert, precisely to bypass this controversy about continuity or discontinuity. Such a term appeared more comprehensive than "ascetical" and "mystical," yet it is questionable whether it does justice to what most people understand by spirituality today. Whether distinguished as ascetical or mystical theology or united as spiritual theology, the approach to the spiritual life that held the field up to the Second Vatican Council had several features with which a contemporary theology would be uncomfortable. First, while not crudely dualistic, this approach often conceived of the supernatural life as distinguishable from or grafted on to the natural. Consequently, it was possible to identify specifically spiritual areas for exclusive treatment. Second, while differing on the classifications and distinctions in the spiritual life, spiritual theologians saw the journey toward perfection in terms of degrees or separate stages. Thus, the ultimately mysterious nature of human experience and existence was reduced to detailed analysis according to predetermined general laws. Finally, there was a tendency to be individualistic, to ignore the social dimensions of the Christian spiritual life, and to reduce the ecclesial aspects of spirituality to participation in the sacraments. Although, in general, this approach withered after Vatican II, there appeared as late as 1980, rather surprisingly, an English-language volume of spiritual theology on the old model, which differed little from Tanquerey and which, apart from some references, appeared to ignore any developments in theology since the Vatican Council.

A writer such as Louis Bouyer must be distinguished carefully from this kind of manual theology. His approach is illustrated mainly through *An Introduction to Spirituality*. Bouyer's work differed substantially from the older manuals in recognizing developments in liturgical theology and biblical study and in his impatience with a multitude of classifications and distinctions. He was also more open to the spirituality of traditions other than the Roman Catholic tradition. Although Bouyers's approach is now dated, it formed an important bridge between the constraints of a narrow neo-scholastic theological approach to spirituality and a more scriptural, liturgical, and ecumenical approach after Vatican II.

One could simply answer that the Western church no longer shares the same cosmologies espoused in patristic, medieval, and modern contexts; therefore, spirituality means an entirely different thing in a postmodern world. However, this argument fails to articulate how Christian spirituality relates to nonviolence. The tradition of just war further complicates this problem.

Western Christian Justification of Violence

As we have learned with Western Christian spirituality, so now we learn with Western violence that the final decision as to the justice of any conflict and the possibility of conscientious participation usually rests upon the individual. Just war points to the problem that if Christian spirituality addresses personal spirituality only to the extent that it enables communal practices of nonviolence, then how can Christianity ever justify the use of violence?

The evolution of the just war concept has its roots in classical antiquity. Plato formulated a code of just war although Aristotle phrased it as "just war." Plato, living in the context of Hellenic wars between city-states, wrestled with the problematic thought that Greeks would wish to exterminate fellow Greeks. He helped to establish the parameters within which rational people would wage war as the ultimate way of settling disputes. The just war was meant to vindicate justice and restore peace. Besides Plato and Aristotle, just war theory is traced back to the Roman orator and statesman Cicero. Ambrose of Milan introduced Cicero's ideas into Christian theology; subsequent church fathers Augustine and Aquinas further developed just war theology as a part of the Christian ethos; and Luther and Calvin carried them into the Protestant Reformation. Pacifism, as a Christian doctrine, was enacted only later through church groups such as Anabaptists and Quakers. But each of these groups gave different emphases to understandings of nonviolence. These marginalized groups are important variations in the historical tradition of the church, which has at times operated firmly in the service of the rulers and at other times struggled to distance itself from oppressive rulers by affirming an alternative liberating tradition.

In Christian history, three attitudes toward war exist: pacifism, just war, and holy war. The early church, persecuted by a pagan state, was pacifist until the time of Constantine, when, through the early church's close association with the state and the threat of the barbarian invasions, Christians took over the classical world's doctrine of just war, especially as St. Ambrose and St. Augustine added Christian elements to understanding just war.[40] In order to fight in a war, the motive had to be love, and the clergy, both secular and monastic, were exempt from fighting in war until the Crusades of the Middle Ages. Just war seems to have become an official church doctrine through the rise of Renaissance Italy's city-states. Perhaps the chief justification for war came through the Reformation, which precipitated wars on religion. For example, Anglicans and Lutherans accepted just war and by and large still do today. As the church grew complicit with colonization in the eighteenth and nineteenth centuries, the interpretation of peace changed on the basis of European churches now defining what should represent peace around

---

[40] It is interesting that Augustine said that justice was nothing but robbery on a large scale. Conditions of just war are also in Summa Theologia of Aquinas: Legitimate authority by due and solemn warning, self defense, restoration of justice, punishment for justice, a just cause (end result will justify evil means).

the world. Then the twentieth century came with two world wars, in which the church's three positions of just war, pacifism, and holy war resurfaced again, but in a different way. Now, the twenty-first century is about to commence a third world war on "terrorism" or "an Axis of Evil."[41] In light of this tragic history, Archbishop Desmond Tutu is helpful in describing his own confusion:

> There is much puzzlement in the black community. Not only did the West go to war with the approval of the church, it lauded to the skies the Underground Resistance movement during World War II and regarded a Dietrich Bonhoeffer as a modern day Christian martyr and saint (and I believe rightly) even though he was involved in a plot to assassinate Hitler, the head of his home country for which involvement he was executed. Most Western countries have their history written in blood. The USA became independent after the thirteen colonies had fought the American War of Independence. But when it comes to the matter of black liberation the West and most of its church wake up and find themselves gone all pacifist.[42]

Desmond Tutu and Just War

Tutu seems to be an adherent of just war theory. As a disciple of Tutu, I always found this to be a disturbing position. Upon more discussion of his position, however, perhaps the reader may make sense of how Tutu's position makes sense in light of the tragic situation of apartheid in South Africa. Tutu constantly illustrates his efforts of seeking nonviolence, but he explains that he often found himself feeling as though there was little alternative to changing those who

---

[41] A phrase made popular by George W. Bush

[42]Tutu, Addresses "Violence and the Church," June 1987.

controlled an apartheid state than through use of violence. Tutu explains:

> And yet how strident is the opposition overwhelmingly from whites to economic sanctions. We blacks cannot vote. Now we must not invoke the non-violent methods which are likely to be the most effective. Then what is left? If sanctions should not be allowed or being applied, fail, then there is no other way left but to fight for the right to be human and to be treated as such. Can someone show us a different conclusion?[43]

In this quotation the reader finds the summation of Tutu's Christian realism, in that the full acknowledgment is made that nonviolence is the Christian norm; however, how does one translate this norm into a hostile world? Other evidence of Tutu's acceptance of the legitimate use of force comes through his following statement: "Should the West fail to impose economic sanctions, it would then be justifiable in my view for blacks to try to overthrow an unjust system violently. But I myself am committed to the way of bringing an end to this tyranny by peaceful means. Should this option fail, the low-intensity civil war I referred to at the beginning of this essay will escalate into a full-scale war."[44]

Again, Tutu is helpful in explaining his complex position that nonviolence is the Christian norm and yet why he would later articulate just war theory. He states, "The peace for which we long is not merely an absence of war or a passive state of tranquility. Peace is the active harmony where all things work together for good."[45] Although I am a disciple of Tutu, I believe that in Christian spirituality, any conceptualization of just war is anachronistic if we

---

[43]Tutu, Addresses "Violence and the Church," June 1987.

[44]Tutu, "Freedom Fighters or Terrorists?" 77; Tutu, Addresses "Violence and the Church," June 1987.

[45]Tutu, "Faith," in *The New World Order*, Sundeep Waslekar (ed.) (New Delhi: Konark Publishers, 1991) 177.

are to unlearn the self-fulfilling prophecy of violence. This requires Christians to constantly practice peace. In other words, talk of just war originally meant something much different than the way we want to use it today. Theologically, the early church expected God's kingdom to dawn imminently amidst the world; it faced a hostile government that sought to eradicate Christianity as a subversive influence in the Roman Empire.

For early Christians, the pertinent question was whether or not to take up arms, either in self-defense or in the service of the state. In the post-Constantinian era, on the other hand, Christians readily fought for the empire under the insignia of Christ. The theological question had changed to what constituted a just war. This theological question has never been answered. How could any Christian formed in the Sermon on the Mount envision a constitution of just war? Christians are formed to make peace, and as Tutu believes, "Peace is achieved through active cooperation."[46] A theological imperative was the establishment of criteria in terms of which a distinction could be made between wars with a just cause and end, and wars of material greed, national pride, vindictiveness, power, and the like. Tutu provides the criteria for just war:[47]

---

[46]Tutu, Foreward, A Gift of Peace, John Hartom & Lisa Blackburn (eds.) Imagine Render, Michigan Art Education Association.

[47]Five criteria of Just War:

1. There must be a just cause

Augustine believed there could only be a defensive war, but it could be aggressive if the aim was to restore what was taken unjustly. Luther was an augustinian. For Calvin, war was a means to ensure peace and social stability, but if a ruler brought chaos then rebellion against such a ruler was in order by a magistrate. Lastly, just cause includes the protection of the innocent, restoration of rights, and re-establishment of just order.

2. There must be a just end.

What is the likelihood of "success" of the war? Barth believed that where the community or person believes before God that the ulitmate goal of war needs to be fought, the cost cannot be regarded as a decisive factor. Of course, blacks and whites would read costs and end differently. Simply put, this criterion means that a just end involves having peace and justice as a goal, rather than mere vengeance or satisfaction of the lust of power.

We try to use the very strict set of criteria that we use to determine when it would be justifiable for Christians to go to war, the so-called "just war" theory.... According [to just war theory] once the criteria have been satisfied, e.g., have all other nonviolent means been exhausted, is the cause just, are the prospects of success good, will the situation that results be better than that which it is intended to replace, are the methods just (in the case of war, will every effort be made to ensure that innocent civilians are not unnecessarily injured and the war is to be declared by a competent authority)?[48]

Soon, a related question emerged concerning the responsibility of Christians regarding tyrannical rule. To what extent were they permitted or obligated as Christians to resort to arms to remove the tyrant? For example, young white males (usually English-speaking white males) asked whether it was theologically legitimate for them to fight in the South African Defense Force since it was involved in the military occupation of Namibia, cross-border raids, and war in the townships. These young white males articulated their protest against being drafted into the South African Defense Force in terms of traditional just war theory. Regarding this matter, Tutu states,

Many resisters, for their part understood how the South African Defense Force was used as a military police within our townships and neighborhoods, and understood the strategic importance of creating an alternative within their ranks....

---

3. Just means ought to be used.

Restraint of weapons, minimizing of suffering and death and the atrocities of war are in order. This is the most difficult criteria to put into practice.

4. War must be a last resort.

5. War must be declared by a legitimate authority.

Yet Augustine, Aquinas, Luther, and Calvin agree that the time comes when the tyrant should no longer be obeyed, if the will of God, the tyrant should be removed. But Villa-Vicencio asks the important question, who is responsible for this removal?

[48]Tutu, Addresses "Violence and the Church," June 1987.

People—and young people specifically—are less and less willing to be used as cannon fodder, fighting to uphold corporate interests or the rule of the elites.... The gap between the countries of the south and north—in areas of wealth, education, health care, etc.—seems only to widen. And understanding of this gap, and its economic and colonial origins, can only help us to formulate solidarity and create a more cooperative internationalism. The children of war, through their networking, summits, and informal dialogues, have already begun this process. We are called upon to follow their lead.[49]

In other words, the problem of defining a just use of violence depends on who is interpreted as oppressor and victim—as terrorist or freedom fighter. After all, President Nelson Mandela was once described as a terrorist and even went to prison under what was known in South Africa as the Terrorist Act to protect the state.

Tutu explains this complexity of who gets to define the just use of violence further: "Polarization in which police and army used against civilian population demanded a response, and yet we are called to beat our swords into plowshares. St. Francis had made us instruments of God's peace."[50] As I have sought in my display of Christian spirituality above, the interpretation of oppressor and victim can never be fully separated if the *raison 'detre* of Christian spirituality is the creation of community. If such spirituality does not truly represent the church, then Christianity will always be individualistically used to justify violence from the perspective of the oppressor. And the cycle of violence will continue from the perspective of the oppressed.

Rewritten from the perspective of the oppressed, theology is rediscovering the significance of traditional theological teaching on

---

[49]Tutu, Draft of Foreword for 1993 Children of War Peace Calendar, War Resisters League, March 13, 1992.

[50] Tutu, Handwritten Undated Address, "Conscientious Objection," Tutu testifies before Court Martial.

who in fact can be named as tyrannical rulers. For example, those who are considered terrorists challenge the assumption that we live in a world at peace. What is terrorism? Terrorism, according to the U.S. Department of Defense, is the unlawful use of force against individuals or property with the intention of intimidating societies for ideological purposes. This definition assumes that wars can be fought by states only. But one person's terrorism is another's martyrdom. For example, what constitutes terrorism, guerilla warfare, or legitimate defense? Those who are considered terrorists challenge the assumption that we live in a world at peace. Tutu describes this duplicity of Western nations in his own South African context when apartheid was still the official rule:

> There is, however, no unequivocal Western support for black South Africans who have for decades tried to change the unjust rule in South Africa non-violently. The white minority government of South Africa cannot be called remotely democratic when seventy-three percent of the population is constitutionally excluded from the electoral process. In this situation one can only understand why some oppressed people resort to the armed struggle. Yet the West castigates them. President Reagan calls the Contras freedom fighters, while labeling the ANC terrorists.[51]

The United States seems in no better position to demonstrate a lawful use of force. Tutu explains further: "The USA supports quite vigorously supports those called Contras in Nicaragua who seek to overthrow a valid government legally decked in what independent observers considered to be free and fair elections. The Reagan administration also supports Dr Jonas Savimbi and his Unita forces which are bent on toppling the MPLA Luanda government."[52]

Tutu's insight in Western bias raises an interesting question: When Christians go to war, what are we defending? The answer

---

[51]Tutu, "Freedom Fighters or Terrorists?" 77.
[52]Tutu, "Freedom Fighters or Terrorists?" 73-74.

usually leaves Christians embarrassed, especially if such Christians are committed to the spirituality of the church in which the formation of community is essential. In Christian spirituality, there can be no unconditional obedience to the principle of violence. Just war assumes one can separate the difference between noncombatants from combatants on the basis of universal evils, but without universal criteria for good and evil there is no way to respond to moral anarchy in war situations. In other words, a double standard morality always exists in just war criteria. Tutu illustrates with the example of a formerly oppressed nation of Afrikaners:

> Let it also be remembered that one of the first acts of the Nationalist government after being elected to power in 1948 was to release Robey Leibrandt who had been sentenced to death for high treason against the Smuts government. Today we are ruled by those guilty of such behaviour who have the gall to read us lessons on patriotism while espousing the virtue of the rule of law and the rejection of all violence.[53]

Christian ethicists such as Stanley Hauerwas disagree with a methodology by which to adjudicate universal evils; namely, Christians respond in war situations not on the basis of universal principles of what is right or wrong nor on the basis of assuming a liberal ideal of freeing a world free of war, but on the basis of the Christian way of life determined by the church, not on the basis of universal evils espoused in just war theory. As Christians, we are a particular kind of people with particular behaviors that should always increase community. Therefore, when one determines a spirituality of war or peace, what is determined is a particular spirituality in which faith commitments are made explicit. Is there an explicit commitment to community as taught and practiced by Jesus? If so, we return to the original question of this paragraph: When Christians go to war, what are we defending? Is it so much that we are defending the justice of anyone but the individual in the Western world? As Hauerwas teaches

---

[53]Tutu, "Freedom Fighters or Terrorists?" 73-74.

us, "People don't go to war because of their evil but because of their loves." And we in the Western world love ourselves the most. For the church, however, to practice peace we must realize that our main love and obligation is to a person who would rather be crucified than take up arms; herein is our difficulty to live peaceably in a world at war.

For Hauerwas, the difficulty is to live peaceably in a world at war. It is difficult to live peaceably because our loves give slant to our vision as to how to behave in the world. Our loves create national interests and motivations for war. In addition, our loves perpetuate the double-standard methodology of believing in justice for all, while justice is practiced by those in power. Tutu displays the double standard: "Many have called on the ANC to renounce violence and have not directed similar demands to the South African government which has destabilised the neighbouring countries. Is it because the perpetrators are white and the victims of injustice black that this selective morality holds sway?"[54]

People don't go to war because of their evil but because of their loves. Herein is the problem with just war theory; namely, it creates a different set of criteria for what Christian spirituality looks like from what Jesus taught in the Sermon on the Mount. For Jesus, the spiritual person is indeed in the world, helping the world to practice peacemaking, meekness, purity, and the kingdom of God. For those who think Jesus' Sermon on the Mount is idealistic or irrelevant, their criteria for living in the world is usually about what is best for the survival of the individual; therefore, heroism becomes the world's chief virtue. We learn from Hauerwas, however, that the problem with heroism is that its unpredictable and successful wars cannot be fought this way. Heroism is an example of mediocre soldiers having the opportunity to shine through as heroes. You should never fight wars for ideals because then they become limitless. The problem with democracies is that you have citizen soldiers who do not know how to fight limited wars. In war there is an organic escalation in which you have moral adjudication lacking in a people incapable of fighting a realistic war.

---

[54]Tutu, Addresses "Violence and the Church," June 1987.

So far, I have presented a short discussion of the rationale of violence in the Western church. The discussion has been easy for me to articulate as I am an advocate of unequivocal nonviolence and believe such a position is the essence of the practice of Christian spirituality. As we all know, however, such a position of unequivocal nonviolence is not assumed by all Christians. More difficult for me to consider, unequivocal nonviolence is not the position of some I consider saints, such as Desmond Tutu:

> Is Violence Justifiable to Topple an Unjust System? I am theologically conservative and traditional. I think the dominant position of my church regarding violence is this: We regard all violence as evil (the violence of an unjust system such as apartheid and the violence of those who seek to overthrow it). That is why we have condemned "necklacing" and car bombs, as well as instances of violence perpetrated by the government and the security forces. This does not mean, however, that the mainstream tradition of the church does not reluctantly allow that violence may in certain situations be necessary. The just war theory...makes this point clearly.[55]

As I have mentioned, Tutu's position on the legitimate use of force challenges what is at the heart of my perception of Christian spirituality. Tutu's vital leadership in South Africa's history, when there could be no official black leadership, forced him into being the sole voice able to articulate pluralism and individual rights, the corrupt public discourse of South Africa at that time. In light of the oppressive and exclusivist discourse of apartheid, Tutu's ecclesiology readily accepts pluralist tendencies. Tutu states,

> One of the first things we should acknowledge is the cultural, religious, and racial pluralism of our day. Consequently, we must be as a Church, as Christians, to make our contribution to the establishment of democracy as part of a

---

[55]Tutu, "Freedom Fighters or Terrorists?" 76.

cooperative venture. The days are past when we operated as if we were the only pebbles on the beach. It was exhilarating for us in South Africa when we marched in Cape Town in September of 1989 to walk with arms linked with a Jewish rabbi on one side and a Muslim imam on the other. That united front forged between peoples of different faiths and ideologies made us more robust as we faced a formidable adversary in the brutal apartheid regime. We must build coalitions and forge alliances. We as Christians should also know that we cannot produce a constitutional blueprint which can be stamped as Christian par excellence. We can say that there is a broad spectrum of options ranging from those barely enshrining the values of the kingdom of God to those which most nearly embody those values and principles.[56]

In other words, in order to understand Tutu's position of just war, one must be fully located in the context of South African apartheid. One must then ask the following question: To what extent could a spirituality of nonviolence become intelligible in an apartheid society? For example, in the South African context, Tutu states,

The elimination of violence is directly related to the elimination of state and institutional oppression. This is seen nowhere more clearly than in a rare exchange of views between P. W. Botha and Nelson Mandela in 1985. Botha offered Mandela his freedom on condition that he reject violence as a political instrument. "I am surprised at the conditions that the government wants to impose on me," Mandela replied. "It was only when all other forms of resistance were no longer open to us that we turned to armed struggle. Let Botha show that he is different to Malan, Strijdom and Verwoerd. Let him say he will dismantle

---

[56]Tutu: "Postcript: To Be Human Is To Be Free," 314.

apartheid.... Let him guarantee free political activity so that
the people may decide who will govern them."[57]

For Tutu, it is not so much a question of his own
acknowledgment of a spirituality of nonviolence, which he maintains;
it became more of a question of being a responsible hybrid leader of
spirituality and politics in the tragic circumstances of apartheid South
Africa, in which the only worldview was, at best, holy war. Tutu's
genius was in showing that the primary violence in South Africa was
the violence of apartheid, a context in which he was called upon to
lead nonviolently, although realistically.[58] Tutu states,

> We must be clear in our stance about violence. The pri-
> mary violence is apartheid. The Government and its sup-
> porters provide the primary violence and terrorism in South
> Africa. But there is the violence on our side. I myself
> condemn all violence as always evil, but I hold too that there
> may come a time when it would be justifiable to use violence
> to overthrow an unjust regime. That is the traditional and
> conservative position of the church. We must prepare people
> to be disciplined in nonviolent action, to disobey unjust
> laws.[59]

Having been a student of Tutu's for about fifteen years, I am
only now beginning to make sense of his complex positions on just
war. This is complex because I believe Tutu to be a de facto
nonviolent resister, and yet a public Christian realist. His following
position on the death penalty helps me explain. In the Lusaka
Statement of the World Council of Churches in May 1987, Tutu
states that he abhors all forms of violence. Tutu continues,

---

[57] *Weekly Mail* article quoted in Villa-Vicencio, 99.
[58] Tutu, "Preamble," 11. See also "Evolution of Apartheid," 10; "Why We Must
Oppose Apartheid."
[59] Tutu, "Koinonia II"

It is important too to point to another form of state violence—the death penalty. I am fundamentally opposed to capital punishment. That is why I appealed for clemency to President Rene of Seychelles when South African mercenaries led by Mr. Hoare tried to engineer a coup in that island and were sentenced to death. Far too many of those in the condemned cell are blacks who tend to fall foul of many laws since they are the victims of so many unfortunate socioeconomic and political circumstances.[60]

Regarding capital punishment, Tutu believes it is erroneous based on a kind of society he envisions the church to be. He states,

Life is a gift from God, and it is sacrilegious to take that life away especially as a judicial act. It seems a nonsense to hold that we have reverence for life and punish those who destroy life by ourselves taking life away. It seems to me that in the kind of society we envision, capital punishment would be taboo. It has not proved its efficacy as a deterrent and brutalizes society which becomes increasingly violent and human life is seen and treated as cheap.[61]

In light of this position on judicial violence, Tutu believes that "sanctions have been the strategy of those who do not have the power of the ballot box and who do not want to use violence."[62] Here, Tutu's genius is in his narration both of the realism of a violent world as well as the narration of nonviolence. He provides this example:

Given the negative results achieved by non-violent protest and resistance it can well be asked how blacks, even at this late hour, can still talk of non-violent methods. Yet they

---

[60]Tutu, Addresses "Violence and the Church," June 1987.

[61]Tutu, "Postcript: To Be Human Is To Be Free," 317.

[62] Tutu, "Church and Prophecy in South Africa Today," *Essex Papers in Theology and Society*, Published by the Centre for the Study of Theology in the University of Essex, 1991, 10.

continue to use such means in stay-aways, in consumer boycotts which have knocked some sense into the heads of white businessmen, and in the rent boycott that has been maintained in many black townships. To this the authorities responded in their usual mailed-fist way. For example, in one area of Soweto the youth erected barricades to stop the security forces from evicting those who refused to pay rent. The police went indiscriminately into homes in the area, ordered the children into the streets and beat them. When the children ran away, they shot them. I went to one such home, where a thirteen-year old boy had been shot dead. His younger brother who had been shot in the stomach was in a critical condition in hospital. The stunned mother sat silently on her chair. She kept wiping her eyes but there were no tears. I tried to talk to her about the love of God and silently asked, "How long, oh Lord?"[63]

Even though Tutu believes one should use all nonviolent means of protest, how does Tutu's spirituality of peacemaking maintain its position when he seems to confess that nonviolent means can never be exhausted, and yet he appears to consent to the necessary evil of "just war"?

Tutu believes there are "remarkable" Christians who believe that no one is ever justified in using violence, even against the most horrendous evil. These are "pacifists," who believe that the gospel of the cross effectively rules out anyone taking up the sword, however just the cause. We hear this in Tutu's own words: "I admire these persons." Tutu states, "Sadly, I must confess that I am made of far less noble stuff."[64] Further, he confesses, "I am not in Gandhi's league."[65] In another statement, Tutu claims, "I am a lover of peace and I try to work for justice because only thus do I believe we could

---

[63]Tutu, "Freedom Fighters or Terrorists?" 75-76.

[64]Tutu, Addresses "Violence and the Church," June 1987.

[65] Catherine Ingram, Interview with Desmond Tutu, Feature Story, Buddhist Peace Fellowship, Fall 1989, 279.

ever hope to establish a durable peace."[66] And finally, he says, "I have agreed to testify before this court-martial because I do hold strong views on the basis of my understanding of the teaching of the Holy Bible and the doctrines and tradition of the church of God as well as the practice to be found in most democratic countries. I will also want to say something in the context of the border war currently being waged on the Christian view of the so-called just war. The unswerving teaching of the Christian church is that a person ought always to obey his conscience."[67] Gandhi is helpful here as he was fond of saying in his old age that his remaining obsession was with the truth. How does one obey the call of truth from moment to moment, no matter how inconsistent it may appear? Gandhi's commitment was to truth, despite its seemingly inconsistent incarnations.

In light of what appears to be inconsistent incarnations of truth, Tutu cites the narratives of God creating human beings in God's own image—that is, freedom, which is an indispensable ingredient of moral responsibility. For Tutu, Jesus always challenges persons to opt to follow him or desert him, to obey him or reject him. We are not robots. In this light, Tutu refers to the parable of the prodigal son, whose conscience developed, although slowly, and needed not to be violated in its development. So, too, St. Paul teaches us in the New Testament that one should allow the ongoing development of conscience concerning food offered to idols. Paul teaches that those who are wise know de facto that there are no such things as idols (that is, idolatry is that which mimics the truth of God) and so can eat this food without spiritual defilement (1 Cor. 8). There are others, however, for whom to eat is to violate their conscience and so to sin. Spiritual decisions are based as far as possible on a sound understanding of all the factors that are relevant to the subject under review. As we shall soon discuss in chapter four, this is why spiritual direction becomes a crucial practice of peacemaking.

---

[66]Tutu, Addresses "Violence and the Church," June 1987.

[67] Tutu, Handwritten Undated Address, "Conscientious Objection," Tutu testifies before Court Martial.

It is from such biblical exegesis that Tutu has come to understand
how one can understand the use of violence on a nation-state level.
One cannot impose spiritual growth on communities; instead, like the
prodigal son, one must allow spiritual maturity to develop naturally
and in due season. More specifically, this exegesis applies to his
position on conscientious objection in the following way. Tutu
believes, based on the above rationale of the freedom of development,
that space and time must always be allowed for Christian maturity.
For Tutu, this means that there is a legitimate Christian principle that
persons are obliged to obey their conscience. This legitimacy is
modeled in most normal democratic countries, where conscription
obtains provision and where space and time are made for
conscientious objectors by the provision of an alternative form of
national service.[68] Tutu states further,

> In the same vein we must insist that the Gospel of Jesus
> Christ demands that each person should obey his conscience
> and that this imperative implies an inalienable right to be able
> to do so. It is pernicious in the extreme therefore for the state
> to force people to violate their consciences, especially for a
> state that claims to be Christian. We must as churches insist
> on the right to conscientious objection to participate in war
> and therefore urge the authorities to provide as a matter of
> considerable urgency for alternative forms of national service
> which need not be less demanding in effort and courage than
> military service. We must salute those persons such as Charles
> Yetas, Peter Moll, Richard Steele and others who at great cost
> to themselves have believed that they must obey their
> Christian consciences.[69]

---

[68] Tutu, Handwritten Undated Address, "Conscientious Objection," Tutu testifies
before Court Martial.

[69] Tutu, "General Secretary's Report to National Conference of the SACC," 1982.

So, for Tutu, just war is intelligible as it hinges on the conscience of a person's development; such a conscience, however, must be intense enough to deal with the reality and inevitability of violence.

Before one concludes entirely that Tutu is a just warrior, one must fully understand Tutu's theological assumptions as I have tried to do through Tutu's biblical exegesis of spiritual growth. More particularly, such an understanding of spiritual growth for Tutu depends upon the character of the community in which the Christian individual is to grow. Tutu explains,

> Trying to make sense of the experience of a particular and definite community of believers in the light of God's revelation of who He is, the cardinal reference point being the man Jesus Christ. Engaged theology is one done with passion and sometimes not paying too much attention to the niceties and delicacies.... Why you see, what you apprehend, depend so much on who you are, on where you are.... When blacks—after many years during which their cautious protest was consistently ignored—opted in desperation for armed struggle, whites dubbed them "terrorists," which meant they could be ruthlessly imprisoned, hanged or shot. The will to be free is not, however, defeated by even the worst kind of violence. Such repressive violence has only succeeded in throwing South Africa into a low-intensity civil war which threatens to escalate into a high-intensity war.[70]

How, then, does one make sense of a saint like Desmond Tutu and his apparent avowal that just war is sometimes necessary? Despite the obvious answer that such sense has been commonly assumed, as St. Augustine and St. Ambrose also espouse just war, I think one makes such sense through how Tutu understands himself and his context of what was apartheid South Africa. Tutu understands himself first and foremost as a church leader, not as a politician. Unlike Martin Luther

---

[70]Tutu, "Freedom Fighters or Terrorists?" 72.

King Jr., Tutu had no legal means by which to appeal for equality of all people:

> What then? I believe that we do have an outside chance that a negotiated settlement could be reached reasonably peacefully if the international community intervene decisively with effective pressure on the South African government to lift the state of emergency, to remove the troops from the black townships, to release all detainees and political prisoners, and to urban black political organizations.[71]

The only appeal for Tutu was the international community. One could even make the argument that Tutu's appeal was, in essence, first to the catholic (universal or international) church and then to the good will of international nation-states. In a letter to Tutu, Rune Forsbeck, general secretary of the Swedish Ecumenical Council, wrote,

> Our dream is that governments around the world will one day finance peace services in their respective countries, and that eventually the UN will be able to take responsibility for these services on a global basis.... In order to make it work, though, huge financial resources must be tapped. This autumn we plan to go out with an appeal to people of goodwill here in Sweden to support Global Peace Service by donating a sum of money, the equivalent of the cost of one lunch, each week. [Tutu responds on paper with handwritten notes.] "We have seen quite breathtaking examples of 'people power' when citizens, often downtrodden for decades, have said 'enough is enough' as they have paraded and demonstrated in the streets massing up against tanks and guns with empty hands or flowers.... We need those who will defuse tense situations and

---

[71]Tutu, Addresses "Violence and the Church," June 1987.

to resolve conflict, and those who will tell us how to cultivate cultures of tolerance."[72]

We see such further appeal to the international community, as Tutu states, "I call for sanctions as a last chance for relatively nonviolent resolution."[73] This means that the last chance for peaceful change for true reconciliation which will come with repentance and justice, "is if the international community is ready to apply effective political, diplomatic but above all economic pressure."[74] Furthermore, "International action and international pressure are our last chance."[75] Tutu states, "If we do not bring about an end to the violence of apartheid soon through the intervention of the international community, as some of us want, then obviously there will be an escalation of violence which will spill over from South Africa into other countries. That is why, when the United Nations says that apartheid is a threat to world peace, it is not just an empty slogan."[76] Tutu concludes, "International action and international pressure are among the few non-violent options left. And yet how strident is the opposition to economic sanctions. Blacks cannot vote. We are driven therefore to invoke a non-violent method which we believe is likely to produce the desired result. If this option is denied us, what then is left? if sanctions should fail there is no other way but to fight."[77]

This appeal to the international community means that Tutu never tried to articulate a systemic justification for war in political discourse; rather, he was always about the articulation of a spirituality of community that could ultimately disinfect apartheid. Such a system has indeed made the church complicit in the sins of nation-states that

[72]Tutu, Preface for a booklet in support of a Global Peace Service, Published by the Swedish Ecumenical Council, August 30, 1991.
[73]Tutu, handwritten, undated.
[74]Tutu, "Christmas Letter 1" 1985-1986, 5f.
[75]Tutu, Addresses "Violence and the Church," June 1987.
[76]Ingram, Interview with Desmon Tutu, 279.
[77]Desmond Tutu, "Freedom Fighters or Terrorists?" in C. Villa-Vicencio (ed.), *Theology and Violence*, 76-77.

adhered to colonialism and the legitimacy of state violence. Therefore, Tutu never saw himself as speaking for the state; instead, his speech was based in the theology and spirituality of the church. As Tutu advocates in his quotation below, he believes in an "engaged theology" that compels him into the world. He states,

> I think what I am trying to do is give an example of engaged theology.... Events such as cross-border raids as in strikes on Livingstone and Maputo, the bomb blast outside of the Johannesburg Magistrate's Court, explosion of the South African van outside a house in Gaborone, Cosatu strikers shot by police during the strike against the South African Transport Services, and "routine" deaths associated with repression in South Africa cannot be theologised about in a value-free or academic manner. Engaged theology cannot be neutral. It is one done with passion.[78]

Secondly, one must come to grips with how Tutu acted as a church agent in the midst of the political context of apartheid. This context is further complicated by the theological justification of apartheid by white South Africans. In such a context, according to Tutu, "It is necessary to underline this fact because many seem unaware that black South Africans through their political organizations such as first the ANC and later the PAC used conventional nonviolent means such as petitions, delegations, demonstrations, protests, boycotts, were the most drastic focus of resistance to which blacks resorted."[79] In other words, political and theological language fused together in apartheid South Africa, and Christians were legitimizing the use of force to kill each other.[80] One can see such inconsistency for how Christians justified killing each

---

[78]Tutu, "Freedom Fighters or Terrorists?" in *Theology & Violence: The South African Debate*, Charles Villa-Vicencio (ed.) (Johannesburg: Skotaville), 1987, 71.

[79]Tutu, "Freedom Fighters or Terrorists?" 73.

[80] See my discussion of this through why Tutu articulates Ubuntu in my book, Michael Battle, *Reconciliation: The Ubuntu Theology of Desmond Tutu* (Cleveland: The Pilgrim Press, 1997).

other through Tutu and Allan Boesak's encounter with F. W. de Klerk, who also declares himself to be Christian. Tutu states,

> I need do no more than tell a story about the first meeting which church leaders had with President F. W. de Klerk in October 1989, shortly after he became State President. During the course of the meeting, the President referred to the task of Government as one of maintaining law and order. Dr Allan Boesak dissented: "No, Mr President," he said, "according to the tradition from which you and I come (the Calvinist tradition) the task of government is the establishment of justice." President de Klerk, acting in the way that we have come to see is characteristic of his willingness to enter into open debate, immediately conceded the point.[81]

Black Christians were in the bind in which there were neither legal means by which to fight for justice, nor theological means to articulate nonviolent resistance since apartheid itself was defined as a theological term to justify the separation of the races. Rhetoric of nonviolence would only serve an apartheid nation-state. Tutu laments,

> Only when liberation movements could no longer operate legally and openly in South Africa, did some members of these organizations believe that they were left with no option but to undertake an armed struggle to liberate the people of South Africa. The aim of this armed struggle is for a new, just, non-racial and democratic South Africa. It is enshrined in the Freedom Charter. Whether those who fight for this goal are "terrorists" or "freedom fighters," depends on which side of the divide you locate yourself.[82]

---

[81]Tutu, Draft of Article mailed to *Woord en Daad* (Word and Action) June 24, 1991.

[82]Tutu, "Freedom Fighters or Terrorists?" 73.

To further articulate the lack of legal appeal, Tutu exposes us to the South African context in which

> Detention without trial is the order of the day, with even children being subjected to the horrendous situation where the police are able to act as both prosecutor and judge. Frequently those who are detained are held in solitary confinement and without access to a doctor of their choice, their lawyer or family. When this is the character of what is "lawful" in a country it is necessary to obey God rather than human authority.... In political trials the death sentence is often passed on people who are dedicated, idealistic and have the best intentions, while those who sit in judgment on them are as a rule totally unsympathetic to the cause of the accused. There is little doubt that the law and the judicial system are weighted against those who seek change to the existing order. When the death sentence is not passed, the sentences imposed are rarely other than viciously excessive. Young students receive twelve months or more for throwing stones.[83]

Tutu seems inconsistent in his nonviolent position of just war because of his need to lead in a particular way spiritually and politically in a particular context of tragic apartheid. Again, rhetoric of nonviolence would only serve an apartheid nation-state, especially in ecclesial sense of acknowledging a capitulated vision of the church in the vision of Afrikaner Calvinists. Tutu's complicated position should not hinder a constructive display for how Christian spirituality is essentially nonviolent in character. Indeed, Tutu's understanding for how to adjudicate spiritual progress among Christians is helpful in understanding how to break cycles of violence. And for Tutu, he remains unequivocally devoted to the role of the church in the world in such an endeavor to break cycles of violence. Regarding the unique

---

[83]Tutu, "Freedom Fighters or Terrorists?" 74-75.

role of the church in a violent world, Tutu states, "The Church must face up to the possibility that it may die in this struggle, but what of that? Did our Lord and Master not tell of a seed that will remain alone unless it falls to the ground and dies (John 12:24)? We can never have an Easter without a Good Friday: there can be no Resurrection without a Crucifixion and death."[84] Tutu's understanding that Christians need space and time to grow gives him his vision for how post-apartheid South Africa is to proceed—in the vision of God's image of peace. South Africa may be like the blind that Jesus healed, whose vision slowly increased with clarity. South Africa is now on the brink of coming to its senses, like the prodigal son who turned back toward his father's direction. We are to understand such direction toward God. Tutu concludes,

> I believe in that great liberator God of the Exodus and of Calvary and so I have no doubt at all that we shall be free in South Africa, black and white, for it is God's intention which cannot be frustrated forever and a new South Africa will emerge, truly democratic, nonracial and just where all, black and white, will be seen as of infinite value because all, black and white, are created in God's image; all, black and white, will strive to dwell amicably together as brothers and sisters as members of one family, the human family, God's family. And for this cause I am ready to give even my life.[85]

In the twentieth century, the church faced nuclear war. How could such war ever be justified or made holy? This leaves the church in its current bewilderment, especially in the face of two Western figures who defined Christian spirituality as irrelevant and useless.

---

[84]Tutu, "God's Strength - In Human Weakness," 23.
[85]Tutu, Addresses "Violence and the Church," June 1987.

Marx and Nietzsche

Essential to my thesis of how spirituality and nonviolence are synonymous is that it is better to view Christian faith and hope as derived from a peacemaking community in which a Christian spirituality of nonviolence does not necessarily have to bless the established order. My argument (seemingly Tutu's as well) is that one learns to see that we need to worry far more that many people are more interested in what Christians have inherited from Pontius Pilate than from Jesus—that is, we have inherited disinterested political interests at the jeopardy of whole communities. What must be articulated from the standpoint of Christian spirituality is that no violence, no war, can ever be just, that no violence, no war, can ever lead to the flourishing of creation and community. In order to know this fully, it is important to know the arguments against my position.

For some, the necessity of violence may be predicated on socio-biological judgments about the genetically and biologically determined character of human nature drawn from analogies with the violence and aggression seen in the animal kingdom.[86] For example, Karl Marx thought life is violent by its very nature as one has to constantly struggle and rebel. In such a worldview, the only way to justice and human dignity is through violence. Since revolution is necessary and good for Marx, the counter force of religion provides the *telos* for Christianity to become essentially functionless and irrelevant for society. In his "Introduction to a Critique of Hegel's Philosophy of Right," Marx criticizes Christianity as "the sigh of the oppressed creature" and "the opium of the people," and he concludes that the concept of Christian religion never escapes these criticisms.[87]

For Marx, religion consoles the oppressed by offering them heaven as that which they are denied upon earth, namely, an abstracted good form of human existence. In that, religion plays

---

[86] See for example the arguments of sociobiologist Edward O. Wilson in *On Human Nature* (Cambridge: Harvard Unvirsity, 1978).

[87] See Karl Marx, *Contributions to the critique of Hegel's Philosophy of Right* Deutsch-Franzosische Jahrbucher, 1844).

somewhat of a progressive role by giving the common people some idea of what a better order would be. But when it becomes possible to realize this better order upon earth, particularly in the form of concrete social structures, then religion becomes wholly reactionary and distracts from establishing a new and possible good society on earth because it engenders among its devotees the need for heaven. As a result of this otherworldly nature, Christianity's sanctification of the existing social order makes it a counterrevolutionary force.

Since revolution is necessary and good for Marx, the counter force of religion provides the *telos* for Christianity to become essentially functionless and irrelevant for society. In Marx's revolutionary end, there will no longer be an exploiting class, nor will the common people stand in need of the state, which also will wither away. It is in this Marxist eschatology that Alasdair MacIntyre sees an internal inconsistency, placing Marxism more on the side of religion than against it. On the one hand, according to MacIntyre, Marx brought down to earth the hitherto metaphysical themes of alienation and used them for solid analysis; on the other hand, by insisting on the possibility of something more than an empiricist understanding of social facts, he became immune to the very disease he saw as religion. Marx became oblivious to the very false consciousness in his own theorizing by falling into the need to project beyond what is perceived as fact. Ironically, this was the problem that, for Marx, was inseparable from religious modes of thought.

Because Marxism succeeds the development of the philosophies of Hegel and Feuerbach, MacIntyre thinks one cannot understand Marxism adequately unless one understands it as a secular version of Christianity. Marxism shares the content and function of Christianity as an interpretation of human existence, in part because it is the historical successor of Christianity. In order to move from the Christian religion to Marxism, there must be a more radical step of social practice.

MacIntyre sees Marx as further developing a secular religion through a humanistic belief in the possibilities and resources of human nature. This belief, without which Marxism as a political movement

would be unintelligible, is a secularized version of a Christian virtue.[88]
Just as Christianity is better at describing the state of fallen humanity
rather than the glories of a redeemed humanity, so Marxism is better
at explaining what human alienation consists of rather than describing
the future nature of unalienated humanity. For Marx, the
eschatological vision describes human alienation transformed in the
work of creative activity that may be judged by aesthetic standards.
But it is in these standards that we find the paradox of Marxism
simultaneously repeating the inconsistencies of Hegel and Feuerbach,
namely, recreating in a Marxist's own conceptions of human nature
the very same religious phenomena against which she or he was
concerned as a critic. Thus it is better to see Christianity and Marxism
as rival religions. MacIntyre suggests, though, that there still remains
a residual complementary between these two "religions." Toward a
common future end of the Year of Jubilee in which amends are made
for the poor, there is a common language for Christianity and
Marxism in which each does not necessarily lose any of its authority
to critique the other.

For MacIntyre, the strength of Marxist critique holds true for a
great deal of Christian thought, and in particular for a great deal of
nineteenth-century Anglican theology. For example, the doctrine of
the Tractarian movement suspiciously enough focuses on priesthood
and apostolic succession just at the time when the state was beginning
to deny in Anglican practice any real difference between
nonconformity and the Church of England. Doubtless, as a result, high
churchmanship replaced any other display of worship as the mark of
true Anglicanism. And any ascetical disciplines commended by the
Tractarians were only accessible to a leisured English class whose
sacramental doctrines often became irrelevant to an industrial society.
In 1838, F. D. Maurice described the inconsistency among the
Tractarians through their view of baptism:

---

[88] Alsdair MacIntyre, *Christianity and Marxism*, 92.

Where is the minister of Christ in London, Birmingham
or Manchester, whom such a doctrine, heartily and inwardly
entertained, would not drive to madness? He is sent to preach
the Gospel. What gospel? Of all the thousands whom he
addresses, he cannot venture to believe that there are ten who,
in Dr. Pusey's sense, retain their baptismal purity. All he can
do, therefore, is to tell wretched creatures, who spend eighteen
hours out of the twenty-four in close factories and bitter toil,
corrupting and being corrupted, that if they spend the
remaining six in prayer—he need not add fasting—they may
possibly be saved. How can we insult God and torment man
with such mockery?[89]

MacIntyre concludes that the benefit of the attraction between
Marxism and Christianity is that it provides attention toward the
rescue of individual lives from the insignificance of finitude. For
MacIntyre, Christianity is able to create an identity that transcends
the identity which existing social order confers upon individuals and
within which it would like to confine them. Marxism is the only
systematic doctrine in the modern world that has been able to
translate, to any important degree, the hopes of people into the
expressions of human possibility and history as a means of liberating
the present from the burdens of the past, and so constructing the
future.[90] Marxism as an historically embodied phenomenon may have
been deformed in a variety of ways, but the Marxist project remains a
viable means for many for reestablishing hope as a social virtue.[91]
    After synthesizing the above complementary between
Christianity and Marxism, MacIntyre critiques those who insist that
Marxism is substantially true and those who insist that Marxism is
essentially false. The first position, which advocates Marxism or its
derivative tendencies, faces the following two major difficulties: the

---

[89]MacIntyre does admit another side to the doctrine of the Tractarians, but of a
great deal of what they taught, he thinks the Marxist critique remains true (115.
    [90]Ibid.
    [91]Ibid., 116.

impotence of Marxist economic theory today and the fate of Marx's predictions, that is, the predicted growth of a revolutionary working class and the predicted smooth transition to socialism among countries of the Eastern European bloc.

For Marx, theory informs and directs human activities; it gives vision and articulates an explicit definition to political and moral stances forced upon individuals in consequence of the positions they occupy in the social system. Therefore, theory is not a set of opinions that individuals may or may not choose to adopt. But this is what Marxism has become, namely, a set of "views" that stand in no kind of organic relationship to an individual's social role or identity. In becoming like this, Marxism is "practiced" in precisely the same way as religious beliefs are practiced in modern secularized societies. Just as Hegel said that reading the newspaper replaced the practice of morning prayer, for the modern radical intellectual holding Marxist views this replacement stands the same as holding certain theological views.[92]

The second position rejects Marxism as false under the rubric that no theory may correctly possess the ability to connect moral attitude and belief about the past and belief in a benign future possibility. The dominant character from which this rejection comes is liberal theory, which asserts that fact and value are logically independent of each other and that ultimate authority must reside in the individual. It is this same belief that underpins the liberal rejection of Christianity as well.

The inherent strength of MacIntyre's maturation through Marxism and Christianity is that he now sees in modernity the liberal intention to make the individual the source of all value, which necessarily legislates in matters of value. Therefore, one's autonomy is only preserved if it is regarded as choice, and that between one's own ultimate principles, unconstrained by any external consideration. As we have seen through MacIntyre's sojourn, this will not suffice for Marxism and Christianity, which both provide ready responses to this

---

[92] Ibid., 123.

question: How is Christian identity both determined by and determinative of boundaries of culture, class, and race? According to MacIntyre, the cost of not properly seeing these frameworks of Christianity and Marxism is only exacerbated in the dangerous tendencies of moral privacy and moral solipsism.

Liberal theory necessarily develops a view of the world as divided and compartmentalized. The most fundamental of the distinctions inherent in liberalism is between the political and the economic. Instead of religious reification, liberalism reifies economic categories. Similar to the view above of the Tractarians, liberalism can combine within itself a drive toward ideals of political equality with an actual fostering of economic inequality. And just as the political sphere is separated from the economic, so morality tends to become a realm apart, a realm concerned only with private relationships. The only salvific thing about Marxist tendencies is that they refuse to separate political, economic, and social aspects of the human identity. The genius of Marx was in his ability to identify conflicts of interest embodied in the very self-descriptions of liberal theory. If left unchecked, these self-descriptions lead to self-deception, which may be observed by uses of liberal theory that make the existence of an overriding common interest appear as independent of contingent social realities. Even though the mature MacIntyre now focuses his attention on the problems of such liberal theory, he offers much guidance in putting Christianity and Marxism in context according to their paradoxical commonality.

Nietzsche's Violent Cosmology

Another major Western intellectual in favor of the means of violence is Friedrich Nietzsche, whose thought is best summarized through the recognition of the inescapability of violence. Though he does not posit genetically or biologically determined accounts of human nature (unlike what many supremacist groups want to claim),[93] he does deploy arguments drawn from analogies with the animal kingdom:

> That lambs dislike great birds of prey does not seem strange: only it gives no ground for reproaching these birds of prey for bearing off little lambs. And if the lambs say among themselves: "these birds of prey are evil; and whoever is least like a bird of prey, but rather its opposite, a lamb—would he not be good?" there is no reason to find fault with this institution of an ideal, escept perhaps that the birds of prey might view it a little ironically and say: "we don't dislike them at all, these good little lambs; we even love them; nothing is more tasty than a tender lamb." To demand of strength that it should not be a desire to overcome, a desire to throw down, a desire to become master, a thirst for enemies and resistances and triumphs, is just as absurd as to demand of weakness that it should express itself as strength.[94]

It is unresolved whether Nietzsche celebrates violence, the predatory strength of masters over their weak and weakened prey. Many people claim adherence to Nietzsche in their avowal for necessary power and even war. Perhaps Nietzsche is correct in his assumption that violence will always be an option in the world, but Christians do not have to take it or practice it. As an African-American male, a descendent of slavery, I know this firsthand. I know

---

[93] Greg Jones provides a good display of Nietzsche's account of gift-giving as distinct power from the power of violence. Gift giving uses the strength of power as a way of minimizing, though never escaping, the reality of violence. From such a perspective, life is sustained by the effective utilization of power, which requires recognition that violence is inescapably part of how things really are in the world. With this mind persons recognize that gift-giving can be a power that is generous in its very being. This reading of Nietzsche moves away from the Nazi glorification of predatory violence to a more sustained ethical and political concern. See Greg Jones, *Embodying Forgiveness* (Grand Rapids, MI: Eerdmans, 1999) 80; Also see Nichohlas Lash, "Not quite Politics or Power?" *Modern Theology* 8/4 (October 1992): 353-364.

[94] Friedrich Nietzsche, *On the Geneology of Morals* tr. Walter Kaufman and R.J. Hollingdale, ed. Walter Kaufman (New York: Vintage, 1989) section 13, 44-45.

that we must not dismiss the profound insight of W. E. B. Dubois, who identifies the seemingly universal problem of racial and economic discrimination in which the darker shade of complexion one is, regardless of race and nationality, the more likely that person will fall under the category of the oppressed in the world.[95] It should be natural for me, in light of my ancestors' context of slavery and in light of my current context of racism, to advocate the use of violence to change oppressive realities. I have learned, however, through practices in Christian spirituality to unlearn a violent worldview. In short, when faced with natural violence, I have learned to refuse such violent struggle, which only incites more violence as it inadvertently lends itself to anarchy, constant war, and a lack of personhood. This, in the end, surely does not construct a Christian spirituality that empowers the oppressed people of the world because such a people will be struggling in Darwinian fashion until they are the only ones left at the end of the world.

My own context as an African American goes back to the US Constitution, in which I was taught to remember that in order to be a peacemaker, I had to learn the valuable lesson of identifying who in fact writes the rules—that often, ironically, the oppressor defines what is good and evil. Many have already learned these lessons simply by being a member of the oppressed group of people who have had to abide by the truth defined by the dominant cultures. Instead of my rightful retaliation against American culture and ideology, I have learned to appeal to more than the U.S. Constitution for how I am to proceed in the world. I name this supererogation as Christian spirituality, in which I claim a formation to break retaliatory cycles of violence. It is in Christian spirituality that we may facilitate more of a constructive enterprise in the need to continue making saints instead of perpetuating enemies. MacIntyre is helpful here as he seems to explain my own intention behind saintmaking:

---

[95] W.E.B. Dubois, *The Souls of Black Folk*, 23, quoted in James Cone, *A Black Theology of Liberation*, (Maryknoll: Orbis Books, 1989) xv.

To anyone who wishes to argue with one about religion one can then only take the argument in cogent, logical terms as far back as his own first principles will allow. But because there comes a point at which such argument must cease, it does not follow that there is nothing more to say. It is no accident that the religious autobiography is a classic form of theological writing for this shows us how a man comes by the premises from which he argues. It goes behind the argument to the arguer. St. Augustine's *Confessions* are the classic document here. Thus it is not mere pious moralizing which connects the rise of unbelief with a lowering of the quality of Christian life. Where the Christian community is incapable of producing lives such as those of the saints, the premises from which I argue will appear rootless and arbitrary.[96]

If we are to maintain such saints, there must be this accounting of a character that is inseparable from violence. Whether it is acknowledged or not, all people represent a spiritual tradition in which there is a kind of order for common life. Particularly for Christians who follow Jesus, this kind of life displays the exercise of spiritual practices that prohibit certain actions that destroy what may be perceived of as our enemy. In Christian spirituality we have learned that we are more like dumb sheep; that is, we have trouble recognizing our enemy, so we depend on a shepherd to define our being and direction. We have trouble recognizing our enemy because most of the time the true enemy is the self. Therefore, instead of assuming that Christians are skilled enough to be peaceful, as Christians we will do well to unlearn violence in the Christian Beatitudes which may in the end redirect attention away from the self in such a way that we may reenter the garden of Eden and resist the temptation of haughty knowledge. Jesus explains this process of unlearning the knowledge of good and evil through his parable of the great judgment:

---

[96]From Alasdair MacIntyre, *Difficulties in Christian Belief* (New York: Philosophical Library, 1959) 118.

When the Son of man comes in his glory, and all the angels with him, then he will sit on his glorious throne. Before him will be gathered all the nations, and he will separate them one from another as a shepherd separates the sheep from the goats, and he will place the sheep at his right hand, but the goats at the left. Then the King will say to those at his right hand, "Come, O blessed of my Father, inherit the kingdom prepared for you from the foundation of the world; for I was hungry and you gave me food, I was a stranger and you welcomed me, I was naked and you clothed me, I was sick and you visited me, I was in prison and you came to me." Then the righteous will answer him, "Lord, when did we see thee hungry and feed thee, or naked and clothe thee? And when did we see thee sick or in prison and visit thee?" (Matt. 25:31–39)

Here, Jesus displays an account of Christians not knowing when they were doing good; instead, Christians are to discover, underneath all the theoretical discourse concerning who is good, that they simply are to pay attention to the sustainer of life, the shepherd who leads them into the way of life. Interestingly enough, this sustainer who provides protection and nourishment for Christians is one who himself was oppressed.

It is interesting to note the particularity of the oppressed in the United States, especially as reported by the Federal Bureau of Prisons Statistics:[97]

Inmates by Gender
Male: 145,897   (93%)
Female: 10,982   (7%)

Inmates by Race
White: 87,796   (56%)

---

[97] These statistics were compiled from both the Department of Justice and the Federal Bureau of Prisons. See websites: Federal Bureau of Prisons (www.bop.gov) and The Department of Justice (www.ojp.usdog.gov/bjs/correct.htm)

Black: 64,238	(40.9%)
Asian: 2,393	(1.5%)
Native American: 2,452	(1.6%)
Hispanic 49,698	(31.7%)

Inmates by Offense

Drugs: 76,096	(55.1%)
Firearms, Explosives, Arson: 12,921	(9.4%)
Immigration: 12,331	(8.9%)
Robbery: 8,716	(6.3%)
Property: 7,228	(5.2%)
Extortion, Fraud, Bribery: 6,599	(4.8%)
Homicide, Aggravated Assault, Kidnapping: 2,681	(1.9%)
White Collar: 1,011	(0.7%)
Sexual: 1,008	(0.7%)

How do Christian sensibilities negotiate the harsh realities of the oppressed and the oppressor? The answer given by Jesus' parable of the great judgment suggests a reordering of power and goodness. Thus, through the mystery of *perichoresis*, in which God is through the relationship of Father, Son, and Spirit, Jesus gives us a deeper meaning of the use of power than Nietzsche provides. There is yet a better *telos*, or goal, both for the individual and the community than to focus on the necessity of physical power. MacIntyre summarizes: "Only if I place my own physical survival lower on the scale of values than other goods, can my self be perfected."[98]

In this spirit in which MacIntyre challenges Nietzsche's worldview, the following Buddhist story provides a counter narrative to that of the eagle and the lamb:

> Once, in a kingdom lying in the foothills of the Himalayas, the Buddha was born as a kind-hearted prince

---

[98] Alasdair MacIntyre, "Can Medicine Dispense with a Theological Perspective on Human Nature," in *Knowledge, Value, and Belief*, II, ed. H. Engelhardt and D. Callahan (Hastings-on-Hudson, N.Y.: Hastings Center Publication, 1977) 34.

called Mahasattva. One year, a terrible drought visited itself upon the kingdom; the people suffered greatly and many wild animals died. Prince Mahasattva was walking in the woods with his two brothers when they came upon a starving tigress and her seven cubs. The cubs were barely alive, and the tigress was so feeble with hunger that she could not even give chase. Mahasattva's brothers quickly ran away, but Mahasattva did not flee.

"I see from the suffering in your eyes and the frailness of your body that you have been many day's without food," he said to the sad, emaciated creature. "What will you do?"

The tigress replied, "It is a terrible thing. My children are half dead. If I cannot find food soon, I must devour them so that at least one of us may live."

Remembering Buddha's teachings on selflessness, Prince Mahasattva replied, "Take my body instead, for it is of little use to me." With that he laid down before her. The tigress and her cubs devoured him, skin, bones, and all. Thereafter, they vowed to honor the prince's sacrifice by living virtuous lives. Then the forest was harmonious.[99]

Of course the Christian perspective is deeply enriched by this Buddhist story as Christians reflect on Christology and the atoning work of Christ to offer to the world his own body and blood so that the world (the forest) is made harmonious.

In conclusion, instead of Nietzsche's eagle, which does not despise the sheep for being a sheep but only sees such sheep as tasty and ready to be eaten, Christian spirituality offers a different paradigm in which creation sees itself as interdependent without the need to kill the other to make sense of one's own existence. St.

---

[99] This story was given to my by Alex Semilof. Its closest appropriation is given in *Generous Wisdom, Commentaries by H.H. The Dalai Lama XIV On The Jatakamala*, 1992, Library of Tibetan Works and Archives, Dharamsala, India and printed at Indraprastha Press (CBT), New Delhi.

Columba and the Crane provides such an example in which a bird of prey begins to understand compassion:

> And another time it befell, while the Saint was living on Iona, that he called one of the brethren to him, to speak to him. "Go thou," he said, "three days from now to the west of this island at dawn, and sit above the shore and wait: for when the third hour before sunset is past, there shall come flying from the northern coast of Ireland a stranger guest, a crane, wind tossed and driven far from her course in the high air; tired out and weary she will fall on the beach at thy feet and lie there, her strength nigh gone: tenderly lift her and carry her to the steading near by: make her welcome there and cherish her with all care for three days and nights; and when the three days are ended, refreshed and loath to tarry longer with us in our exile, she shall take flight again towards that old sweet land of Ireland whence she came, in pride of strength once more: and if I commend her so earnestly to thy charge, it is that in that countryside where thou and I were reared, she too was nested." The brother obeyed: and on the third day, when the third hour before sunset was past, stood she was bidden, in wait for the coming of the promised guest: and when she had come and lay fallen on the beach, he lifted her and carried her ailing to the steading, and fed her, famished as she was. And on his return that evening to the monastery the Saint spoke to him, not as one questioning but as one speaks of a thing past. "May God bless thee, my son," said he, "for thy kind tending of this pilgrim guest: that shall make no long stay in her exile, but when three suns have set shall turn back to her own land." And the thing fell out even as the Saint had foretold. For when her three days housing was ended, and as her host stood by, she rose in first flight from the earth into high heaven, and after a while at gaze to spy out her aerial

way, took her straight flight above the quiet sea, and so to Ireland through the tranquil weather.[100]

In conclusion, Christians need to be aware of the challenges posed by Marx and Nietzsche, but Marx and Nietzsche should not be followed. Whether the argument is the inescapability of violence or the ontology of violence, Christians claim to follow one who could easily have been a bird of prey, wreaking havoc on creation as if such havoc would be normal existence, but instead Jesus came as the Lamb of God to show how to permanently end violent existence. Both Marx and Nietzsche wanted to "unwrite" this Christian narrative in which they thought Christianity glorified weakness and dulled people's truely heroic excellence. John Milbank even suggests that Nietzsche's *Geneology of Morals* is an attempt to counter the narrative told by Augustine in *The City of God*.[101] Augustine emphasizes the priority of God's gift of peaceableness in creation, but Nietzsche wanted to subvert that by stressing that the beginning was violent, not peaceful. It is important for Christians to learn to respond to Nietzsche, who represents a controversial and important example of the position that violence is inescapable because it is inscribed in the way things are, in the very nature of the world.[102] Such an ingrained understanding of a violent world is like the humorous assumptions we all make, exemplified in the following Garrison Keillor jokes:

> What's the difference between mechanical engineers and civil engineers?
> Mechanical engineers build weapons. Civil engineers build targets.

> Two cannibals sit by a fire; one says he hates his mother-in-law, and the other says, "Well, try these potatoes."[103]

---

[100]Helen Waddell, *Beasts and Saints*, 40-41.

[101] See John Milbank, *Theology and Social Theory* (Oxford: Blackwell, 1990) 389.

[102] See Greg Jones, *Embodying Forgiveness*, (Grand Rapids: Eerdmans) 79-81.

[103] Garrison Keillor, Prairie Home Companion Radio Broadcast of Jokes.

It is important to respond to Nietzsche and Marx; otherwise, Christians may slowly discover that they are believing one way yet behaving as if Nietzsche and Marx are right. Such deception can be illustrated by the fascinating statistic given by social psychologists that an average child laughs 300 times a day, whereas an adult laughs only 17 times a day. Does this data suggest that we inevitably succumb to the recognition that this is just a violent existence? Iris Murdoch believes we inherit a cosmology from Nietzsche that is seldom broken. As C. S. Lewis articulated so well, "A fish does not know it's wet."[104] In the same manner, Western Christian spirituality does not know its own complicity with a violent universe: "How is one to connect the realism which must involve a clear-eyed contemplation of the misery and evil of the world with a sense of an uncorrupted good without the latter idea becoming the merest consolatory dream?"[105] Tutu further illustrates what seems to be the merest consolatory dream of peace in South Africa's context:

> Apartheid causes untold and unnecessary suffering "by law." By depriving black people of their South African citizenship, the South African government has been able to uproot over three million people, disrupting stable communities, demolishing habitable dwellings, destroying schools, churches, small businesses and clinics. These people are dumped in poverty-stricken resettlement camps and their children are made to starve, not because there is no food in South Africa, but in order to satisfy government ideology. Young people are hindered in their development and old people are made to suffer. This is legalized, structural violence. It is violence used to uphold an unjust and repressive system, augmented by repressive laws.[106]

---

[104] C.S. Lewis, *Mere Christianity*.

[105] Iris Murdoch, *The Sovereignty Of Good* (New York: Schocken, 1971) 61.

[106] Tutu, "Freedom Fighters or Terrorists?" 74-75.

Peacemaking, the essence of building community, should always be at the heart of Christian spirituality. Indeed, this is not a passive peace, but one that proactively builds community and births the kingdom of God.

2

PNEUMATOLOGY:

A DEFINITION OF COMMUNAL SPIRITUALITY

The Holy Spirit elicits the connotation of peace. As we learned in chapter one, Sheldrake is correct in showing a dialogical form of spirituality, especially in his insight of the residual effects of the current divorce between spirituality and human experience. I would encourage Sheldrake's argument toward the transformation of his dialogical image into a conversational one. Namely, Christian spirituality is about the Spirit, who implies more than dialogue. God's Spirit continually creates conversation with more than two persons; therefore, the Trinity makes spirituality conversational in respect to the possibility of always creating community. It is toward the perfection of Christian community that we now turn in order to define spirituality further.

The need to define Christian spirituality alongside pneumatology is akin to the need of a person to touch physically another person. If Christian spirituality is to be intelligible it needs to be able to touch others and to be touched by others; therefore, defining spirituality carries with it the concomitant task of articulating what life in God's Spirit looks like. Josef Sudbrack is correct that the "banality...of the word [spirituality]...is only the product of our own time, as also is unfortunately, the anemic unreality which is almost always connected with the word spirituality."[1] When we articulate life in the Spirit, persons catch a glimpse beyond Western individualism toward the flourishing community or shalom. Bernard Haring facilitates an understanding for the Spirit's role: "If we look at our weaknesses, at our inheritance of individualism and group egoism, our tight grasp on old customs and formulas, and on the other hand at our often weak and cowardly, subservient spirit, we would be forced to despair. But our confidence is not our own. It comes from the Spirit of Pentecost."[2]

Much of the Christian revelation about God's Spirit comes from Scripture. Christian theologians point to a gradual unfolding in the Old Testament of the doctrine of the "spiration" (not generation) of the Spirit's procession in the Godhead. Spiration, as opposed to generation, is important in order to avoid the heresy of Filioque, in which the Spirit and the Son are generated from God the Father. Generation of these two persons subordinates the Spirit according to Orthodox theology. The Trinity is not the result of a process, but a primordial given. God has no need to reveal himself to himself by a sort of Hegelian wakening of consciousness of the Father within the Son and the Spirit. Revelation is thinkable only in relation to the other-than-God, that is to say, within creation. Just as the Trinitarian existence is not the result of an act of the will, it is impossible to see here the process of an internal necessity. The Triune God is plenitude of love that does not have to be poured out to others, since the other is already in God. Thus, an Aristotelian schema of cause and effect has no relevance when trying to locate the three hypostases in their absolute diversity because there must be no possibility of establishing any subordinate order among the Godhead (hence the rejection of Filioque). From our perspective below, the Spirit leads us through the Son to the Father, and this becomes the way the Eastern Church discovers the unity of the three. On the other hand, Vladimir Lossky

---

[1] Josef Sudbrack, "Spirituality," Sacramentum Mudni, Karl Rahner with Cornelius Ernst and Kevin Smyth, eds. (New York: Herder and Herder, 1970) 149.

[2] Haring, 88.

suggests that many conceptual problems in Western theology are caused from the emphasis upon the one essence in order to arrive at the Three Persons.[3]

The Father is the source, the Son the manifestation, the Spirit the force that manifests. Thus, the Father is the source of love; the Son, love that reveals itself; the Spirit, love realized in us. The Spirit does not have the character of a work that is subordinate and in some sense functional in relation to that of the Son. The work of Christ concerns human nature, which he recapitulates in his hypostasis. The work of the Holy Spirit, on the other hand, concerns persons, being applied to each one separately. Within the church the Holy Spirit imparts to human hypostases the fullness of deity after a manner that is unique and "personal"—appropriate to everyone as a person created in the image of God.

Thus, the work of Christ unifies, and the work of the Holy Spirit diversifies. One work is impossible without the other. Herein abide two aspects of the church: the body of Christ becomes the nature of the church, and the fullness of the Holy Spirit ordains the multiplicity of human hypostases, each one of whom represents not merely a part but a whole.[4] The union accomplished in the person of Christ must be fulfilled in our persons by the Holy Spirit and our own freedom; hence, the two aspects of the church—that of fulfillment and that of becoming: "It is in the light of the dogma of the Holy Trinity that the most wonderful attribute of the Church—that of catholicity—is disclosed in its true and properly Christian sense, which cannot be translated by the abstract term of universality. For the highly concrete sense of the word 'catholicity' comprehends not only unity but also multiplicity."[5]

Typically, biblical images, both Hebrew and Greek, that describe "the Spirit" of God are connected to "wind" or "breath." These images are good metaphors for the mysterious and invisible operation of the Holy Spirit because, like the wind, the Spirit is better known by

---

[3] MTEC, 52.
[4] MTEC, 174.
[5] MTEC, 176.

the results of the Spirit's presence than by our ability to see or discern such presence or operations. As a Christian strains to feel the effects of the Holy Spirit, St. Augustine points us to the role of interconnection as that which also helps to identify the presence of the Spirit of God. Commenting on John 3, Augustine wrote, "No one sees the Spirit; how do we hear the voice of the Spirit? A Psalm is sung, it is the voice of the Spirit; the Gospel is read, it is the voice of the Spirit; the Word is preached, it is the voice of the Spirit. You hear His voice but you know not whence it comes or wither it goes."[6] In a similar way, the "spiritual birth" that Jesus enjoined upon Nicodemus (John 3) comes to us through the Word and sacrament of God.[7] The voice of the Spirit is heard in the human soul as it connects to the truth of being related to God. It is in this connectedness that I display how the pneumatology informs the connotation of nonviolence in Christian spirituality.

The Holy Spirit connects persons to the union of God. It is in this connection that Christians learn their identities as more than mere creatures of a Creator and how to relate to one another in the peace of Christ as children of God. For John Wesley, "the witness of the Spirit" "is an inward impression on the soul that I am 'a child of God'; that Jesus Christ hath loved me, and given himself for me; that all my sins are blotted out, and I, even I am reconciled to God."[8] This familial communication between the human spirit and the Spirit of God, as child to parent, was precisely the premise of Catherine of Siena's *The Dialogue* and numerous other significant works. Through the Holy Spirit, Christians come to believe and practice the tangible presence of being related to God as children.

To practice Christian spirituality in the Western context, however, requires a sensibility that does not always come easy in relating to God as a child. Much of the incentive to believe in God as a child would believe in God has been lost in Western Christianity. The

---

[6] Mary Clark, ed., *Augustine of Hippo* (New York: Paulist Press, 1984) 285.
[7] Clark, *Augustine of Hippo*, 285.
[8] Albert Outler ed., *The Works of John Wesley*, vol. I, Sermons (Nashville, Tenn: Abingdon Press, 1984) Sermon #10, "The Witness of the Spirit," 274.

following account illustrates what I mean: "Frightened in the night, a little boy waits. His mother goes into his dark room to comfort him: 'It's all right, son; God is with you.' The son replies, 'But, Mom, I want someone with skin on.'" In many ways, the communal practices of God's presence are no longer discernable in what has come to be defined as Christian spirituality. I propose that the discernment of God's presence in a Western setting is only intelligible through spiritual practices like intercessory prayer, retreat, and Eucharist.[9] Since I make synonymous intercessory prayer and God's Spirit, I challenge the notion that Spirit is irrelevant to the concept of nonviolence and relationality.

I prefaced earlier the difficulty in naming Christian spirituality; indeed, we need more of a concerted effort to display a discourse in Christian spirituality that can move us beyond the relative purity of one person's heart's experience. The typical understanding of Christian spirituality as personal journey must be challenged in order to understand the work of the Spirit. For example, John Tyson invites his readers into an understanding of the breadth of Christian spirituality as he uses the image of a banquet. He then lapses into a typical understanding of Western spirituality as personal spirituality: "The texts presented in this collection serve as an invitation to a great feast, and yet each person's meal involves matters of personal 'taste' and selection; each person's pilgrimage is distinctly his or her own pilgrimage."[10] Christian spirituality is not about relativizing personal journeys of faith, as if the locus of authority of knowing God is given to the individual alone. In other words, we do not know God privately as if to maintain individual autonomy. We cannot know God

---

[9] It is ironic how Duke University Medical School seems to be more of a leading voice on the discourse of prayer than the Divinity School. See the Medical School's recent empirical studies on prayer. See H. G. Koenig, et al, *Religion and Health: A Century of Research*, rev. ed. (New York: Oxford University Press, 2000) and H. G. Koenig, et al, "Does Religious Attendance Prolong Survival?: A Six-Year Follow-Up Sutdy of 3,968 older Adults." Journal of Gerontology: Medical Sciences, Spring 1999.

[10] John Tyson, ed., *Invitation to Christian Spirituality: An ecumenical Anthology* (New York: Oxford University Press, 1999) 3.

this way because God is not an individual monad existing eccentrically in some other galaxy. Holmes is helpful here:

> Plato said that to be is to be in relation and Aristotle defined the human being as a political animal, zoe politike. This term is sometimes translated "social animal," but it literally means a creature who lives in a city (polis). In other words, for us to be we must exist in a community, in which our identity does not stop with our skin, but extends into the corporate reality. We are our community or the multiple communities of which we are a part.[11]

Individualistic understandings of God also lead to obsession with personal salvation. Spiritually, God saved us by the cross of Christ, yet the body that died was material, and the body that rose was real. Although the effect was wondrously spiritual, the world in which Christ lived was emphatically this one: air and soil and rivers and streams and trees—and smashed cars. God so loved the world that even though unworthy of love, God granted us salvation in which we could live.

In order to demonstrate my thesis that Spirit is crucial to a Christian's conceptualization of nonviolence, the following methodology is set forth in this chapter: First, I locate pneumatology in biblical discourse as the crucial agent of intercessory prayer. By gaining a clearer vision of Spirit and intercessory prayer, the reader is led to my second step of defining pneumatology as the ceaseless peacemaking of the Holy Spirit's presence. Pneumatology then illuminates how ceaseless prayer is crucial for our healthy relationship with God as opposed to fragmented or nonfunctional prayers of individualistic forms of Christian spirituality. To pray as if to worship self or to be trapped in individualistic spirituality dries up prayer and causes prayer to cease when it is not practiced in community. How pneumatology displays the function of ceaseless prayer leads me to my third step of displaying the concept of covenant as a form of ceaseless prayer that is practiced through the maintenance of

---

[11] *Spirituality for Ministry*, 12.

authentic community. My last step, therefore, is a display of what such community looks like in the church.

The Holy Spirit in Biblical Discourse

In Christian theology, some have summarized the role of the Spirit in the Old Testament as "the Divine Power immanent in human history.... It is immanent only because it is essentially transcendent, coming forth out of the supernatural life of God who deals directly with men."[12] In the Old Testament there is the notion of the "Spirit" as Ruach. Ruach is the instrument of divine action, both in nature and in the human heart. The Spirit of God was already operative at the creation, brooding on the face of the waters (Gen. 1:2). In early times, the Hebrews saw evidence of the Spirit's action in deeds of valor and prowess. For example, the Divine Spirit inspired the artistic skill of Bezaleel (Exod. 36:1f), the successes of Joshua (Deut. 34:9), and the strength of Samson (Judg. 14:6). In particular, the Spirit was bestowed upon those appointed to communicate divine truth and especially on the prophets (Isa. 61:1f). The Spirit is also the chief power for making moral purity and holiness (Ps. 51:11). Above all, the Spirit was to be the possession of the coming Davidic king (Isa. 11:2) and of the servant of the Lord (Isa. 42:1); and in the Messianic Age there would be a large extension of the Spirit's activities and power (Jer. 31:31ff; Ezek. 36:26f). In the later Old Testament writings the Spirit was increasingly seen as the bestower of intellectual capacities. It is the spirit of understanding that fills the devout person (Eccles. 39:6) and conveys to humanity wisdom and religious knowledge (Wisd. 7:7; 9:17).

In the New Testament, the Old Testament teaching on the Spirit is further developed. It was through the overshadowing of the Spirit that Mary conceived the Savior (Luke 1:35; cf. Matt. 1:18–20). The Spirit descended upon Christ at his baptism (Mark 1:10). The Spirit

---

[12] George Johnston, "Spirit," in Alan Richardson, ed., *A Theological Word Book of the Bible* (New York: Macmillan, 1950) 236-37.

led Jesus in the wilderness in conflict with Satan (1:12), but was an operative power throughout Jesus' ministry and miracles. Teaching on the Spirit receives an especially characteristic form in John's Gospel, where the Spirit is "another Paraclete" (John 14:26; 15:26).

Pentecost, where the fullness of the Holy Spirit was poured out on the church, is described in Acts 2:1–13. It was marked by the gift of tongues, and St. Peter saw in this outpouring of the Spirit the new dispensation prophesied by Joel (Acts 2:16f; cf Joel 2:28–32). Luke emphasizes the extent to which the early church was possessed by the belief of the Spirit's operation. Deception of the apostles was deception of the Holy Spirit and lying to God (Acts 5:3–9). The apostles were conscious of receiving direct communication from the Spirit (Acts 11:12, 16; 16:6f), and the Holy Spirit shared in the deliberations of the apostles on the question of the law (Acts 15:28). And the gift of the Spirit was so far entrusted to the apostles that it was conveyed to others through the imposition of their hands (Acts 8:15f; 19:6).

In the theology of Paul, the thought of the Spirit is central. Indeed he associates the exalted Christ so closely with the Spirit that Christ and the Spirit often seem almost identical. In Scripture we learn from Paul that spirituality (that is, "to walk according to the Spirit") is the Christian process of being fully united with Christ. To follow Jesus, therefore, means that the Christian also walks in the power of the Holy Spirit because to be united with Christ is to be united with Christ's spirit (1 Cor. 6:17). Paul's vision of this connatural identity in Christ and the Spirit creates his vision of new creation in which the old has passed away and the new has come (2 Cor. 5:17). This connatural identity in Christ and the Spirit creates new desires that conform to the lifestyle of Christ (Phil 2:3–11). Therefore, the goal of Christian spirituality is unitive in that the Christian disciple becomes more and more like Christ through the power of the Spirit. The goal of Christian spirituality is union with God. Such union, however, is rarely displayed in the Christian life.

The Christian life as the life "in the Spirit" (alternately, life "in Christ") is sharply contrasted with life "in the flesh," and it is the presence of the Holy Spirit that makes the Christian's body the temple of God (1 Cor 3:16; 6:17). The Spirit is our intercessor with the Father (Rom. 8:26f). The Spirit divides her gifts to us as she wills (1 Cor. 12:11), and the fruit and gifts of the Spirit are described (Gal. 5:22f). Hereafter, the Spirit will raise up our bodies as "spiritual bodies" in the likeliness of Christ's resurrection (1 Cor. 15:42–44; cf. Rom. 8:11). The synoptic Gospels built upon and extended the Old Testament teaching by demonstrating that the Spirit authenticated (Matt. 3:16–17) and directed Jesus' ministry (Matt. 4:1). The Gospel According to John delineates the theological connection between Jesus and the Holy Spirit; the "Spirit of truth," whom Jesus sent upon his ascension, is "another counselor" (Greek, *paracletos*, "helper," "advocate") and made the ascended Christ present among his disciples (John 14:15–24).

John 14:15-31 is the passage of Scripture where Jesus describes the office of the Holy Spirit for his disciples. First, the Holy Spirit will be another counselor to them, and thereby the physical absence of Jesus will be rectified by the presence of the Holy Spirit (John 14:15–16). Second, the Spirit will call to mind the things of Christ (14:25–26), will bear witness to Christ (15:26), and will glorify Christ (16:12–16). And third, the Holy Spirit will convince them of sin and righteousness (16:8–12).

Perhaps during the patristic period, one learned to connect the connotations of peace with the Holy Spirit. For example, the Cappodocian Fathers interpreted the sending of the Holy Spirit as being synonymous with sending Christ's peace among his disciples. As reflection upon the Holy Spirit proceeded into the patristic period, Gregory Nazianzus aptly noted that the Holy Spirit "came after Christ that a Comforter should not be lacking unto us; but another comforter, that you might acknowledge His co-equality. For 'another' is not said...of different kinds, but of things consubstantial."[13] The Holy Spirit as comforter and peacemaker becomes a controlling metaphor. The Cappodocian interpretation of Scripture envisioned

---

[13] Gregory of Nazianzen, "Orations on Pentecost," in Philip Schaff and Henry Wace, eds., *A Select Library of Nicene and Post-Nicene Fathers of the Christian Church*, Series Two, vol. VII, 383.

Jesus teaching his disciples that the comforting Spirit "will teach you all things, and bring to your remind you of all that I have said to you" (John 14:26). In a similar way, the "Spirit of truth, who proceeds from the Father" will "bear witness" to Christ (John 15:26) and "will convince the world concerning sin and righteousness and judgment" (John 16:8). In the end, the "Spirit of truth," when she comes, will "guide" the disciples of Jesus "into all truth; for he will not speak on his own authority.... He will glorify me [Christ], for he will take what is mine and declare it to you" (John 16:14).

The doctrine of the Spirit in a theologically elaborated form, though implicit in the New Testament, was not reached for some centuries. An important stage was reached in Tertullian. The Montanists showed the need to distinguish between true and false operations of the Holy Spirit; despite the insistence of the Montanists on the Spirit's activities, their strange conceptions of the operation of the Spirit have not left any permanent mark on the development of the doctrine. Origen emphasized that the characteristic sphere of the Spirit's operation was the church, as contrasted with the whole of creation, which was that of the Word. From AD 360 onward the doctrine of the Spirit became a matter of acute controversy. A group of theologians known as the Macedonians, while maintaining against the Arians the full divinity of the Son, denied that of the Spirit. The most considerable work provoked by these discussions was Basil's *De Spiritu Sancto*. At the Council of Constantinople of 381, Macedonianism was finally repudiated and the full doctrine of the Spirit received authoritative acceptance in the church. In the West, this doctrine was elaborated by Augustine in his *De Trinitate*, notably by his conception of the Spirit as the bond of union in the Holy Trinity.

What is meant by the comforting and peaceful presence of the Spirit is multifaceted. It is by the power of the Holy Spirit that Christians confess Jesus as God incarnate (1 John 4:4) and as Lord (1 Cor. 12:3). The Spirit aids Christians in their prayers for "adoption" as God's children and for "the redemption of our bodies" (Rom. 8:22–27), as well as for the "perseverance" of the saints through the proclamation of the gospel (Eph. 6:18). The Spirit creates a sense of belonging to God in the heart of the Christian, which Paul characterized as those who, led by the Spirit of God are children of God, who cry "Abba, Father!" (Gal. 4:6; Rom. 8:16). Paul teaches that "it is the very Spirit bearing witness with our spirit that we are children of God" (Rom. 8:16) (see also 1 John 3:12–24; 4:3–5:12). It is through this understanding of the Spirit that one comes to understand a deeper meaning of connectedness and belonging.

Christian spirituality carries the epistemological burden of defining what a flourishing spirit looks like. Such a flourishing spirit is about the full relationships of living organisms to their habitat. Aren't we saying as Christians that our ultimate habitat is a utopian existence of heaven in which the lion shall lie down with the lamb and children will play harmlessly with the most poisonous of snakes? There is a problem, however, with how the Spirit of God flourishes. We often seem to have a different picture of what the spiritual life should like, a picture that is often different than what is given to us as U.S. citizens. Desmond Tutu helps me explain:

> The last mark of the operation of the Spirit seems to be that those who are chosen to be special instruments are destined for suffering.... Those who are God's friends are distinguished by the fact that they suffer.... There is an unbroken link in the mystery of service and suffering, witness and persecution, stretching from the Old Testament to the New Testament.... A church that does not suffer cannot be the Church of Jesus Christ, the suffering servant of the Lord.[14]

Through pneumatology Christians are said to able to "rejoice" in their sufferings. Suffering produces endurance, Christian character, and hope because "God's love has been poured into our hearts through the Holy Spirit which has been given to us" (Rom. 5:5). The Holy Spirit not only enables us to begin Christian life, by confessing Christ, but creates Christian life within us by its witness, perseverance, and love.

---

[14] Tutu, "The Holy Spirit and South Africa"

In a similar way the Holy Spirit deepens the concept of peace beyond self-contained spirituality in which the goal is personal peace. This deepening of peace to include relationality can be seen through how Catherine of Siena describes the Holy Spirit as sanctifying Christians by enabling them to "believe in the name of [God's] gifts and graces."[15] It is by the power of the Holy Spirit that Christians are changed into the likeness of Christ from one "degree of glory to another...for this comes from the Lord who is the Spirit" (2 Cor. 3:18). The Spirit produces "varieties of gifts" (Greek, *charismata*) for "varieties of service" in the body of believers. Among these gifts are proclamation, spiritual guidance, and healing (1 Cor. 12:4–14). At various points in the history of the church the Spirit has given gifts such as prophetic utterance, "speaking in tongues" (glossolalia, 1 Cor. 14), and "the working of miracles" (1 Cor. 12:10). The most abiding of these spiritual gifts, however, are faith, hope, and love, "but the greatest of these is love" (1 Cor. 13:13). St. Augustine's comment on the phrase "varieties of service" is illuminating: "Various duties are harmoniously allotted to the various members.... Despite these members being different, they rejoice in the common equal health (1 Cor. 12:26) all together, not separately, no one with more, another with less."[16] Intercessory prayer is understood in this way in which the body of Christ is gifted by the Spirit to intercede on others' behalf (Eph. 6:18). It is as if the Holy Spirit conducts a symphony of gifts working in harmony to make "melody to the Lord" with "psalms, hymns, and spiritual songs" (Eph. 5:18–20).

Contemplation is made possible by the Holy Spirit. The Spirit looks like grace, which grips and sanctifies human persons into whole persons and community (John 16:13f). In the community or body of Christ, we are anointed (1 John 2:27) by the all-knowing Spirit and we are given complete knowledge that needs no further teaching.. The Spirit, who alone knows the "hidden things of God," who "searches everything, even the depths of God," has in principle opened up these

---

[15] Catherine of Siena, *Dialogue*, translated by Suzanne Noffke, O.P. (New York: Paulist Press, 1980) 146.

[16] Mary Clark, ed., *Augustine of Hippo* (New York: Paulist Press, 1984) 146.

depths to the "spiritual," to "those who possess the Spirit," who "have the mind of Christ." They have access to these and all the mysteries that "no eye has seen, nor ear heard"; no one who has not received the Spirit "is able to understand them because they are spiritually discerned." The image of spiritual discernment is that of the "pouring" of the divine Spirit into our hearts (Rom. 5:5; cf. Gal. 4:6), or the Spirit "sealing" the innermost core of our spirit (Eph. 1:13).

Spirit and Ceaseless Prayer

St. Paul's first epistle to the Thessalonians helps me explain what I mean by ceaseless prayer:

> But we appeal to you, brothers and sisters, to respect those who labor among you, and have charge of you in the Lord and admonish you; esteem them very highly in love because of their work. Be at peace among yourselves. And we urge you, beloved to admonish the idlers, encourage the faint hearted, help the weak, be patient with all of them. See that none of you repays evil for evil, but always seek to do good to one another and to all. Rejoice always, pray without ceasing, give thanks in all circumstances; for this the will of God in Christ Jesus for you. Do not quench the Spirit. Do not despise the words of the prophets, but test everything; hold fast to what is good; abstain from every form of evil. (1 Thess. 5:12–22)

Paul's understanding of a discerning community that prays without ceasing presents a way of praying that is difficult for an individualistic culture to grasp: that there is such thing as ongoing communal discernment.

I will later argue that much of the problem with Westernized Christian spirituality is that it has lost the meaning and value of covenants. Paul teaches the church that to pray without ceasing assumes the covenants of always seeking the other's good, never repaying evil for evil, rejoicing always, always being thankful, being at peace, and helping the weak. For Paul, to understand prayer is to understand prayer in relationship with one another and not in some kind of Western system of personal salvation in which one can pray to God alone. Without covenants, ceaseless prayer remains unintelligible. Prayer need not be understood in an individualistic sense, and an expanded understanding of prayer without ceasing has increased my vocational awareness of peacemaking. Brother Lawrence says:

> Our sanctification depended not upon changing our works but in doing for God what we ordinarily do for ourselves.... [He found] that the best way of reaching God was by doing ordinary tasks, which he was obliged to perform under obedience, entirely for the love of God and not for the human attitude toward them. [For him] it was a great delusion to think that time set aside for prayer should be different from other times...[since] we were equally obliged to be united to God by work in the time assigned to work as by prayer during prayer time.[17]

Through covenant, Jesus taught his disciples that prayer must become their way of life in seeking the Father's best intentions not only for their life but for the lives of those they served. The emphasis is not simply upon asking and receiving for self alone, as some popular evangelists are wont to say about Matthew 7:7, but upon the way of life of Jesus' disciples who have learned to negotiate God's presence always with them. This means that prayer is more accurately understood as our disposition toward God, than as our words of petition. This is what Jesus taught Nicodemus:

> Now there was a Pharisee named Nicodemus, a leader of the Jews. He came to Jesus by night and said to him, "Rabbi, we know that you are a teacher who has come from God; for no one can do these signs that you do apart from the presence

---

[17] *The Practice of the Presence of God*, 49,50.

of God." Jesus answered him, "Very truly, I tell you, no one can see the Kingdom of God without being born from above." Nicodemus said to him, "How can anyone be born after having grown old? Can one enter a second time into the mother's womb and be born?" Jesus answered, "Very truly, I tell you, no one can enter the kingdom of God without being born of water and Spirit. What is born of the flesh is flesh, and what is born of the Spirit is spirit. Do not be astonished that I said to you, 'You must be born from above.' The wind blows where it chooses, and you hear the sound of it, but you do not know where it comes from or where it goes. So it is with everyone who is born of the Spirit." Nicodemus said to him, "How can these things be?" Jesus answered him, "Are you a teacher of Israel, and yet you do not understand these things?" (John 3:1–10)

Nicodemus's violent world forced him to the uniqueness of Jesus who taught lessons more profound than he had ever heard. Jesus became Nicodemus's epiphany to reintegrate the life of spirit back into perfunctory beliefs. Those who separate the environments of prayer, spirit, and ministry fail to make the connections between Christian spirituality and the nonviolent life. The assumption that prayer is more our way of life in practicing the presence of God facilitates our needed growth of all that we are—body, spirit and intellect. The practice of such integrated growth toward God, as a grapevine grows toward sunlight, is what I define as ceaseless prayer.

Pastors, priests, and ministers are essential to such growth in others because they have been given the talent to articulate God's presence on behalf of the Christian community. I learned firsthand the problem of a Western determination of individualistic prayer. When I was a seminarian at Princeton, I attended a Presbyterian church in which the pastor proceeded to take out his clipboard during the intercessions. I did not know what was about to occur, but I thought to myself that whatever was about to happen would leave an indelible impression on me. The pastor asked the congregation for "the prayer requests from the body." He then began to jot down notes and record the antiphonal responses from the congregation. I noticed that most of the prayer requests did not reveal intimate knowledge about the particular person who spoke. The prayer requests were usually to "pray for the mailman who needed Jesus" or to "pray for my great-grandmother who entered the hospital." No one ever requested prayers for deliverance from sexual temptation or prayers that they would fill out their tax return to the best of their knowledge. Once the antiphony of superficial requests came from "the body" the pastor proceeded to "lift them up in prayer." He proceeded to inform God about things God did not know. It was as if the pastor needed to wake God up from God's slumber: "Dear God, we just want to ask you right now to be with us, to bring the news of your flock, to help the mailman who is struggling with his faith, to visit Jenny's great-grandmother who just entered the hospital."

As a result of such a redundant understanding of God's presence, I now teach my students, who lead their congregations in prayer, that if prayer is to be intelligible, prayer must be understood as continuous and communal. My mantra in teaching is that prayer, as "my personal relationship with God," is the bane of Western spirituality. Holmes is helpful here:

> Our understanding of the meaning of prayer has very much to do with our understanding of God. The New Testament common verbs for prayer, *euchomai* and more especially *proseuchomai*, mean to pray as to wish for something. The implication is that God is the source of what we might desire and prayer consists largely of a "wish list." Such an understanding of prayer rises all kinds of questions about God, if we understand him as he who foreordains all things and knows all that shall come to pass. It is as if one prayed each day for the sun to rise the next.[18]

In order to counter individualistic assumptions of Western Christian spirituality, I have learned through my experience to define prayer apophatically. To define what prayer is does not help my

---

[18] Holmes, *Spirituality for Ministry*, 19.

students, formed in an individualistic culture, to understand their complicity with superficial practices of God's presence. The apophatic method toward God is helpful in respect to delivering one from self because the apophatic method makes one look past self into a deep dazzling darkness. Alan Jones states, "The more I follow the apophatic way, the more I need to be nourished by the images from the Bible and from the Liturgy. These images point me in the direction I wish to go, but they are not the way itself."[19]

Of course the best practices of prayer are both conceptual (cataphatic) and critical (apophatic), but I privilege apophatic prayer in my context because it helps my Western students see that the Apostle Paul's understanding of ceaseless prayer makes sense through the practices of recognizing God's presence. Apophatic prayer is the process of stripping cultural and anthropomorphic images of God so to remind the community that what we think of as God is not the living God. God is always much more than we can think or imagine. Since we will always be cultural and communal beings, aphophatic prayer must be a continuous and ceaseless process of reminding Christian disciples that God is not our creation.

Prayer Defined Apophatically

Apophatic prayer is prayer without ceasing, a spiritual discipline that requires our constant attention of removing stagnant images and concepts that often replace the presence of the living God. Simone Weil helps me explain how apophatic prayer is ceaseless prayer through her concept of attention. Weil believes that our love for God is cultivated in an increased attention span for God. The concept of attention for Weil, however, does not necessarily end in Pelagianism because she believes that love does not seek to produce anything greater than ourselves. Love only produces mutuality. Any effort of love stretched toward God does not reach God without God's grace. For Weil, it is only after a long and fruitless effort that ends in

---

[19] Jones, *Soul Making,* 28.

despair, when we can no longer expect anything, that from outside ourselves, the gift of vision of God comes as a marvelous surprise. This stripping process is needed because it provides a history in which we can recognize the false sense of fullness and finally recognize God's presence. In other words, we cannot know God without a history of mutuality. This is also Augustine's understanding that "to know God is to love God."

Weil's concept of attention helps me see that the call (avocation) of Christ is to love God and others even through despair. Our love for God, which produces our knowledge of God, makes us long to increase our attention span for God's presence. This need to seek God in all things facilitates a coherent understanding of my vocation as priest and professor in which I no longer polarize academy and church. In other words, I no longer see my vocation in either the church or the academy. I can no longer accept the concept of the church that by an onrush of emotion the skepticism of the academy can be permanently dissolved, and that of the current academy that skepticism is as virtuous as critical thinking. It is a false dichotomy to think that there is either an academic divinity school or a church institution that trains pastors. No longer do we believe that only by careful scientific method is truth obtained.

In order to solve this problem between church and academy, at least in terms of how prayer presents a solution to the false dichotomy between church and academy, I propose that prayer contains elements both of hope and despair, faith and skepticism. Our restlessness for God contains within it the tensions that often represent both the church and the academy. In prayer, I learn as a priest and professor that I must constantly be attentive to God in our midst without necessarily fixing that reality as God. In other words, I learn to appropriate God's presence apophatically, which ironically becomes a contentment I have not had before. I learn the contentment that I need not simply play the role of a professor or the role of a priest. Practicing the living presence of God through apophatic prayer allows me also to understand my dynamic vocation of teaching others to love God so that they may know God.

Apophatic prayer, however, requires both a history and a community in order for it to be understood.

Apophatic prayer requires a history in the sense that the student learns to recognize God, an anamnesis in which one practices God's presence retrospectively. More particularly to my own narrative of leaving a position as assistant professor of spiritual and moral theology at the School of Theology at the University of the South and now assistant professor of spirituality and black church studies at Duke University, a history has to occur in which I can see how I have responded to God and my neighbors as priest and professor. From such a history my experience has been that people identify either to my priestly vocation or my professorial vocation. Perhaps I just don't know what it would mean or look like for someone to relate to me as both priest and professor. To be granted such cohesion to my vocation, however, to be both priest and professor, is a matter of grace because the academy and the church are usually vying for sole vocational allegiance between prayer and scholarship. In other words, the academy and the church rarely allow full histories to occur in which individuals are simultaneously understood as priest and professor.

Apophatic prayer assumes and requires a community in the sense that it is not just my experience of God that determines God's reality, but others' mutual experiences with God. Through such mutuality I gain a better understanding of a cohesive vocation as priest and professor in which I am able to answer why I teach certain courses and read and write certain books. And what I understand as authentic community is largely understood through my particular narrative as priest and professor, who understands unity in diversity, especially as such unity relates to a broad spectrum of instructional techniques in a classroom. A theological institution can focus on many different aspects of instructional design but must ultimately come back to the classroom. As diversity becomes a more significant concern, the teacher's attention toward God, three persons in one nature, will inevitably turn to how she or he can maximize the performance of diverse students in one classroom.

Spirit and Covenant

Most of our images of God are inherited through communal ways of knowing, and this communal way of knowing is the way that Jesus teaches us how we are to know God. But this communal way of knowing is not easy, as Tutu explained earlier: "Those who are God's friends are distinguished by the fact that they suffer." In some sense, we are taught in mystical literature that a living death is required of us to even know ourselves. In our egalitarian milieu, this spiritual truth of death and resurrection may seem incommensurate with our understanding of individual wholeness and well-being, but as Tutu continues, "Who says that death is the worst thing that could happen to a Christian?"[20] Instead, our spiritual journeys are kenotic in the sense that in order to really know anything, much less God and ourselves, we need to learn how to see experience of God and self in light of how such a relationship creates mutuality. Mutuality as spiritual concept for Western Christians is extremely difficult to comprehend without reverting to language of heresy and schism.

Tom Shaw, Episcopal bishop of Massachusetts, shows the need to be trained in knowing how to see God in our experience. Shaw tells the story of how he practices early arrivals to the churches for whom he performs confirmations. One particular Sunday, Shaw learned how to see his experience of God in a much different way. On this Sunday, Shaw showed up early as usual, but the candidates for confirmation were not present. Shaw waited until he had to leave the church classroom in time to make the procession for the Sunday service. On his way to the front of the church, one of the candidates, a black boy, ran up to Shaw. The young boy was dressed in a white tuxedo. Shaw said, "You're late. I waited for you and all the others to make sure that you all learned what you will be professing this morning. Now that the service is beginning, I have a question which I'd like you to answer. What does baptism mean to you?" The boy responded, "Doesn't that mean that God loves you so much that he worships you?"

---

[20] Tutu, handwritten notes, Undated.

Shaw's story helps us see that the questioning discourse of Christian spirituality is not the modern method in which there is interrogation of data but that spiritual discourse provides the space and context in which there is interrogation of us. It is the intractable strangeness of the ground of belief that must constantly be allowed to challenge the fixed assumptions of religiosity and psychotherapy. So far, my argument has been that Christian spirituality is not about the typical Western obsession of an aggregate of individuals in pursuit of his or her experience of God; rather, spirituality is an impossible lifestyle only achievable through a communal way of knowing in which Christian pilgrims and disciples are trained to see God in experience. In other words, Christians are trained to make peace, trained to make that which is impossible possible. At this point, I want to move to where this training occurs.

The Spirit: Where Christian Spirituality Occurs

In the kingdom of heaven we will discover the great mystery that we need others to know God and ourselves. For example, we need others to discover the concepts of beauty, language, and faith. I need someone else to know if I am handsome or ugly, to know if I have intelligence. I need a community to make sense of myself. I also need to know saints to make sense of how God exists in a world such as this. Because of our reliance on others, both in knowing God and our own experience of God, Christian spirituality becomes the communal practice of staying awake in the presence of God. In other words, Christian spirituality looks like a community of saints who know themselves through the deep awareness of each other's presence. And such a community is knowledgeable of itself as Christian through the awareness of the greatest other, God, revealed in Jesus Christ. Such Christian communal awareness is not static, however; it is an ongoing, dynamic knowledge that depends upon spiritual practices of God's revelation in Jesus. Since Jesus' own immediate disciples had trouble practicing Jesus' ways, and most of all had trouble staying awake with

Christ, we all the more need to be aware of a practiced Christian spirituality of community.

There are certain assumptions that the church gives us in terms of understanding spirituality as a practiced revelation. These assumptions facilitate our training in the divine mystery of the church that I mentioned before, that we know self through the other. Such divine knowledge is practiced. For example, in order to recognize angelic presence, the late Alexander Schmemann, a distinguished Orthodox priest and teacher, once told a group of students why he believed Christians have to practice the revelation of angels. When he was a young man living in Paris, he was traveling on the Metro one day with his fiancée. They were very much in love and bound up only in each other. The train stopped, and an elderly, very ugly woman got on. She was dressed in the uniform of the Salvation Army and she came and sat near them to their disgust. The young lovers began to whisper to each other in their Russian language, exclaiming to each other about the grossness and ugliness of the old woman. The train came to a stop. The old woman got up, and as she passed the two young people, she said to them in perfect Russian, "I wasn't always ugly!" That person, insisted Father Schmemann, was an angel of God. She brought the shock of revelation, the shock that was needed for him to see that what was there was much more than an ugly old woman. Next time, he would be able to look at an unattractive person in a self-effacing, uninterfering way. It takes practice, however, to spot angelic presences, just like it takes practice to recognize God. But practice alone is not enough, unless one has a great threshold for living in the paradox of practicing being surprised.[21] We need both spiritual practices and community in order to have a vibrant Christian spirituality.

Another example of spirituality as practiced revelation comes from Thomas Merton, a fascinating Cistercian Monk, who discovered that true spirituality meant the difficult attachments to community.

---

[21] See Alan Jones' astute discussion of Alexander Schmemann in Alan Jones, *Soul Making: The Desert Way of Spirituality* (San Francisco: Harper & Row, 1985) 53-54.

In 1958, a decade and a half after his decision to remove himself from "the world," the monk learned this same lesson. When he went to the city of Louisville, Kentucky, to see about printing a postulant's guide for this monastery, Merton had an epiphany that brought about Schmemann's shock of revolution to his entire outlook on life. This epiphany, the defining moment of his life, caused him to be transformed and brought him to a deeper understanding of God: "In Louisville, at the corner of Fourth and Walnut, in the center of the shopping district, I was suddenly overwhelmed with the realization that I loved all those people, that they were mine and I theirs, that we could not be alien to one another even though we were total strangers."[22] Merton understood he could no longer turn his back on the world—and although he maintained his vocation as a monk, his renewed commitment to people resulted in a new form of spirituality, which led him to embrace the world beyond his monastic walls. "To think," wrote Merton, "that for sixteen or seventeen years I have been taking seriously this pure illusion [a separate holiness] that is implicit in so much of our monastic thinking."[23] With this reorientation Merton became an active voice for peace, justice, and racial reconciliation during the Cold War—all the while maintaining a transformed monastic life.

Merton wrote as clearly on this subject of peace as anyone. He made it clear that the issue for the Christian is not pacifism. It is the question of how the church might meet most effectively the evil in the world, which stands in the way of the Christian goal: God's reign over creation. Persons are recruited into God's strategy to redeem creation by resisting evil (that is, violence). This may require force on occasion, although Merton argued that the most effective tactic in the resistance of evil is nonviolence. But first we must be clear about the objective, which is peace, the health and wholeness of society. Then—and only then—we have to affirm what logically follows: that the Christian's goal on this earth is to resist evil through practices of

---

[22] Thomas Merton, *Conjectures of a Guilty Bystander* (New York: Doubleday, 1966) 156.
[23] Merton, *Conjectures of a Guilty Bystander,* 157.

nonviolence. The issue for every Christian finally becomes how evil is best resisted. If with Merton we conclude that the best tactic is nonviolence, we must never confuse nonviolence with nonresistance.

In the supportive community of Gethsemani, Merton grew to understand the seeds of contemplation that God had spread in his life and that blossomed into his monastic vocation. Carefully, he charted the meaning of a life consciously lived before God. In one of his most famous passages, Merton teaches Christians how to remain available to the life of God:

> Every moment and every event of every man's life on earth plants something in his soul. For just as the wind carries thousands of invisible and visible winged seeds, so the stream of time brings with it germs of spiritual vitality that come to rest imperceptibly in the minds and wills of men. Most of these unnumbered seeds perish and are lost, because men are not prepared to receive them: for such seeds as these cannot spring up anywhere except in the good soil of liberty and desire.[24]

In his lifetime Merton reached out to millions with his books. But the more people discovered his writings, the more he seemed to be drawn to deeper solitude. He became not only a monk, but a hermit, retiring to a secluded cottage on the monastery grounds. In the year or so just before his death, Merton's friends began to feel uneasy when they visited him. He seemed distant, beyond their reach: "No matter how much you talked," one said, "you got the feeling that he was always apart." Two of his oldest friends, Edward Rice and Robert Lax, found themselves sharing their impressions when they met. As Rice remembers, "I told Lax that I thought the Old Bos (which was what we called him) wasn't relating to people; Lax agreed. Now, I wonder if he was not literally in another world."[25]

---

[24] Thomas Merton, *Seeds of Contemplation* (New York: Dell, 1949) 11.
[25] Edward Rice, *The Man in the Sycamore Tree* (Garden City, NY: Doubleday, Image Books, 1972) 176.

Necessary for contemporary forms of Christian spirituality are communal practices of God's presence that inform how a person moves beyond Western definitions of spirituality, which are often self-contained with little understanding of relationality. To move spiritual discourse beyond a Western infatuation with self is a difficult task because the impetus to be spiritual in Western cultures comes from the so-called personal or subjective sphere. For example, the dominant question in our Bible Belt is, "Do you have a personal relationship with Jesus?" But how many times is a Western person asked, "Do you have a communal relationship with Jesus?" Especially, how many times are they asked this question in the same soteriological or salvific importance as the previous question? In other words, does a communal relationship with Jesus matter just as much as a personal relationship with Jesus in matters of salvation? I would be so bold as to volunteer the answer of no, not really—that Western Christian conceptions of salvation are normally confined to one's own personal relationship with Jesus. Therefore, Christian spirituality is usually about one's own personal journey.

My task, however, is to show how Christian spirituality is personal only to the extent that it is practiced communally. Personal spirituality is recognizable and intelligible only to the extent that it is relational and relates fully to one's neighbor. And who is one's neighbor? The answer to this question is only discovered, as taught by Jesus, through hospitality and sacrifice. In other words, Jesus teaches a specific kind of spirituality through the story of the Good Samaritan, that one cannot know who is neighborly unless such a relationship is demonstrated through practices such as rescuing and feeding the dying. In the same way of practicing being good neighbors, so too must we discover the obvious definition of Christian spirituality through spiritual practices such as prayer, fasting, confession, and reconciliation in which we recognize God's presence on earth as it is in heaven. In other words, Christian spirituality is obvious in its practices.

The problem of practicing God's presence, however, is that God is not always obvious. We create a scandal of the cross and stumble over God, nailing God to a cross. We often even see our own misinformed actions as providential. Unfortunately, we still mistake God in our midst for an enemy. This lack of discernment of God's presence correlates to a lack of ongoing spiritual practices that prepare us to meet and recognize our Maker. What these ongoing spiritual practices entail are the tasks of prayer in which trust and faithfulness build a Christian character able to withstand the truth of God. In a Western cultural definition of spirituality, however, many people practice a form of spirituality in which there is no conceptual space to confess that there is someone much greater than oneself. As a result, the truth of God that scared most biblical characters rarely frightens Western Christians, who easily define God through a personal relationship.

Further still, in Western Christian spirituality there seems to be space enough only for the fulfillment of personal salvation. For example, the concept of heaven in the Western world is only intelligible in light of some form of individual, existential bliss. If one thinks hard, however, on this side of heaven, how could anyone be existentially in heaven, fully cognizant of the other in hell? This question is not often asked in the Western world with its disconnect between personal salvation and communal salvation. Traditions such as the Eastern Orthodox and the Anglican Church in Africa are much more in touch with how complete bliss, joy, and heaven are only intelligible through communal awareness. With the kind of Christian spirituality that most of us practice in the Western world, I would dare say that we worship ourselves more than God. What we often call a personal relationship with God is shorthand for our own version of God. Instead of seeing ourselves made in the image of God, we, like the German sociologist Emil Durkheim, see that God is made in our image. Someone described such a God as an individualistic deity contemplating suicide at the edge of the universe.

Christian spirituality should be different from this. Christian spirituality should be a communal ability to practice the image of God in whom three persons are one nature. The image of God is community. Such a communal ability is revealed through our participation in the Spirit of God, who is not individualistic or psychotic, contemplating suicide at the edge of the universe. Christian spirituality becomes intelligible through God's image of relational personhood: three persons in one nature.

Vladimir Lossky helps me explain how we fit into the image of God through the Holy Spirit. For Lossky, there is a theological problem in the doctrine of God. He reflects upon how the Holy Spirit is now unknown due to the absence of a reciprocal image; for example, the Son is the image of the Father and the Holy Spirit the image of the Son, but as of yet there is no image of the Holy Spirit. Lossky displays the beautiful insight that since the Holy Spirit is made manifest in us as deified persons, the multitude of the saints will be the Spirit's image. Through the coming of the Holy Spirit the Trinity dwells within us and deifies us, confers upon us the uncreated energies of which we must partake. The Holy Spirit mysteriously identifies herself with human persons while remaining incommunicable. She substitutes herself for ourselves and cries on our behalf. In the Holy Spirit the will of God is no longer external to ourselves. She confers grace inwardly, manifesting such grace within our very person insofar as our human will remains in accord with the divine will and cooperates with it in making grace our own. This is the way of deification.

But deification and theosis are difficult to explain, impossible apart from the initiatives of the Holy Spirit, the Spirit who is no longer external to ourselves.[26] In short, the church is the image of the Holy Spirit. This is both good and bad news, however: good news as the church basks in the image of Holy Spirit who through Pentecost helps the church celebrate diversity as unity and unity as diversity, but bad news in the sense that the church betrays the image of God to be other than God is. In other words, we make God look atrocious through our practices of greed, disunity, and victimization. The Western church further endangers blasphemy against the Holy Spirit as it locates the spiritual life in a private, separate sphere of existence.

In Christian spirituality we begin with the mystery of the church's deepest experience—a mystery because the church's origin is

---

[26] *Orthodox Theology*, 173.

deeper than our minds can take us. By the time the church became conscious of her experience, God had already become an experience of an experience; therefore, the church constructs an image of a reality that in itself occurs before her normal, historical awareness can become operational to describe it. In other words, what we know at the deepest place of the church, we know not with the clarity of our cognitive minds but through what is often seen as the obscure hermeneutics of particular communities calling themselves the church. I name this "knowing through obscurity" because the church, since her beginning, has had to seek God in unknowing. Only a few in the church have claimed an immediacy of contemplative intuition.

Even as we attempt this description of something sensed called spirituality, even more particularly Christian spirituality, we find ourselves bringing our cognitive, categorizing faculty of knowing into operation, as opposed to affective ways of knowing by heart, the heart as defined by the core of one's being where one is most truly oneself. To reiterate, Christian spirituality cannot be when our minds seek explanation of its existence, of its experience, because to do so would be like the dog who thinks itself born to turn in circles to chase its own tail. Herein, in this chase to define Christian spiritual experience, I argue that a discourse in Christian spirituality carries with it the daily need of habits and skills given to Christian individuals through the church. There can be no experience of God solely as an individual's experience per se, as if God's presence resides only in the personal realm (you all have heard the saying that you must have a personal relationship with your Lord and Savior, and if you were the only one alive, God would still come and die for you — but this way of naming relationship with God is individualistic and unintelligible to the way that Jesus taught us how to pray); instead, Christian spirituality articulates our image of God as diverse persons in an unified nature of the church. Christian spirituality immediately becomes problematic when it is conceived of as outside of community. Community is the image of God.

In the desert tradition, the African desert father Abba Moses tells the story of a disciple who wanted salvation that he could achieve on his own. The disciple came to Abba Moses seeking such salvation

autonomously achieved through asceticism. Abba Moses instructed the
disciple first to go and curse the dead. The disciple did as he was told.
"You are the most vile of souls!" the disciple proclaimed in a
graveyard. Upon the disciple's return, Abba Moses asked, "What did
they say back to you?" The disciple said, "There was no reply." Abba
Moses then instructed the disciple to return, this time to praise the
dead. "You are the most beatific of souls!" the disciple proclaimed in
the graveyard. Upon the disciple's return, Abba Moses asked, "What
did they say back to you?" The disciple said, "Not a word. They were
as silent as before." Abba Moses said to the disciple, "In order to be
saved, you must be like the dead, beyond cursing and praise." Abba
Moses teaches Christian disciples that our pursuit of a personal
heaven that disregards the living, that disregards the other, is a
spirituality not worth having. In order to be like the Christian image
Abba Moses leaves us with, the Christian disciple must mature beyond
the infantile conceptualization of "me" and "mine" into the
contemplation of the communal ways of knowing God. From this
communal understanding of spirituality we can better understand the
following assumptions of the Christian spiritual life:

(1) The practice of prayer makes real the revelation that life
is a gift.
(2) The practice of prayer eventually reveals the mystery
that God is the one praying in us.
(3) The practice of prayer makes real the axiom that all
manner of things will be made well.
(4) The practice of prayer informs us of the truth that all
that is concealed will be revealed; nothing can be hidden from
God.
(5) The practice of prayer reveals that all of life contains the
possibility of meeting God.
(6) The practice of prayer reveals that Scripture and
tradition are privileged mediators of God's presence; however,
God is not contained by any single word, image, idea, or
experience.

(7) The practice of prayer reveals that as one's relationship with God changes, so will its expression in prayer. Persons need to continue to grow in the presence of God.

(8) The practice of prayer reveals how God turns us into friends through the mystery of mutuality between Creator and creature.

(9) The practice of prayer reveals that any form of spirituality must always serve relationality and be reflective of it.

(10) Ultimately, the practice of prayer reveals that the one who prays is a symphonic voice, a voice that cannot be heard without the relation of other voices.

In order to counter individualistic understandings of prayer, a word must be said about how prayer assumes community. Jesus taught the disciples that prayer occurs where two or three gather; in other words, prayer is not a monologue between an individual and God. Instead, prayer is more like a form of covenant among a community. Particularly, ceaseless prayer is understood and practiced through covenants because we learn the authenticity of our prayers through our covenants with each other. In other words, to know if our prayers make sense, we need to test them in a community. In this sense, the Presbyterian pastor may have rendered a good service to his congregation by helping them test their prayers. Where that pastor could improve that congregation's life of prayer is through a more rigorous theology in which God is not deistic or in need of information about their condition. The pastor's role is to facilitate a history of common prayer in which the congregation learns to discern an authentic presence of God.

As a community recognizes its history of prayer together, they will see retrospectively where their prayers were authentic or where they were simply entertained by their own monologues and shopping lists. From a history of common prayer my experience has been that people's prayers are either flavored with hope or despair. Prayers are hopeful as the "pray-er" looks back, with the help of community, and discovers personal symmetry with God's will. More and more, I am convinced that prayer is understood retrospectively. In other words, prayer is *anamnesis*, something that can only be recalled through communal covenant. Jesus taught the disciples that his presence is discovered through covenant: "Again, truly I tell you, if two of you agree on earth about anything you ask, it will be done for you by my Father in heaven. For where two or three are gathered in my name, I am there among them" (Matt. 18:19–20) An historical covenant has to occur in which I can see what I needed and how I survived the situation in which I was praying.

Prayer requires mutual covenant because no one can know God alone. To know God is to love three persons in one nature, an image of God that disallows individualistic spirituality. Our requirement to love God with all of who we are and to love our neighbor as ourselves is our required covenant that makes sense of ceaseless prayer. As I discuss below regarding a diverse classroom, the greatest difficulty is practicing this covenant in which we must pray with and for those who are much different than ourselves. The constant vocation to love those we would rather not love becomes a ceaseless prayer. Therefore, the covenant to love God and neighbor is indistinguishable from our call to prayer. Walter Wangerin states, "You discover *what* the covenant is in the painful, passionate business of living it out. And, if the covenant is real, if the commitment is real—even not knowing the future, even though we have no idea what the covenant is going to be—then a third being comes to exist between us (the parties who make the covenant)."[27]

Prayer derived from covenant has a life of its own, and it will grow given the opportunity. But covenants take time; in fact, they require time. There must be trust that the other person is not going to cut and run. But when an individualistic society lacks communal sensibility, covenants cannot flourish. Community is important to a definition of covenant because community acts like a buffer against the inevitable suffering that will come under the covenant and with the covenant. But it is not a wasted suffering; often, it is a generative suffering. Wangerin states, "But if [suffering] arises out of covenant, then those who have made the covenant can grow wise and strong.

---

[27] Walter, Wangerin in "The Door Interview," *The Wittenburg Door*, 1989, 15.

They can grow into something different from what either one of them were, because the suffering forced them into new territory. Then the covenant becomes the blessing."[28]

This is why the community is crucial to an understanding of prayer without ceasing. Not only must an individual make a covenant between the self and God, but the individual must enter community in order to solidify the covenants we have with God and our neighbor. Through community we determine through grace and gritted teeth to what extent our covenant with God and each other is real. Indeed, we discover such reality or illusion in the confines of the church. Our covenant with God is a blessing from the beginning even though it feels like imprisonment at certain times. Our journey is difficult because we find it hard to believe that there is such a thing as covenant anymore. It blesses individuals into community because it holds a communal attention together while individuals discover what the covenant is and what the communal relationship is going to be. The covenant describes a new and different world in which one discovers and works out what may seem like disparate relationships. Hence, covenants require time. When Westernized students are too eager to retreat into individualistic modes of education, covenants cannot flourish.

I learned from C. S. Lewis's insight that friendship cannot be chosen. People do not select their deepest relationships; they are discovered in life's journey. So, too, persons discover God's continual presence through the communal process in which one may look back and reflect that there was an abiding presence of God. Nonviolence is a communal process that relies upon the desire to move from pretense to authenticity and from ignorance to understanding. In the Christian mystical tradition, the movement of prayer contained three levels of ascending order: purgation, illumination, and union. In this regard, Paul illustrates my meaning of ceaseless prayer through the following pneumatology: "Likewise the Spirit helps us in our weakness [ignorance]; for we do not know how to pray as we ought, but that very Spirit intercedes with sighs too deep for words. And God, who

---

[28] Ibid., 16.

searches the heart, knows what is the mind of the Spirit, because the Spirit intercedes for the saints according to the will of God" (Rom. 8:26–27). It is my conviction that such a vision of ceaseless prayer becomes vital to sustaining Christian spirituality through nonviolence.

In the end, instead of the typical Western dualisms of rationality and faith, freedom and will, I have an affinity for the Eastern Church, which places revelatory emphasis upon our relation to what God has already revealed in the world. Most importantly, God's Spirit reveals the salvation of the world, but such a revelation does not require control or domination on our part; neither does it claim a banal observation of a "new heaven and new earth" already complete on earth. God created us to be responsible for others—in fact, to know one's identity through others—because God so desired that our movement toward God's life be a movement of participation in the divine life, a life that implies freedom. The problem then becomes how to stay motivated in a Christian vocation of nonviolence in which we know our rewards are few and far between.

Lack of the Spirit

My argument has been that Christian spirituality is not about an aggregate of individuals in pursuit of his or her experience of God but that it is a communal way of knowing in which Christian pilgrims and disciples are trained to see God in experience. Now, I want to talk about where this training occurs.

In the kingdom of heaven we will discover a great mystery. Because of our reliance on others, both in knowing God and our own experience of God, there are certain assumptions that the church gives us to help facilitate our training in the divine mystery of the church:

> Then they prayed and said, "Lord, you know everyone's heart. Show us which of these two you have chosen to take the place in this ministry and apostleship from which Judas turned aside to go to this own place." And they cast lots for

them, and the lot fell on Matthias; and he was added to the
eleven apostles. When the day of Pentecost had come, they
were all together in one place. And suddenly from heaven
there came a sound like the rush of a violent wind, and it filled
the entire house where they were sitting. Divided tongues, as
of fire, appeared among them, and a tongue rested on each of
them. All of them were filled with the Holy Spirit and began
to speak in other languages, as the Spirit gave them ability.
(Acts 1:24–2:4)

Vladimir Lossky explains that the Holy Spirit is now unknown
due to the absence of a reciprocal image; for example, the Son is the
image of the Father and the Holy Spirit the image of the Son, but as
of yet there is no image of the Holy Spirit. Lossky displays the
beautiful insight that since the Holy Spirit manifests self in us as
deified persons, the multitude of the saints will be the Spirit's image.[29]

Through the coming of the Holy Spirit the Trinity dwells within
us and deifies us, confers upon us the uncreated energies of which we
must partake. The Holy Spirit mysteriously identifies herself with
human persons while remaining incommunicable. She substitutes
herself for ourselves and cries on our behalf. In the Holy Spirit the
will of God is no longer external to ourselves. She confers grace
inwardly, manifesting itself within our very person insofar as our
human will remains in accord with the divine will and cooperates with
it in making grace our own. This is the way of deification. But
deification and theosis are difficult to explain, impossible apart from
the initiatives of the Holy Spirit, the Spirit who is no longer external
to ourselves. The Spirit acts as the nexus between person and
community.[30]

---

[29] OT, 173.

[30] Susan Rakoczy, IHM, "Unity, Diversity, and Uniqueness: Foundations of
Cross-Cultural Direction. Rakoczy's references are: David Augsburger *Pastoral
Counseling Acress Cultures* (Philadelphia: Westminster Press, 1986). Augsburger is
good with the third way between sympathy and empathy, he calls it interpathy: a
progressively deeper experience of presence and psychological-spiritual bonding
with people who come in all their uniqueness. quoted in Rakoczy, 18. Mbiti, John. S.
African Religions and philosphy (London: Heinemann Eduational Books, 1969).

Pneumatology suggests that the word "spirituality" expresses the conscious human response to God that is both personal and ecclesial.[31] When we pray (contemplating life in the Spirit), we are often struck dumb by the impossible beauty of grace—and this not until we actually experience a love we know we do not deserve. The impossible truths we meet in our experience, we meet them, are changed by them and learn to appropriate them. But this transformation does not come without death and resurrection—death to our sin and resurrection of our new life in Christ. It is by simply looking upon the possibility of the impossible that we are healed to this new life, indeed, to this "life in the Spirit." Within this simple working definition, we may then approach particular periods with a number of questions in mind. First, was there an understanding of communal spirituality that dealt specifically with how individuals matured in the life of the Spirit? Secondly, what was the relationship between the personal and communal dimensions of prayer as viewed through the patristic period? Lastly, was there a distinction between what we now think of as spirituality and pneumatology?[32]

Spirit teaches the church how to pray. How does the church inform a person's view of prayer? My purpose of asking this question is to take seriously what you and I say we do when we pray. Christian understandings of prayer come mainly through the Western narrative of cognitive prayer, in which prayer, study, and contemplation are all synonymous terms. I want to go a step further in defining prayer as more than a cognitive function. According to Aquinas, sight is the highest and most spiritual sense, and therefore most akin to the

---

John Pobee, *Toward an African Theology* (Nashville: Abingdon, 1979). Benjamin Ray, *African Religions: Symbol, Ritual and Community* (Englewood Cliffs, NJ: Prentice-hall, 1976). Twesigye, Emmanuel Common Ground: Christianity, African Religion and Philosophy (New York: Peter Lang, 1987).

[31] See E. Schweizer, "Pneuma," in The Theological Dictionary of the New Testament, 10 Vols. Edited by Gerhard Friedrich (Grand Rapids, Mich: Eerdmans, 1968) VI: 332-455 (especially 415-36 on Paul's understanding of Spirit. Josef Sudbrack, "Spirituality," in Sacramentum Mundi, edited by Karl Rahner et. Al. (New York: Herder and Herder, 1970), VI:148-49, a good survey of the Holy Spirit in Christian Spirituality

[32] Sheldrake, *Spirit & Histor,* 37

intellect. It is for this reason that intellectual knowledge is called sight (*visio*). Because bodily sight is not effected without light, those things that serve for the perfection of intellectual vision are called light. Aristotle compares the agent intellect to light because the agent intellect makes things actually intelligible, even as light somehow makes things visible. Thomism continues nature into supernature and when it has described the total human, and not merely the human soul, as the immediate object of morality or theology, it goes on to deal with our destiny in heaven. It is a destiny not merely of the human soul but of the total person. God is this destiny, and even on earth we are being made to abide with him in heaven. So beware:

> It is a serious thing to live in a society of possible gods and goddesses, to remember that the dullest and most uninteresting person you can talk to may one day be a creature which, if you saw it now, you would be strongly tempted to worship, or else a horror and a corruption such as you now meet, if at all, only in a nightmare. All day long we are, in some degree, helping each other to one or other of these destinations.... There are no ordinary people. You have never talked to a mere mortal. Nations, cultures, arts, civilisations—these are mortal, and their life is to ours as the life of a gnat. But it is immortals whom we joke with, work with, marry, snub, and exploit—immortal horrors or everlasting splendours.[33]

Spiritual masters are aware of the difficulty of keeping human attention in the divine realm. Human beings have a greater propensity for perpetuating and continuing what facilitates our needs as rational animals. Therefore, what captures our attention the most are goods and services that contribute to our survival. Too often, such benefits are relegated to a material understanding of the earth. But innate to human language is the awareness that we are more than rational animals, or at least we are able to describe ourselves as more.

---

[33] C.S. Lewis, *The Weight of Glory* (New York: Macmillan, 1949) 14-15.

The Spirit opens rationality beyond MacIntyre's critique of incommensurate difference. In the Trinity we do not see the monster of personal disorder, but the ability to be an individual in social relationship. Here is pure participation for the other in such a way that uniqueness is demonstrated by virtue of the other. In the Father, Son, and Holy Spirit there is no pain or absence, no incomplete character. And here, O'Donovan's attention to the subjective realty of the presence of the Spirit in the believer and in the church makes sense in the dialectic of freedom and authority as the form of the Christian moral life. The Spirit turns our screams and cries into language by getting us to see through Christian character, an objective moral order that was accomplished by the work of Christ. Confession is the means to continually match who you are with what you are, becoming in such a way to see and be truth simultaneously, to be in the position to benefit consciously from this objective moral order of the Trinity. And confession exorcises the schizophrenia of not being who we are, though some remain schizoids. John's Gospel shows this by going to the true encounter of Jesus and his oneness with the Father (ch. 18).

Jesus stood before a frail man, Pilate: "So you are the king?" Jesus answered, "You say that I am a king. For this I was born, and for this I have come into the world, to bear witness to the truth. Everyone who is of the truth hears my voice." There before Pilate stood the greatest integration between creed and deed; there before him was the cohabitation of heaven. And yet Pilate reverted to theory in order to cling to the pain and absence of God, in order to deny the being before him. All he could do was mumble, "What is truth?"

I claim that prayer is the entire capacity of human beings to be present to God and creation. In other words, prayer is our attention span for God and others. Rowan Williams is helpful:

> To say that knowing creatures in a "contemplative" fashion is to know God is a point of some considerable signi- ficance; it may lead us back to Gregory of Nyssa's insistence that the receptivity of the self before the ungraspable

mysteriousness of creatures is not different in kind from the receptivity of the self before God. And perhaps it also looks forward to the theme beloved of Simone Weil, that the practice of selfless attention, self-forgetful attention, to any task is a proper preparation for contemplating God. To be absorbed in the sheer otherness of any created order of beauty is to open the door to God, because it involves that basic displacement of the dominating ego without which there can be no spiritual growth.[34]

The concept of prayer as our attention for God and creation does not necessarily drive us toward Pelagianism because we cannot produce anything greater than ourselves. Any effort stretched toward goodness does not reach: "It is after long, fruitless effort which ends in despair, when we can no longer expect anything, that, from outside ourselves, the gift comes as a marvelous surprise."[35] These efforts are needed because they destroy the false sense of fullness. The call of Christ is to believe *through* affliction. In response to seeing a "new level of poverty and squalor" in Calcutta, Tutu states,

I was truly devastated by what I had experienced. I wondered about God, about the reality of His love and caring. Why should so much unmitigated and seemingly pointless suffering be happening, especially when one looked on potbellied urchins who looked so dissipated and exhausted so prematurely? Was there any point in human existence? Now these and similar questions I could have asked in almost identical settings at home in South Africa.... So much avoidable suffering could happen just because human beings appeared to be incorrigibly selfish, for in my home country one had the distressing spectacle of the squalor and poverty of a Crossroads, a black slum near Cape Town, existing almost obscenely cheek by jowl with the affluence of white suburbia. Where *was* God in all of this? Was it all just sound and fury

---

[34] William, *The Wound of Knowledge*, 179-180.
[35] Simone Weil, *Gravity and Grace.* (New York Putnam 1952) 41.

signifying nothing? Did human beings really count? Why did
justice, righteousness and all the worthwhile things seem to
bite the dust so comprehensively and often so ignominiously
when their opposites strutted about arrogantly?[36]

Belief must percolate the skepticism of affliction. Instead of the
assumption of much modern religious thought that by an onrush of
emotion, skepticism can be permanently dissolved, there must be a
true confrontation of evil; otherwise, life is lived in a dangerous
illusion. Percolation of faith within affliction involves *attente*,
attention on God, an operation that cannot be hurried. For Weil, this
is the subjective counterpart of the operation of grace itself:
"'Humility is endless,' and *attente* is humility in action."[37]

Prayer tests the intentions of the person praying; that is, true
attention to God disallows the treatment of others as means for ends.
In this respect, Maggie Ross's concept of God's kenosis also proves
helpful in that *attente* is important due to our lack of skill in
recognizing God. Her thesis is that we often look for power in
association with God, but such power does not show God's presence.
God does not force creation, although God allowed God's Second
Person to be forced by it. Christian consciousness is formed by this
narrative of God's interaction with creation, whether they
acknowledge it or not. Salvation comes in the turning toward God,
who acts in such ways so as know where God is acting to be cleansed
by God's presence. Therefore, forgiveness is not so much what we
choose to do as what we become. Without forgiveness, we can never
rise above affliction. In forgiveness the wound of creation is slowly
transfigured toward a new heaven and earth.

Weil's spiritual writings provide special insight into prayer, as
she states,

The key to a Christian conception of studies is the realization that prayer consists of attention. It is the orientation
of all the attention of which the soul is capable toward God.

---

[36]Tutu, "My Credo," 231-232.
[37]Tomlin, 60.

The quality of the attention counts for much in the quality of the prayer. Warmth of heart cannot make up for it. The highest part of the attention only makes contact with God, when prayer is intense and pure enough for such a contact to be established; but the whole attention is turned toward God.[38]

True prayer trains persons beyond the contradictions of survival and grace. Whether a person can maintain the fixed attitude of "attention" which, as Weil remarks in her essay on "The Right Use of School Studies," depends not so much on the goal of knowing God as an object of prayer as to be known by God. Howard Thurman accentuates this point when he states, "It may be that the experience of which we speak is not possible unless and until the individual sees himself as being contained or held by something so much more than he is that his life is brought into a focus of self-conscious meaning and value."[39] Herein, it was Weil's desire to be passive and recipient rather than seeker and pursuer of truth that made her reject the "consolations of religion."[40] Creation is at the point where love is just possible—a "love," for Weil, that was "not a state but a direction."[41] It is a love in proportion to the distance created between God and creature. Tutu states,

> At the heart of things is an ultimate reality that is good and loving, concerned to see that justice and goodness and love will prevail. This ultimate reality I believe to be personal, a being with whom I can enter into intimate personal relationship. Despite all appearances to the contrary this ultimate reality, God, is in charge, but in charge in a way that does not cancel out our autonomy as persons. God gives us space to be persons who are moral agents, with the capacity to respond freely, to love or not to love, to obey or not to

---

[38]Weil, "Reflections on the Right use of School Studies with a View to the Love of God," in *Simone Weil Reader*, 44.

[39] Walter Fluker, ed., *A Strange Freedom: The Best of Howard Thurman on Religious Experience and Public Life* (Boston: Beacon Press, 1998) 249-250.

[40]Weil, *Gravity and Grace*, 13.

[41]Weil, *Waiting on God*, 77.

obey, free to be good or to be vicious. God has such a profound reverence for our autonomy and freedom that He had much rather see us go freely to hell than compel us to go to heaven. As they say, the doctrine of hell is God's greatest complement to us as humans.[42]

Howard Thurman provides the additional illustration of the life of African Americans after slavery

A man who had been called "J. B." all his life and who knew no other name had to make a name for himself out of the initials. Think of what it meant to this man who had been regarded by his society as without name or significance to find himself suddenly on the receiving end of personal attention from the vast federal government. Now his name was known, his address duly noted, and his intention to be a consumer of certain goods such as meat, sugar, gasoline, and automobile tires was registered. An entirely fresh dimension of personal awareness opened out before him. He began to experience himself as a human being.[43]

Prayer without ceasing can be seen in how Thurman describes the moment of insight into a new idea. Thurman states,

The impact upon the individual when he experiences himself as a human being is to regard himself as being of infinite worth. Such a sense of worth is not confined by narrow limits of the self so that worth may be determined by contrast with something of someone of less worth. No, this is a specious basis for ascertaining worth. Such a sense of worth is rooted in one's own consciousness which expands and expands until there is involved the totality of life itself. As important as is the clue to one's self—estimate, as found in the attitude of others in the environment, this is not now what is at issue. To experience oneself as a human being is to

---

[42]Tutu, "Credo," 234.
[43] Fluker, ed., *A Strange Freedom*, 247.

feel life moving through one and claiming one as a part of it. It is like the moment of insight into a new idea or an aspect of truth. What initially is grasped by the mind and held there for meaning begins slowly or suddenly to hold the mind as if the mind itself is being thought by a vaster and greater Mind. It is like the thing that happens when you are trying to explain something to a child and you finally succeed in doing so. Then the child says, "I see." In that moment you are no longer there in fact. The barrier that stood between the child's comprehension of the idea and the idea itself has been removed. There is a flowing together, as if the child and the idea were alone in all the universe.[44]

Violence: The Problem of Maturation in the Spirit

Blasphemy against the Holy Spirit is the sin for which there is no forgiveness (Mark 3:29). I interpret such blasphemy against the Holy Spirit as the capacity to depersonalize. Gandhi provides the following analysis of Christian missions as late as 1939: "Up till now [Christian missionaries] have come as teachers and preachers with queer notions about India and India's great religions. We have been described as a nation of superstitious heathens, knowing nothing, denying God.... To me this is a negation of the spirit of Christ."[45] Gandhi helps us see a different picture of the Spirit as unalterable love capable of connecting disparate realities. Spiritual practices like forgiveness illustrate such pneumatology in which the Spirit breaks down boundaries. Maggie Ross states, "Forgiveness: To live in forgiveness, to sin in the Face of unalterable Love, is much more painful than to sin in the face of an implacable authority."[46] Forgiveness is a perfectly free gift of the spiritual life. And grace transforms the

---

[44] Fluker, ed., *A Strange Freedom*, 248.
[45] Harijan, January 7, 1939.
[46] Maggie Ross, *Pillars of Flame: Power, Priesthood, and Spiritual Maturity* (San Francisco: Harper & Row , 1988) 121.

penitent, for God's love makes that which previously seemed incommensurate whole again.

The Holy Spirit communicates to persons, marking each member of the church with a seal of personal and unique relationship to the Trinity, becoming present in each person. The aggressive intellect demands a proper epistemology in which it may decipher how such a personal seal is enacted. But this unique relationship between God and humanity remains a mystery—the mystery of the self-emptying and of the kenosis of the Holy Spirit's coming into the world. Just as the Son emptied himself to remain under the form of a servant, the Holy Spirit remains hidden so that the gift he imparts may be fully ours, adapted to our persons.[47] But how does creation adapt to the Spirit's gifts without jeopardizing our freedom as persons?

Personhood is freedom in relation to nature, a freedom that cannot be categorized as psychological or moral:

> Personal uniqueness is what remains when one takes away all cosmic context, social and individual—all, indeed, that may be conceptualized. Eluding concepts, personhood cannot be defined. It is the incomparable, the wholly-other. One can only add up individuals, not persons. Their person is always unique. The concept objectifies and collects. Only a thought methodically "deconceptualized" by apophasis can evoke the mystery of personhood.... For the approach to personhood is penetration into a personal universe, at once assumed and open-ended: that of the highest artistic creations, that above all, sometimes very humble but always unique, of a life offered and mastered.[48]

Since personhood can be evoked only through its relation with another, the only way to distinguish the persons of the Trinity is by making precise their relationships, of the Father, the generation of the Son, and the procession of the Holy Spirit are all relationships

---

[47] MTEC, 168.

[48] Vladimir Lossky, *Orthodox Theology* (Crestwood, NY: St. Vladimir's Seminary Press, 1978) 42-43.

which allow distinction among the persons. This view of personhood helps solve the problem mentioned above concerning creation, namely, somehow God is able to relate creation ex nihilo to the possibility of being co-eternal with that which is without origin. Even though God has the freedom not to create, the Trinity "imposes" on created beings the necessity to exist, and to exist for ever: contingent to God, creation is necessary to itself, because God freely makes of the created being what it must be. Therefore, every being has its "reason" in God, in the thought of the Creator who produces not through caprice, but with "reason" (which is yet another meaning of Logos). It is in this reason that Lossky defines the image of God in us to be the ability to be personal, a free responsible being. God has taken our finite nature and opened it up even to the capacity to love more than our own nature, indeed more than our own life: "Thus the mystery of the singular and plural in man reflects the mystery of the singular and plural in God: in the same way that the personal principle in God demands that the one nature express itself in the diversity of persons, likewise in man, created in the image of God."[49]

In the kingdom of heaven we will discover a great mystery. Lossky explains that the Holy Spirit is now unknown due to the absence of a reciprocal image; for example, the Son is the image of the Father and the Holy Spirit the image of the Son, but as of yet there is no image of the Holy Spirit. Here, Lossky exhibits the beautiful insight that since the Holy Spirit manifests himself in us as deified persons, the multitude of the saints will be his image (Orthodox Theology, p.173.

In Lossky's "theandric" church and through a sacramental existence, we enter into union with the divine nature and uniqueness of the Son. But it is necessary that every person of this one nature of Christ's body cooperate with the Second Adam, uniting created nature with the fullness of uncreated grace. This is the work of the Holy Spirit. Yet if our nature finds itself in the body of Christ, human persons are in no way caught up in a blind physical process of deification that abolishes freedom and annihilates the personality.

---

[49] Ibid. 56.

Therefore, Lossky does not adhere to a mysticism of absorption that is so commonly followed in the Eastern religions, nor does he accept the aridity of Spanish spirituality that seems more fixated upon separation from God.[50] Lossky's appeal to mystical theology holds somewhat of a system in theology in that it allows the intellect to have a proper theological language that would prefer silence before uttering what has not yet been revealed.

---

[50] Vladimir Lossky, *The Mystical Theology of the Eastern Church* (London, J. Clark 1957) 226.

3

GANDHIAN SPIRITUALITY: A CORRECTIVE TO WESTERN INDIVIDUALISM

How does one relate the particularity of Christian spirituality to the particularity of Gandhian spirituality? The answer to this question may prove useful in seeing the need to hold both particularities together in synthesis and paradox. Interestingly enough, lessons learned about how spirit promotes nonviolence now lead us to one named Mahatma, "The Great Spirited One." In a post-9/11 world, it is urgent to remember the genius of Mahatma Gandhi, who articulated how a nation-state could avert religious wars. For example, Christian and Muslim tensions in Nigeria and the plight of Pakistani Christians point toward a resurgence for justifying violence in the name of religion.[1] Gandhi understands this synthesis and paradox as he stated, "The finer Christian minds have, in fact, in every age...come in contact with the outside races, whether in their literature or face to face, to realize at once that the 'impassable gulf' theory between one

---

[1] See Paul Wiseman, "Christians 'paying price' for War" in *USA Today*, October 4, 2002. In this general article, the informative account of the shift toward violence toward minority Christians is taking place. For example, the four Christian women killed August 9, 2002 when Islamic militants burst into their hospital compound throwing grenades at nurses, paramedics and clerical workers.

religion and another was false to life and to the soul."[2] As one learns
from Gandhi's encounter with Christianity, one sees that nonviolence
is the catalyst that synthesizes Gandhi's thought with Christianity.
Therefore, what holds Gandhian spirituality and Western Christian
spirituality together is the insistence of both to reject all forms of
violence. In order to display this thesis, I need to display the
differences and similarities between Gandhi and Christianity. Bouyer's
description of two spiritualities is helpful:

> Two spiritualities, two ways of life, each differing from
> the other in its goal, intentions, and practical details. Yet
> different as they are, neither can long continue without the
> other. They are joined as a flower is joined to the bulb from
> which it grows. The bulb, misshapen and uninteresting, lies
> buried a full year in the soil, until from it grows a brilliant
> flower. In the same way it is always from the community,
> bland and routine as it seems, that grows the passionate
> searching of life on the edge. And just as it is through the
> flower that the bulb is able to reproduce itself, it is through the
> prophetic spirituality of life on the edge that communities are
> changed and new ones formed.[3]

Gandhi's Context and Background

It is my understanding that Christian spirituality may indeed gain
some clarity by using means outside of its own system.[4] Therefore, I
will briefly display Gandhi's narrative outside the Western system,
which doubtlessly sheds light on how individuals and communities may
proceed to face historical injustice without this history destroying

---

[2]M. Gandhi, *The Collected Works of Mahatma Gandhi* (New Delhi: The
Publications Division, Navajivan Trust, Ahmedabad, 1961) 5:49. Hereafter cited
CWMG.

[3] Bouyer, *A Way in the World*, 30.

[4] Gandhi is outside the Western system, although he was educated within
Western institutions as I discuss below.

their futures. During Gandhi's lifetime, political mass movements occurred around the world in a wide variety of cultures, politicizing millions of people. India's struggle for freedom from British colonial rule was one of the longest and largest of these movements. It began formally in 1885 with the creation of the Indian National Congress and reached a transition when India achieved independence in 1947. Gandhi assumed leadership of this movement in 1919, rapidly transforming it into a mass organization that mobilized India's grassroots. The participation of a huge peasant population significantly included women at every level. The most unique aspect of the Indian movement is that it wielded power nonviolently. Gandhi conceived his method of *satyagraha* (nonviolent power) in a culture that, stereotypes notwithstanding, is no less violent than American society. Martin Luther King Jr. articulated the influence of *satyagraha* on his own life:

> Then I came upon the life and teachings of Mahatma Gandhi. As I read his works I became deeply fascinated by his campaigns of nonviolent resistance. The whole Gandhian concept of satyagraha (*satya* is truth which equals love, and *graha* is force; *satyagraha* thus means truth-force or love force) was profoundly significant to me. As I delved deeper into the philosophy of Gandhi my skepticism concerning the power of love gradually diminished, and I came to see for the first time that the Christian doctrine of love operating through the Gandhian method of nonviolence was one of the most potent weapons available to oppressed people in their struggle for freedom. At this time, however, I had a merely intellectual understanding and appreciation of the position, with no firm determination to organize it in a socially effective situation.[5]

[5] Martin Luther King, Jr., "Pilgrimage to Nonviolence," in *I Have a Dream: Writings and Speeches that Changed the World*, ed., James M. Washington (Harper SanFrancisco, 1986) 59.

Today, India, as in Gandhi's era, is torn by cultural division. American journalist A. M. Rosenthal, exploring the violence in India between Hindus and Muslims, observed that "Gandhi, founder of Indian freedom, used religion to combat bigotry, not to promote it."[6] The syncretic spirit of Hinduism allowed him to define "religion…in its broadest sense, meaning thereby self-realization or knowledge of self."[7] On one hand, Gandhi writes "that [he] had learned to be tolerant of other religions"; on the other, he was critical of dogmatic practices in Hinduism, particularly the institution of untouchability.[8] More precisely, he used nonviolence to combat the violence of both political extremism and religious fanaticism. Gandhi perceived early that India's real enemy was not merely imperialism but violence. To all those who promoted it—terrorists, communists, fascists—Gandhi replied, "I do not believe in short-violent-cuts to success. I am an uncompromising opponent of violent methods even to serve the noblest causes. There is, therefore, really no meeting ground between the school of violence and myself."[9] Gandhi's sojourn to realize this defining insight is fascinating.

Mohandas Karamhand Gandhi was born on 2 October 1869, into a Hindu family of moderate means in the town of Porbandar, on the west coast of India. He was the youngest of five children. His father, Kaba Gandhi, was an influential political figure, having served in several public positions. Gandhi describes his father as "truthful, brave and generous, but short-tempered." His mother is portrayed as faultless: "deeply religious" to the point of "saintliness," yet with a "strong common sense." She impressed him most with her spirit of self-sacrifice. As a devout Hindu in pursuit of self-purification, she

---

[6] A.M. Rosenthal, "Hindus Against Hindus," *New York Times*, March 5, 1993, A29.

[7] CWMG, 39:31.

[8] Gandhi relates in his Autobiography that early in his South African experience, "Hindu defects were pressingly visible to me. If untouchability could be a part of Hinduism, it could but be a rotten part or an excrescence." His total opposition to untouchability was evident then and never ceased to be a central issue in his program of social reforms. CWMG 39:113.

[9] CWMG 25:424.

would take the hardest vows and keep them without flinching.... "To keep two or three consecutive fasts was nothing to her."[10]

Gandhi clarified that the decisive influence on his life came from his mother. From an excruciating conflict with his father came redemption through "clean confession," producing a sudden and unexpected "object-lesson in Ahimsa (nonviolence)." Gandhi writes, "When such Ahimsa becomes all-embracing, it transforms everything it touches. There is no limit to its power."[11] In many ways Gandhi's *ahimsa* had formed him by age eighteen, as he prepared to leave India for England. By his mid-teens, he saw through his religion the relationship between truth and nonviolence. He concluded, first, that "truth is the substance of all morality. Truth became my sole objective. It began to grow in magnitude every day, and my definition of it also has been ever widening."[12] This understanding of truth as one's "sole objective" means that the supreme aim of human experience is knowledge of what Gandhi calls "the essential unity of man and for that matter of all that lives."[13]

The connection Gandhi made between truth and nonviolent conduct was crucial for his nonviolent resistance. If the highest truth is to perceive the unity of all being, then violence is impermissible because humanity is, by definition, individuals composed of one another; thus, to harm a person is to inflict injury on oneself. This realization came early in his education. He recalled a poem he learned in grammar school, "But the truly noble know all men as one / And return with gladness good for evil done." Gandhi writes that these "wonderful lines gripped my mind and heart and became such a passion with me that I began numerous experiments in it."[14] It is no wonder that a few years later, as a student in London reading the Bible, he would find and cherish "the Sermon on the Mount which went straight to my heart."[15]

---

[10] CWMG, 39:7-9
[11] CWMG, 39: 28
[12] CWMG, 39: 33-34
[13] CWMG, 25:390
[14] CWMG, 39:34
[15] CWMG, 39:61

Gandhi's journey took him from an obsessive emulation of English values in his twenties and thirties to a radical rejection of Western civilization in his forties, and finally to a mature realization of what we identify today as his inclusive vision of humanity. Gandhi's value system, then, was not realized all at once; he struggled to develop it through constant reexamination, striving for a right fit between his evolving personal values and modes of political leadership. Gandhi left India for London to study law in September 1888, one month before turning nineteen. He recalled, "It was an uncommon thing for a young man of Rajkot [his locality] to go to England." His family, however, had determined that a British law degree would advance their interests, and they pooled their resources to finance it. Gandhi's high school curriculum, dictated and dominated by English masters, had induced in him an awe of British civilization. Once the prospect of studying in London materialized, a sense of adventure overtook him. His mother required that he take three vows: Not to touch wine, women and meat," solemn oaths, he said, to "keep me safe."[16]

Gandhi eventually embraced his own culture and heritage. At first he thought his clothes were unsuitable due to English sensibilities:

I got new ones.... I also went in for a chimney-pot hat costing nineteen shillings—an excessive price in those days. Not content with this, I wasted ten pounds on an evening suit made in Bond Street, the centre of fashionable life in London. I wasted ten minutes every day before a huge mirror, watching myself arranging my tie and parting my hair in the correct fashion. My hair was by no means soft, and every day it meant a regular struggle with the brush to keep it in position. Each time the hat was put on and off, the hand would automatically move towards the head to adjust the hair, not to mention the other civilized habit of the hand every now and then operating for the same purpose when sitting in polished society. As if all of this were not enough to make me look the

---

[16] CWMG, 39: 37-38.

thing, I directed my attention to other details that were supposed to go towards the making of an English gentleman. I was told it was necessary for me to take lessons in dancing, French and elocution.[17]

Countless confessions have come from other such victims of colonialism or racism, writes Denison Dalton in his work on Gandhi. Dalton's introduction on Gandhi describes the lethal process of trying to gain self-respect in a way that only brings self-alienation. This dilemma of self-respect and alienation is also described profoundly by Malcolm X in his autobiography. For example, Malcolm X describes, after pouring lye on his "kinky hair" to make it "real red—as straight as any white man's":[18]

> How ridiculous I was! Stupid enough to stand there simply lost in admiration of my hair now looking "white."… This was my first really big step toward self-degradation: when I endured all that pain, literally burning my flesh to have it look like a white man's hair. I had that multitude of Negro men and women in America who are brainwashed into believing that the black people are "inferior" and white people "superior" that they will even mutilate their God-created bodies to try to look "pretty" by white standards…. It makes you wonder if the Negro has completely lost his sense of identity, lost touch with himself.[19]

In 1893, London law degree in hand, Gandhi went to South Africa to pursue a legal career by representing members of the Indian community, at a safe distance from the expectations and restrictions of his relatives in Rajkot. The first big transformation came from his

---

[17] CWMG, 39: 46-47

[18] Denison Dalton makes an apt comparison between Malcom X and Gandhi, especially his insight that both had to pass through separatist stages before finally accepting more of an inclusive humanity. See Denison Dalton,. (1996). *Mahatma Gandhi: Selected Political Writings*. Indianapolis: Hackett Publishing Company 7-9.

[19] Malcolm X, *The Autobiography of Malcolm X* (New York: Balantine, 1973) 54.

disillusionment with the British, whose empire then included South Africa. Tutu states:

> It must never be forgotten that Afrikaners, who today form the bulk of the white ruling class, themselves rebelled against the British and fought what they like to call their *Vryheidsoorloe* (Wars of Liberation) at the turn of the century. And when General Jan Smuts led South Africa into the Second World War on the side of the Allies, there were those among his *volk* who opposed the war. They formed organisations such as the *Ossewabrandwag*, a pro-Nazi organisation which carried out acts of sabotage to undermine and oppose the Smuts government. Many who in time became leading Afrikaner politicians were members of the *Ossewabrandwag* and interned for their pro-Nazi sympathies and activities. A former State President and Prime Minister, Mr B.J. Vorster, was interned, and the current State President was himself a member of the *Ossewabrandwag*. Were they terrorists or were they freedom fighters? It depends on which side of the political divide you find yourself.[20]

Gandhi had encountered racist abuse from the first days of his arrival in Durban. His emulative attitude of the British went very deep, and for years he excused such abuses as unrepresentative of the real spirit of British civilization, which he characterized as inherently just and fair. Tutu believes, "Gandhi's way did succeed because the British were under a kind of moral imperative."[21] As late as 1905, after having practiced law in South Africa for twelve years, Gandhi urged his Indian community, "We should not envy [Britain], but emulate its example."[22] By 1909, however, Gandhi, now forty, had changed drastically: "If India copies England, it is my firm conviction that she will be ruined."[23]

---

[20]Tutu, Addresses "Violence and the Church," June 1987.
[21]Ingram, 279.
[22] CWMG, 5:117
[23] CWMG, 10:18

What explains this about-face? Gandhi's separatism began in the summer of 1906, with the British response to the "Zulu rebellion," an uprising that British soldiers suppressed with shocking brutality. Gandhi entered that summer so loyal to his colonial rulers that he volunteered to serve as a medic with the government against the Zulus. He soon discovered that what the British had characterized as a rebellion was really a massacre, often of innocent civilians. Gandhi at first consoled himself by attending to wounded Zulus, but soon his assumptions about English civilization, fixed for decades, completely collapsed.[24] Erik Erikson, in his psychobiography of Gandhi, incisively describes this moment: "The experience of witnessing the outrages perpetuated on black bodies by white he-men aroused in Gandhi both a deeper identification with the maltreated, and a stronger aversion against all male sadism—including such sexual sadism as he had probably felt from childhood to be part of all exploitation of women by men."[25]

The precise event that many biographers describe as triggering Gandhi's civil disobedience came only a month after the defeat of the Zulus. In August 1906, the British colonial government in Johannesburg gave notice of new legislation. All Indians were required to register with the police by giving fingerprints and noting other marks of identification. A substantial fine or three months in prison penalized those who failed to comply. Among Indians, the law quickly became known as the "Black Act." Gandhi, as a leader of his community, branded the new legislation discriminatory and humiliating because Indians were regarded as common criminals. He called a meeting of 3,000 Transvaal Indians in September 1909, in Johannesburg, and they resolved to protest through mass civil disobedience. He made clear in moving the resolution that it was far different than any passed before: "It is a very grave resolution that we are making, as our existence in South Africa depends upon our fully

---

[24] In one of the chapters in his Autobiography on Zulu rebellion ("Heart Searchngs") Gandhi relates how this event, unlike his earlier experience in the Boar War (1899-1902), "brought home to me the horrors of war." CWMG, 39:252.

[25] Erik Erikson, *Gandhi's Truth*, (New York: W.W. Norton, 1969 194.

observing it."[26] He insisted that it was so serious that it must be sealed by each person with an oath before God. Much later Gandhi would refer to the events surrounding this meeting as the "advent of *satyagraha*," that is, the birth of his method of nonviolent action. The main ingredients were present here: a common perception of an extreme injustice and a conviction that civil disobedience could offer a remedy. Gandhi reflects on such conviction:

> Writs are impossible when they are confined to a few recalcitrants. They are troublesome when they have to be executed against many high-souled persons who have done no wrong and who refuse payment to vindicate a principle. They may not attract much notice when isolated individuals resort to this method of multiplying themselves. They bear publicity and the sufferers instead of incurring odium receive congratulations. Men like Thoreau brought about the abolition of slavery by their personal examples.[27]

Gandhi was well aware of the heroic words of Thoreau, which challenged the institution of slavery through the concept of civil disobedience:

> I know this well, that if one thousand, if one hundred, if ten men whom I could name—if ten honest men only—aye, if one honest man, in this state of Massachusetts ceasing to hold slaves were actually to withdraw from this copartnership and be locked up in the country jail therefore, it would be the abolition of slavery in America. For it matters not how small the beginning may seem to be, what is once well done is done forever.[28]

The idea of civil disobedience utilizes the potentiality of non-cooperation to paralyze unjust systems and bring attention-ready

---

[26] CWMG, 5:419-20

[27] Gandhi in Krishnalal Shridharani, *War without Violence* (New York: Harcourt, Brace and Co, 1939) 183-184.

[28] Henry David Thoreau, *Civil Disobedience* (Chicago: The Great Books Foundation, 1955) 12.

solutions. The method of civil disobedience constitutes one important stratagem in Gandhi's *satyagraha* that will be discussed later. Gandhi also enlarged upon non-cooperation as a means to destroy a corrupt state. Martin Luther King Jr., of course, never attempted to destroy the state, only the state's corrupt laws. In the Montgomery bus boycott, King combined Thoreau's idea of civil disobedience with Gandhi's technique of nonviolent resistance. This kind nonviolent direct action or "empowerment" meant, from the moment it was conceived, a community's overcoming of fear and recovery of self-respect could come through collective nonviolence. Tutu is helpful here in understanding the effectiveness of *satyagraha*:

> Even where such a minimum moral level exists the nonviolent path is a hazardous one requiring considerable courage and moral uprightness. Having said that I still believe that it was perhaps possible for a Gandhi to arouse moral indignation and thus support for his cause against the British Raj because there were those back in England who were morally outraged to see the treatment meted out by the army to peaceful demonstrators.[29]

Gandhi's new method was initially described as "passive resistance," but within a year Gandhi rejected that term because it did not convey the active power of nonviolence. He then coined the term *satyagraha*, defined as the "force" of truth and love.[30] Interestingly enough, *satyagraha* was born in South Africa. Tutu states,

> There was even a passive resistance campaign a la Gandhi in an effort initially to bring the plight of blacks to the attention of the authorities who it was naively believed would ameliorate that situation. Later it was in order to bring about a radical change in the circumstances of the black people. Thus commitment of the ANC to nonviolence for the first 50 years of its existence was rewarded when one of its Presidents,

---

[29]Tutu, Addresses "Violence and the Church," June 1987.
[30] CWMG, 16:368-69; and 29: 254-55

Chief Albert Luthuli, was awarded the Nobel Peace Prize. Is it all singular that the only South African to have won the Nobel Peace Prize have both been black?

It was whilst blacks were protesting peacefully against the much hated Pass Laws that the Sharpeville massacre happened when 69 protestors were killed by the police, most of them being shot in the back as they were running away. The world was shocked by Sharpeville, but by and large white South Africa remained relatively unmoved. Some white politicians even commended the police action and called for more of the same. Sharpeville served as a paradigm that has sadly been repeated only too often.[31]

From the outset, therefore, Gandhi wanted to emphasize the special power of *satyagraha* by distinguishing it from passive resistance or what he called *duragraha*, "the force of bias." *Duragraha* is the counterfeit of *satyagraha* because it implies a wrong use of power, coming from a selfish obstinacy. The passive resister, or *duragrahi*, may avoid physical violence yet still harbor enmity and anger within, using nonviolence as a tactic but lacking commitment to its core values of understanding, openness, and respect for the adversary.[32] Martin Luther King Jr. understood this distinction when, following Gandhi, he rejected "passive resistance" as a misnomer. *Satyagraha*, King wrote,

avoids not only external physical violence but also violence of spirit. The nonviolent resister not only refuses to shoot his opponent but he also refuses to hate him.... In the struggle for human dignity, the oppressed people of the world must not succumb to the temptation of becoming bitter or indulging in hate campaigns.... Along the way of life, someone must have sense enough and morality enough to cut off the

---

[31]Tutu, Addresses "Violence and the Church," June 1987.
[32] CWMG, 14:63-65.

chain of hate. This can be done by projecting the ethic of love to the center of our lives.[33]

Having returned to India in 1914, Gandhi graciously endorsed the British cause in the war against the central powers, believing that the struggle was against autocracy and militarism. Disillusioned by the Rawlatt Acts and shocked by the Amritsar massacre, Gandhi repudiated the new India constitution of 1919 and persuaded the India National Congress to adopt a program of non-cooperation with the government. No longer would Gandhi tolerate the dominion of the British Empire. It must also be said, however, that British rule meant nothing if it was not preceded by social reform within Indian society. In 1922 Gandhi saw the launching of his first mass campaign of nonviolent resistance for "civil disobedience" in India. The movement was suspended after a few weeks because it was being used by terrorists to injure life and property.

Gandhi's second mass campaign of nonviolent resistance was launched in the spring of 1930. Indians resigned from public office, stopped buying foreign goods, picketed shops and courts, and even refused to pay taxes. The dramatic event was Gandhi's "march to the sea." After walking to the sea, Gandhi's followers filled pans with sea water and let it evaporate to make salt, breaking the law by evading the salt tax and defying a government monopoly. Gandhi's aim was to resist demonizing the British, to make them participate in a process of discernment and moral transformation. Gandhi had combined a political issue with a moral principle, thus putting his opponents in an embarrassing position. Gandhi managed to reinterpret the Bhagavad Gita, which was read by many of his contemporaries as a call to war, as an argument for nonviolence and continuous conscious awareness of truth.

A few months after India's long-delayed independence in 1947, Gandhi was assassinated by a Hindu Brahmin named Nathuiam Godse, who was exasperated by Gandhi's leadership. In a statement in court, Godse explained that he killed Gandhi in order to cleanse India of

---

[33] Martin Luther King, Jr., *Stride Toward Freedom* (New York: Harper and Row, 1958) 103-4.

superstition. Godse concluded that Gandhi was leading India toward
ruin. Godse sought to free India from ruin by returning to Hindu
control.

In retrospect, Gandhi appears to have possessed a peculiarly
instinctive grasp on the needs of India. The idealists spoke of the
syncretic civilization of India, of the essential unity between Hindus
and Muslims. But Gandhi understood more than most how intense the
animosity and distrust was between Hindus and Muslims, especially
under British rule—an insight sadly manifest in the partition of India
and Pakistan. There is great irony in the last lonely months of
Gandhi's life, as the violence between Hindus and Muslims intensified,
that Muslims continued to think of him as a promoter of Hindu
interests, while Hindus accused him of being partial to Muslims.

Dalton shows Gandhi's political theory at its most original when
contributing two ideas that are quintessentially Gandhi's own: the
first, for which he is renowned, his conception of the power of
nonviolence or *satyagraha*; the second, integrally related, his theory
of freedom or *swaraj*. The Sanskrit word *swaraj* carried two distinct
meanings in ancient India. It could denote, in a political sense, a
sovereign kingdom's freedom from external control. It could also
mean being liberated in an internal, spiritual, or psychological sense,
as being free from illusion and ignorance, free to gain greater self-
knowledge and consequent self-mastery. Obsessions with money and
property or with ways of manipulating people are then seen as
addictive forms of human bondage. The Bhagavad Gita views freedom
as spiritual liberation. It describes the free person as one who "acts
without craving, possessiveness," and who "finds peace" in awareness
of the "infinite spirit," thereby being "freed from delusion."[34] In 2
Corinthians 3:17, Paul provides the Christian view of freedom when
he states, "Now the Lord is the Spirit, and where the Spirit of the
Lord is, there is freedom." The Spirit is the key to see beyond the
illusion of separateness, to gain a vision of the unity of all being or
the oneness of life. The prerequisite for this attainment of freedom is

---

[34] *The Bhagavad-Gita* 2: 71-72, translated by Barbara Stoler Miller (New York:
Bantam, 1986) 39.

self-discipline. Perhaps now one may understand the Spirit's urgings to the desert so that we may find perfect freedom.

In active nonviolence, one must exercise self-control to focus on the essential nature of reality and distinguish it from transient illusions, from the myriad temptations and fleeting distractions that surround us. In the Hindu tradition, the Bhagavad Gita acclaimed the liberated sage as the person of discipline and affirmed: "Arming himself with discipline, seeing everything with an equal eye, he sees the self in all creatures and all creatures in the self."[35] This philosophy of freedom came from India's classical tradition to shape Gandhi's idea of *swaraj*. *Swaraj* gave primary attention to the internal and external aspect of freedom, permitting a higher consciousness attained through disciplined pursuit of self-awareness and knowledge of the other. Herein is the transition and the connection to Christian spirituality—namely, Gandhi offers a corrective to the individualism in Western Christian spirituality in that what is defined as external preferences cannot be distinguished from internal preferences. In other words, personal freedom will always carry a dual sense, having political and spiritual sides.

What mattered most to Gandhi was how *swaraj* could be connected to a whole nexus of other concepts, but especially to *satyagraha*, his idea of nonviolent power and truth. These theories were initially developed in Gandhi's first major writing, *Hind Swaraj* (Indian Independence), published in 1909, three years after the civil disobedience movement in South Africa had begun. Several years after *Hind Swaraj*, Gandhi reflected on the original purpose of this written work:

It was written...in answer to the Indian school of violence, and its prototype in South Africa. I came in contact with every known Indian anarchist in London. Their bravery impressed me, but I feel that their zeal was misguided. I felt that violence was no remedy for India's ills, and that her civilization required the use of a different and higher

---

[35] *The Bhagavad-Gita*, 6:29,66; and 8:30, 119.

weapon.... [*Hind Swaraj*] teaches the gospel of love in place
of that of hate. It replaces violence with self-sacrifice. It pits
soul-force [*satyagraha*] against brute-force.[36]

This short treatise consolidates his theories of freedom and
power. Real *swaraj*, he proclaimed, demands "self-rule or self-control.
The way to it is *satyagraha*: the power of truth and love."[37] "Power
is of two kinds," Gandhi believed. "One is obtained by the fear of
punishment and other by acts of love. Power based on love is a
thousand times more effective."[38]

Nonviolence is not only spiritually superior to violence, but it
also can be proven to be more effective in secular societies. The force
of nonviolence, however, when it is diluted or contaminated by anger
or enmity, is undermined. Gandhi tried to explain the problem of
using nonviolent power:

> The word *satyagraha* is often most loosely used and is
> made to cover veiled violence. But as the author of the word I
> may be allowed to say that it excludes every form of violence,
> direct or indirect, and whether in thought, word or deed. It is a
> breach of *satyagraha* to wish ill to an opponent or to say a
> harsh word...with the intention of doing harm. And often the
> evil thought or the evil word may, in terms of *satyagraha*, be
> more dangerous than actual violence used in the heat to the
> moment. *Satyagraha* is gentle, it never wounds. It must not
> be the result of anger or malice. It was conceived as a
> complete substitute for violence.[39]

For Gandhi, peacemaking is always *in medias res* in the sense
that one always has to make peace. It is from this perspective that
Gandhi describes his four meta-principles of peace: truth, ahimsa,

---

[36] CWMG 19:277
[37] CWMG 10:64. Although Gandhi usually translated *satyagraha* as the "force"
of truth or of love, power seems a preferable translation because force is often
associated with violence.
[38] CWMG, 25: 563. January 8, 1925.
[39] CWMG, 54: 416-17. April 15, 1933.

talent, and constructive action. These four principles guard against Gandhi's seven deadly sins: (1) wealth without work, (2) pleasure without conscience, (3) knowledge without character, (4) commerce without morality, (5) science without humanity, (6) worship without sacrifice, and (7) politics without principle. In many ways, what Gandhi means by peace is the larger framework of human relationships capable of flourishing. In order for relationships to flourish they must experience these four sequential movements: respect, understanding, acceptance, appreciation.

In Gandhi's framework of nonviolence one gains the perspective from which to see why I am interested in Gandhi's connection to Christian spirituality. The incipient idea particularly for this work came from a discussion I had with Arun Gandhi, the grandson of Mohandas. I currently serve on Arun's board of the M. K. Gandhi Institute for Nonviolence based at Christian Brothers University in Memphis, Tennessee. Interestingly enough, Arun told me in the middle of one of our conversations that his grandfather's chief practice of truth-telling is essential to the maintenance of nonviolence because without it there is perpetuated *duragraha*, which is the counterfeit of *satyagraha*. By practicing deception and lies, persons practice *duragraha* through a wrong use of power, coming from a selfish obstinacy. The passive resister, or *duragrahi*, may avoid physical violence through practices of nonviolence while still harboring enmity and anger within. In other words, those who fail to practice truth-telling may use nonviolence as a tactic but will inevitably lack commitment to the core understanding of nonviolence, openness, and respect for the adversary. All of this especially relates to Gandhian spirituality concerning the Harijan, the children of God (and yet the caste in which they are considered untouchable).

I set out here to simply tell a brief story of Gandhi's impact of nonviolence, both opponent and proponent perspectives, and then display a brief context of Gandhi in which the reader may understand why I think Gandhi has authority to address Christian spirituality. Gandhi offers a third perspective in the bifurcated Enlightenment approach to religion, in that what is defined as external practices of religion by Nietzsche and Marx is often undistinguished from internal religion privatized and ineffectual. In other words, there is truth on both sides—on one hand, the need to address the historical oppression of certain peoples; on the other, the need for those oppressed to construct a new existence. In the end I conclude that Gandhi's concept of *swaraj* facilitates this third perspective through a definition of freedom that carries a dual sense, having political and spiritual sides, both of which give attention to the internal and external aspects of freedom. *Swaraj* produces a higher consciousness attained through disciplined pursuit of self-awareness and knowledge of the other.

Gandhi's Eclectic Nature

Gandhi did not develop a novel technique of nonviolence; rather, he drew from the available resources of his time and molded a spirituality that would fit the situation with which he was confronted. In Gandhian spirituality, there is an eclectic nature. Gandhi drew his philosophy from many sources as he developed the technique of nonviolent resistance, or *satyagraha*. For example, one could see how Gandhi was influenced by Thoreau regarding civil disobedience. Leo Tolstoy also made a profound impression on Gandhi's life. Having said this, however, Gandhi was first a Hindu. Though he studied in the West and was very familiar with Christianity, Islam, and Zoroastrianism, the main source of Gandhi's inspiration was Hinduism. One, therefore, cannot disregard the influence of the Vedas, Upanishads, Jainism, Buddhism, Asokanism, and medieval mysticism of India. In Gandhi's early life, however, he was affected by Jesus' Sermon on the Mount. The principle of nonviolence as applied to social problems is couched in Jesus' conviction that spiritual force is the only force by which progress is made (for example, Jesus' Sermon on the Mount).

One can discover the emergence of *satyagraha* as India simultaneously moved from under the yoke of British domination. The Indian people pondered the question of how to cast off the foreign yoke for over 200 years. Gandhi's technique of *satygraha* was one of many methods presented in answer to the problem of British colonialism. The people responded to Gandhi's method rather than the method of violence. There are a couple reasons why the Indians refused the method of violent resistance. First, they were completely disarmed. Second, there is the long religious tradition of nonviolence as evidenced in the daily behavior patterns of the people.[40]

In his book *War Without Violence*, Krishnalal Shridharani commented on the adoption of *satyagraha*, or nonviolent resistance, as a method:

> The condition of general disarmament interacting upon the "ethos" that has molded the attitudes of the Indian people appears to have produced the technique of *satyagraha*. Non-violent direct action, likewise, seems to be a culmination of Indian Culture and the military disability of the Indians.... *Satyagraha*, over and above being a movement of the Indian people, is also a technique of solving social conflict, applicable to other countries as well. While such a technique would naturally arise out of such a condition-tradition complex as exists in India, and people possessing such attitudes are apt to adopt more readily the group of social processes called *satyagraha*, nevertheless these culture-traits and conditional restrictions are not indispensable for the successful operation of *satyagraha*. *Satyagraha*, as a technique pure and simple, can be adopted by any people.[41]

Gandhi said that "non-violence is the greatest force" at humankind's disposal. It is mightier than the mightiest weapon of destruction devised by human ingenuity. Perhaps most profound to the understanding of *satyagraha* is the full knowledge that destruction is not the law of the human persons. The evidence of the ultimate freedom of human beings is seen through their readiness to die, if need

---

[40] See Krishnalal Shridharani, *War Without Violence* (New York: Harcourt, Brace and Co, 1939) 189-208.

[41] Shridharani, 209-210.

be, at the hands of sisters and brothers, but never by killing them. Gandhi concludes, "Every murder or other injury, no matter for what cause, committed or inflicted on another is a crime against humanity."[42]

Harijan: Children of God

The most specific example of how Gandhi models *satyagraha* and offers a corrective to Western spiritualities of individualism can be seen in his work to counter the system of untouchability. Gandhi issued a series of press statements and a stream of letters to his numerous correspondents to educate the public on the evils of untouchability. He arranged for the publication of a weekly paper, *Harijan*, to promote this campaign. *Harijan* means "children of God"; it was Gandhi's name for the untouchables. Since the *Sanatanists* (orthodox Hindus) relied upon the texts of Hindu scriptures, Gandhi doubted whether there was any support in them for untouchability. Gandhi wrote, "It is not our position that there is not untouchability at all in the Shastras.... They (the orthodox) are expected to prove that untouchability as at present practised has sanctions in the Shastras. It is an impossible task to perform honestly." Even if it were possible to prove a sanction for this tyranny from some ancient manuscript, Gandhi would not have felt bound by it. Eternal truth, he asserted, could not be confined within the covers of a book, however sacred. Every scripture, he argued, had certain permanent elements—certain universal truths—but it also contained injunctions relevant to the contemporary society. If interpretations of scripture did violence to human dignity, they could be ignored. Gandhi writes, "All the religions of the world describe God pre-eminently the Friend of the friendless, and Help of the helpless, and the Protector of the weak. Who can be more friendless or helpless or weaker than the

---

[42] Mohandas K. Gandhi, *All Men Are Brothers* (New York: Columbia University Press) 1958, 85.

forty million or more Hindus of India, classified as untouchables?"[43]
Archbishop Desmond Tutu agrees with this kind of hermeneutic.
According to many voices, a person's pigmentation or a person's
sexual orientation should determine whether her or his status is high
or low on the social pyramid. These voices proclaim that there should
be both God's judgment and grace deciding "with a rigidity unknown
even in the strictest Calvinistic predestinationism where you are born
and where you can live."[44] Tutu states further, "We have in this land
a pyramid of power and privilege based on colour—the lighter you are
of pigmentation, the higher you stand on the pyramid of privilege and
power. In this pyramid blacks are the broad base of the exploited and
oppressed. Next is the so called coloureds and then next Indians and
right at the top Makulubaas, white. It is a pigmentocracy."[45]

Why is this true not just in South Africa, but also on a global
scale—the darker a person is in skin pigment the more likely that
person is poor or oppressed? Tutu states, "I would say to [South
African expatriates], they are not going to escape the turmoil,
wherever they go. Really. If they go to western Europe, racism is
rearing its ugly head there. And why go through the hoop twice, when
having done it once, you can now relax?"[46] Also, Tutu seems to
reflect on the theodicy question of racism as he reflects on his
international travel:

> I have had the privilege of seeing that resilience in many
> places: among Black people in Brazil, among those in African
> countries who suffer from starvation, civil war, and repressive
> government, among the Nicaraguans and the Palestinians.
> Traveling to these places, I have often wondered how I can
> minister effectively to people who are suffering so much.

---

[43] Gandhi, Harijan, publication of a weekly paper, quoted in B.R. Nanda,
Mahatma Gandhi: A Biography, (Oxford: Oxford University Press) 1989, 352.

[44] Tutu, "Preface," *To Reap a Whirlwind*, a Collection of Essays in a book
scientifically describing what it means to be born into an apartheid society when
Tutu was Bishop of Johannesburg, March 20, 1986.

[45] Tutu, Handwritten Undated Address #5.

[46] Ross Dunn, "A loud, strong voice for peace," *Age*, Melbourne October 4, 1993.

When I have arrived there, I have always found that they have ministered to me.[47]

If God is omnipotent and good, then why evil, and since God is both omnipotent and good, then why should blacks suffer so signally? In light of the problem of racial oppression, Tutu asks, "God, on whose side are you?"[48] For Tutu it almost seems as if God wanted to let those who doubt God's presence have a "field day and give sleepless nights to those of His worshippers desperate to provide meaningful theodicies to a skeptical world."[49] God intends to transfigure and transform the world so that it will not disappear into nothingness, so that the world will enter the eschatological dimensions of the new heaven and earth when all manner of things will be made well.

Like Tutu, Gandhi believed in conversion, not compulsion, "so that the opponents of today might become the reformers of tomorrow." On 7 November 1933, Gandhi set out on a countrywide tour to promote the *Harijan* cause. He covered 12,500 miles, penetrating some of the remotest parts of the country. He called on caste Hindus to purge themselves of prejudice against the *Harijans*, and he urged the *Harijans* to shake off the vices (drugs and drink) that hindered their absorption into Hindu society. Gandhi did not favor legal aids to fight social evils.[50] He pleaded for the opening of temples to *Harijans*: "Temples are for sinners, not for saints; but who is to judge where no man is without sin?" He ridiculed the superstition that anybody could be unclean by birth or that the shadow or touch on one human being could defile another human being. On the *Harijan* tour Gandhi was attacking age-old tyranny and long-established vested interests. Then *Sanatanists* accused him of a dangerous heresy; they organized black-flag demonstrations; they heckled him and disrupted the meetings he addressed. If Gandhi's followers would have retaliated

---

[47] Tutu, "Introduction," in *Icarus 2*, Spring 1991, (New York: The Rosen Publishing Group).

[48] Tutu, Address "The Nature and Value of Theology," undated.

[49] Tutu, Heading: Matthew chapter 5 verse 13, USA?

[50] B.R. Nanda, 353.

in kind or summoned the police, Gandhi's embarrassment would have been completed. On 25 June, in Poona, a bomb was thrown at his party; seven persons were injured, but Gandhi was unhurt. "I am not aching for martyrdom," Gandhi said, "but if it comes in my way in the prosecution of what I consider to be the supreme duty in defense of the faith I hold in common with [*Harijans*], I shall have well earned it."[51]

Gandhi claimed that the politician in him had never dominated a single decision of his,[52] that he had sacrificed no principle to gain a political advantage,[53] that he was used to misrepresentation all his life,[54] that his leadership was not of his seeking but a "a fruit of faithful service."[55] Gandhi writes, "Most religious men I have met are politicians in disguise. I, however, who wear the guise of a politician, am at heart a religious man."[56] Gandhi was not a politician in the sense that he might well have failed in the practical business of government and that he never sought or held any political office—not even the official leadership of any party.[57] Politics was to him not a profession but a vocation, and he was a politician only in the sense that he was conscious of a mission to serve the masses in the political and social sphere and to inspire warring communities with love of the common ideal. Gandhi was more concerned with the purification of political life through the monastic ideal of *ashrama* into politics. He repeatedly insisted that politics cannot be isolated from the deepest things of life. When he visited London in 1931, Laurance Houseman said at a reception at Friends House that in churches we are all sinners while in politics everyone else is a sinner, and that Gandhi had shown the way of unification of politics and

[51] B.R. Nanda, 356.
[52] Young India, vol. II, Ganesan, 568.
[53] YI, March 1925.
[54] YI, March 1927.
[55] YI, March 1927.
[56] *Speeches and Writings of Mahatma Gandhi*, 2nd edition, Natesan, 1918, xxiv.
[57] At twenty-five he held the Secretaryship of the Natal Indian Congress which he founded—the closest he came to holding any political office, apart from presiding over the Belgium Congress in 1924.

religion through constant heart-searching and the concern to define and declare one's private faith.

In an address at Guildhall, Gandhi spoke about the vow of voluntary poverty for a politician. He said that when he found himself drawn into the political coil, he asked himself what was necessary to remain untouched by immorality, untruth, and political gain, and he decided that a servant of the people must discard all wealth and private possessions. What would this ideal look like in the midst of the affirmative action debate—that all politicians would discard all wealth? Gandhi told a group of missionaries in 1938, "I could not be leading a religious life unless I identified myself with the whole of mankind and that I could not do unless I took part in politics. The whole gamut of man's activities today constitutes an indivisible whole.... I do not know of any religion apart from activity. It provides a moral basis to all other activities without which life would be a maze of sound and fury signifying nothing."[58]

Gandhi was certain that he could never be a votary of principles that depended for their existence upon politics or anything else.[59] While even social work is not possible without touching politics, political work must never be looked upon in terms of social and moral progress.[60] Power resides in the people, not in legislative assemblies.[61]

Gandhi and Christianity

Central to the thesis of my work is that there can be no Christian spirituality outside the embodiment of nonviolent practices. It is unfortunate that some feel that the particularity of Christian faith necessarily rules out the common discourse of nonviolence. Gandhi helps me explain: "Though I cannot claim to be a Christian in the sectarian sense, the example of Jesus' sufferings is a factor in the

---

[58] V.K. Jhaveri and D.G. Tendulkar, *Mahatma* (in eight volumes), original edition, 1951-1954, 387-88.

[59] *Mahatma*, 4:190.

[60] *Mahatma*, 7: 254.

[61] *Mahatma*, 6: 23.

composition of my undying faith in non-violence which rules all my actions, worldly and temporal. And I know that there are hundreds of Christians who believe likewise. Jesus lived and died in vain if he did not teach us to regulate the whole of life by the eternal Law of love."[62]

This is unfortunate because the particularity of the Christian faith has become so atomized that it is irrelevant to the world. Unlike Gandhian spirituality, Western Christian spirituality is given to the dominance of psychological discourse of defining the self. It is a misinterpretation of Christian spirituality, however, to see it embodied in enlightenment notions of the self that are defined over and against the other. In other words, Christian spirituality is more itself as a spirituality of community than a personal spirituality. The Reverend Emmanuel Charles McCarthy helps me explain this:

> So, also rejection of violence, love of enemies, and prayer for the persecutors are an irrevocable part of the history, scripture, and authentic memory of the Sacrifice of Love on Calvary. Refusing the protection of the sword (Mt 26:62), healing the ear of the armed man who was to take Him to His death (Lk 22:51) and crying out for God's forgiveness for those who were destroying Him (Lk 23:34) is the memory the Gospels give to humanity of the victimization of Christ.[63]

Western Christianity has the most to gain from an encounter with Gandhian spirituality in that for too long there have been feeble efforts by Western Christians to construct peaceful relationships. Instead, post-Constantinian Christianity has elided power with faith in such a way that active nonviolence becomes an oxymoron. McCarthy continues: "Catholics, Orthodox, and Protestants all believe they have authentic Eucharistic communion within their own churches. This, however, has not prevented them from sojourning into the

---

[62] Harijan, 7-1-1939; CWMG, 68: 278.
[63] Reverened Emmanuel Charles McCarthy, "The Nonviolent Eucharist," Center for Christian Nonviolence, Buxter, Minnesota.

human bloodletting of their own and other Christians on a grand scale and then exonerating themselves by some fantastic manipulation of the Gospel."[64]

Gandhi provides the church the kind of exegesis of peacemaking that allows for a better understanding of how Jesus engages the world, an engagement that is not through the use of force. François Mauriac, in his work *The Eucharist: the Mystery of Holy Thursday*, states,

> Twelve frightened men, who feel that death is hovering over, crowd around the Son of Man whose hand is lifted over a piece of bread and over a cup. Of what value is this gesture, of what use can it be? How futile it seems when already a mob is arming itself with clubs, when in a few hours Jesus will be delivered to the courts, ranked among transgressors, tortured, disfigured, laughed at by His enemies, pitiable to those who love Him, and shown to be powerless before all. However, this Man, condemned to death does not offer any defense; He does nothing but bless the bread and wine and, with eyes raised, pronounces a few words.[65]

Mauriac's image of Jesus helps us see that sacrifice is essential in understanding active nonviolence. Bernard Haring illustrates, "It is not possible to speak of Christ's sacrifice while ignoring the role of nonviolence." Jesus' sacrifice is our ability to experience perichoresis, the act of knowing your own personhood in the other. Interestingly enough, perichoresis is derived from the same verb that gives us the term choreography.[66] Jesus explains perichoresis when he states: "The one who sees me sees the Father" (John 14:9).

Are the elements of Gandhianism Christian? This question is posed to open our quest into the Christian influence on Gandhianism. Such a quest will enable us to understand why Gandhianism was attractive to King. This suggests that there is a commonality between

---

[64] Ibid.

[65] François Mauriac,. *The Eucharist: the Mystery of Holy Thursday* (New York : D. McKay) c1944..

[66] Christopher Morse, *Not Every Spirit*, 131.

the elements of Gandhianism and Christianity. An analysis of *satyagraha* and *ahimsa* will bring the point into focus.

Satyagraha is the determination of truth. Literally, it means truth, but it is also the name given to the technique of non-violent resistance Gandhi wrote, "In the application of satyagraha, I discovered in the earliest states that pursuit of truth did not admit of violence being inflicted on one's opponent but that he must be weaned from error by patience and sympathy. For what appears to be truth tot he one may appear to be error to the another. And patience means self-suffering. So the doctrine came to mean vindication of truth, not by infliction of suffering on the opponent, but on one's self."[67]

Jesus and his teachings are an important source of Gandhi's philosophy of *satyagraha*. The New Testament, particularly the Sermon on the Mount, provided a foundation for the rightness and value of *satyagraha*: "With my known partiality for the Sermon on the Mount and my repeated declarations that its author was one of the greatest among the teachers of mankind, I could not suspect that there would be any charge against me of underrating Christianity."[68] Thus we see the key link between Gandhi and Christianity.

Why did the Sermon on the Mount appeal to Gandhi? It appealed to him because Jesus condemned the use of physical force and preached the law of love or nonresistance. His life and death were a living example. Jesus bore witness to the power of love and nonresistance—the Christian way of overcoming evil. He raised love from the level of natural impulse to that of deliberate intention. This love rules out the use of force in all its forms.[69]

Satyagraha is the prevention of confusion. Accepting nonviolence as a way of life implies that the individual must be nonviolent in relation to others, particularly when resisting evil and injustice. One is put to the test during the stress and strain of conflict.

[67] Gandhi, *All Men Are Brothers*, 88.

[68] Gandhi, is this quoted in Brenton T. Bradley, *The Solitary Throne* (Baltimore: The Stockton Press, 1932) 66.

[69] G. Dhawan, *The Political Philosophy of Mahatma Gandhi* (Bombay: Popular Book Depot, 1946) 26.

One must eliminate personal injustice before seeking to correct the injustices of others. There must be self-discipline: "This self-discipline which includes control of thoughts and emotions develops in the satyagraha the inner strength, the soul-force that becomes irresistible."[70] With this approach confusion can be kept to a minimum.

Ahimsa is the renunciation of the will to kill or to damage. It is "positively the practice of love."[71] It is the way of nonviolence. Gandhi wrote,

> Ahimsa is a comprehensive principle. We are helpless mortals caught in the conflagration of ahimsa. The saying that life has a deep meaning in it. Men cannot for a moment live without consciously or unconsciously committing outward himsa. The very fact of his living—eating, drinking and moving about—necessarily involves some ahimsa, destruction of life, be it ever so minute. A votary of ahimsa therefore remains true to his faith if the spring of all his action is compassion, if shuns to the best of his ability the destruction of the tiniest creature, tries to save it, and thus incessantly strives to be free from the deadly coil of himsa. He will be constantly growing in self-restraint and compassion, but he can never become entirely free from outward ahimsa.[72]

Gandhi believed that love was implicitly in *ahimsa* and professed to see profound similarities between the Bhagavad Gita and the Sermon on the Mount. William Miller notes,

> In his [Gandhi's] reinterpretation of the Gita as the "gospel of selfless action" and in his blending of the Hindu concept of Brahman as impersonal cosmic truth with the biblical understanding of God as love, Gandhi achieved nothing less than a religious reformation in Hinduism. Thus the ahimsa which Gandhi identified with the love spoken of by Paul is no

---

[70] Dhawan, 124.
[71] Gandhi, *All Men are Brothers*, 181.
[72] Gandhi, *All Men are Brothers*, 94.

longer the unalloyed "nonharm" of the ancient or the orthodox Hinduism; it is already a Gandhian concept profoundly
influenced by the New Testament.[73]

Gandhian spirituality, then, contains elements of Christian
spirituality. The elements of Gandhian spirituality are not themselves
Christian but Indian and Hindu. In Gandhian spirituality, self-suffering
is required. Gandhi developed a conviction regarding suffering:
"Things of fundamental importance to the people are not secured by
reason alone but have to be purchased with their suffering. Suffering is
the law of human beings; war is the law of the jungle. But suffering is
infinitely more powerful than the law of the jungle for converting the
opponent and opening his ears, which are otherwise shut, tot he voice
of reason."[74] This basic attitude toward suffering prevailed in the
campaigns of nonviolent resistance that Gandhi led. Without this
attitude toward suffering, Gandhi and his people would have
experienced great difficulty in retaining their nonviolent posture.
Perhaps this character of endurance in spite of suffering was the
greatest gift that Gandhi gave to Christian leaders like Martin Luther
King Jr. Although Gandhi would point to Jesus' nonviolence, one can
easily conclude that Gandhi was a harbinger of the Civil Rights
movement.

Gandhi's Influence on Christian Leaders

To consciously mark the beginning of the history of nonviolence in
the struggle for racial equality in the United States, one could begin
with the year 1942. At that time the first component of the Congress
of Racial Equality conducted its first sit-in at a Chicago restaurant.
Bayard Rustin and others carried out the first integrated "freedom
ride" in 1947. Shortly thereafter came the Montgomery bus boycott
of 1956 in which nonviolence became an accepted method of social

---

[73] William Robert Miller, *Nonviolence: A Christian Interpretation* (New York:
Association Press, 1964) 25.

[74] Gandhi, *All men Are Brothers*, 91.

change. Martin Luther King Jr. became the prominent voice for nonviolence at that time, although others had called for the use of nonviolent resistance.

King had a philosophical acquaintance with the philosophy of nonviolence from the time he was an undergraduate at Morehouse College in Atlanta. Dr. Benjamin E. Mays, the president of Morehouse, and the Reverend Dr. Howard Thurman, dean of the chapel and professor of religion at Morehouse, had both visited Gandhi in the late 1930s. Both of these spiritual leaders and educators played major roles in encouraging debate about the possibility of using spirituality as the means to solve political crisis. Mays and Thurman saw Gandhi's spiritual leadership as providing the most effective resistance against British rule in India through the use of nonviolence. Such spiritual leadership made Gandhi a significant hero among many African Americans on college campuses. King was one of them, and he was quite aware of Gandhi's achievement.[75] It is interesting that just a few weeks after Gandhi was assassinated in 1948, King, at the age of eighteen, was ordained at Ebenezer Baptist Church in Atlanta to the Christian ministry. During the month of September 1948 two devotees of nonviolent direct action, Dr. Abraham J. Muste, head of the Fellowship of Reconciliation, and the Reverend Dr. Mordecai Johnson, president of Howard University, preached on the life and teachings of Gandhi at Crozer Theological Seminary in Chester, Pennsylvania. King had just entered that notable Baptist seminary to work toward his bachelor of divinity degree. There, King began a serious study of Gandhi, though he remained unconvinced about how well nonviolence would work in the midst of the violence of white racists in the United States.

During the Montgomery campaign in 1956, Reverend Glen Smiley and Bayard Rustin, both representatives of the Fellowship of

---

[75] King's favorite work on Gandhi appears to be F.B. Fisher's That Strange Little Brown Man, Gandhi (1932) as evidenced by King's paraphrase of the title, "a little brown man in India" in King, "A Realistic Look at the Question of Progress in the Area of Race Relations" (The library Boston Collection at the Boston University Library containing a large collection of unpublished papers by King, 1954-1964), 7. and "the little brown saint of India" quoted by King in STF, 85.

Reconciliation, convinced King to make nonviolent resistance the center of the Montgomery movement. Indeed, this spirituality became the cornerstone of the Southern Christian Leadership Conference (SCLC) when it was formed in 1957. Between 2 February and 10 March 1959, Dr. and Mrs. King toured India with Dr. Lawrence D. Reddick, a black professor of history at Alabama State University in Montgomery, to study Gandhi's spirituality and techniques of nonviolence. They were guests of Indian Prime Minister Jawaharlal Nehru, one of Gandhi's disciples.

King states, "While the Montgomery boycott was going on, India's Gandhi was the guiding light of our technique of nonviolent social change. We spoke of him often. So as soon as our victory over bus segregation was won, some of my friends said, "Why don't you go to India and see for yourself what the Mahatma, whom you so admire, has wrought."[76] King recounts how he was able to

> talk with [Gandhi's] son, his grandsons, his cousins and other relatives; to share the reminiscences of his close comrades, to visit his ashrama, to see the countless memorials for him and finally to lay a wreath on his entombed ashes at Rajghat.... I left India more convinced than ever before that nonviolent resistance is the most potent weapon available to oppressed people in their struggle for freedom.[77]

It was after King's trip to India that his most profound teaching on nonviolence was recorded. The contest was the increasing disenchantment within the black community, especially among the youth, who advocated for militant black self-defense. The United States was also awaiting the results of the presidential election between Nixon and Kennedy, and King had submitted his resignation as pastor of the Dexter Avenue Baptist Church in Montgomery, Alabama, in order to devote himself to the presidency of the Southern Christian Leadership Conference. It was in this context that King

---

[76] Martin Luther King, Jr., "My Trip to the Land of Gandhi," 1959, in *I Have a Dream: Writings and Speeches that Changed the World*, ed., James M. Washington, (SanFrancisco: Harper, 1986) 40.

[77] "My Trip to the Land of Gandhi," 43.

gave his most explicit thoughts on why nonviolent resistance could be the only effective method in America for African Americans. King states, "It is axiomatic in social life that the imposition of frustrations leads to two kinds of reactions. One is the development of a wholesome social organization to resist with effective, firm measures any efforts to impede progress. The other is a confused, anger-motivated drive to strike back violently, to inflict damage. Primarily, it seeks to cause injury to retaliate for wrongful suffering. Secondarily, it seeks real progress. It is punitive—not radical or constructive." King goes on to say that "calls for violence" are rooted in the latter. He then three responses to violence: nonviolence, self-defense, and violence. King states his case plainly:

> The Negro people can organize socially to initiate many forms of struggle which can drive their enemies back without resort to futile and harmful violence. In the history of the movement for racial advancement, many creative forms have been developed—the mass boycott, sit-down protests and strikes, sit-ins—refusal to pay fines and bail for unjust arrests—mass marches—mass meetings—prayer pilgrimages, etc.... There is more power in socially organized masses on the march than there is in guns in the hands of a few desperate men. Our enemies would prefer to deal with a small armed group rather than with a huge, unarmed but resolute mass of people. However, it is necessary that the mass-action method be persistent and unyielding. Gandhi said the Indian people must "never let them rest," referring to the British. He urged them to keep protesting daily and weekly, in a variety of ways. This method inspired and organized the Indian masses and disorganized and demobilized the British. It educates its myriad participants, socially and morally. All history teaches us that like a turbulent ocean beating great cliffs into fragments of rock, the determined movement of people incessantly demanding their rights always disintegrates the old order.... Our present urgent necessity is to cease our internal fighting and turn outward to the enemy—using every form of

mass action yet known—create new forms—and resolve never to let them rest. This is the social lever which will force open the door to freedom. Our powerful weapons are the voices, the feet, and the bodies of dedicated, united people, moving without rest toward a just goal. Greater tyrants than southern segregationists have been subdued and defeated by this form of struggle. We have not yet used it, and it would be tragic if we spurn it because we have failed to perceive its dynamic strength and power.[78]

This was one of King's most explicit statements on the strategy of nonviolence to end the oppression of African Americans. In his book *Stride Toward Freedom*, King detailed his understanding of the philosophy of nonviolence.[79] First, nonviolent resistance is not a method for cowards because, as Gandhi taught the world, suffering was required to make nonviolence work. Though nonviolence assumes passive resistance, the method of nonviolence is extremely active. Second, the objective of nonviolence is not to defeat or humiliate the opponent, but to win the friendship and understanding of one's enemy. Third, active nonviolence is directed against forces of evil rather than against persons who happen to be doing the evil. Fourth, there must be a willingness to accept suffering without retaliation. Fifth, external physical violence and internal violence of spirit must be avoided. This is implemented by projecting the ethic of love to the center of one's life. Sixth, nonviolent resistance is based on the conviction that the universe is always on the side of justice. Therefore, adherents to this method must have deep faith in the future.

King's explicit fusion of Christian love with nonviolence became another distinctive mark of his leadership. The people involved were familiar with the terminology of Christian love, as well as the moral

---

[78] Martin Luther King, Jr., "The Social Organization of Nonviolence," in *I Have a Dream: Writings and Speeches that Changed the World*, ed., James M. Washington (San Francisco: Harper, 1986) 51-53.

[79] King, *Stride Toward Freedom*, 81-86.

justification for civil disobedience. King states, "It was the Sermon on the Mount, rather than a doctrine of passive resistance, that initially inspired the Negroes of Montgomery to dignified social action. It was Jesus of Nazareth that stirred the Negroes to protest with the creative weapon of love."[80] King constantly faced the dual problem of both inspiring people to resist racial oppression and keeping their fervor within controllable Christian bounds. He states, "Emphasizing the Christian doctrine of love, our actions must be guided by the deepest principles of our Christian faith. Love must be our regulating ideal. Once again we must hear the words of Jesus echoing across the centuries: 'Love your enemies, bless them that curse you, and pray for them that despitefully use you.'" Matthew 5:43, 44

King conceived of love as understanding, redemptive goodwill. He defines love in terms of *agape*, one of the three Greek words for love.[81] King writes,

> Agape means understanding, redeeming good will for all.... It is an overflowing love which is purely spontaneous, unmotivated, groundless, and creative. It is not set in motion by any quality or function of its object. It is the love of God operating in the human heart. ... Agape is not a weak, passive love. It is love in action. Agape is love seeking to preserve and create community.... Love, agape, is the only cement that could hold this broken community together. When I am commanded to love, I am commanded to restore community, to resist injustice, and to meet the needs of my brothers.[82]

King's definition of love obviously has a social dimension. Love's goal should be community. For King, "Christ furnished the spirit and motivation" for nonviolent action, while Gandhi furnished the explicit method of nonviolence in which King fused Christian

---

[80] *Stride Toward Freedom*, 67.

[81] For an excellent discussion of King's theological interpretations agape, See Kenneth L. Smith and Ira G. Zepp, Jr., *Search for the Beloved Community: The Thinking of Martin Luther King, Jr.* (Valley Forge: Judson Press, 1974) 63-69.

[82] *Stride Toward Freedom,* 83-85

love with nonviolence.[83] King states, "I had come to see early that the Christian doctrine of love operating through the Gandhian method of nonviolence was one of the most potent weapons available to the Negro in his struggle for freedom."[84] By his own confession, King did not fully understand Christian love until he saw love expressed in Jesus through the eyes of Gandhi: "Prior to reading Gandhi, I had about concluded that the ethics of Jesus were only effective in individual relationship. The 'turn the other cheek' philosophy and 'love your enemies' philosophy were only valid, I felt, when individuals were in conflict with other individuals; when racial groups and nations were in conflict a more realistic approach seemed necessary. But after reading Gandhi, I saw how utterly mistaken I was."[85] Ultimately and ironically, Gandhi, a practicing Hindu, revealed to King the potency of Christ's love in the area of social reform.

Is the fusion of Christian love with nonviolence valid? Joseph Washington, in his book *Black Religion*, answers no. King viewed love as "passive" and nonviolence as "resistance" and attempted to wed what he had earlier called two "apparent irreconcilables."[86] Washington contends that the two are irreconcilable because love and the strategy of nonviolence are two different forces. Love and nonviolence can be described as "passionate resistance": Washington observes, "Love and nonviolence may work together but they cannot be fused. The root of love is in God, interrelated through theology. The root of nonviolence is in philosophy and it need not rely upon God. Love and theology need philosophy to operate in the context of the human community, to determine the content and quality of justice. But love and theology always transcend, or bear a corrective on philosophy."[87]

---

[83] *Stride Toward Freedom*, 67.

[84] *Stride Toward Freedom*, 67

[85] *Stride Toward Freedom*, 77

[86] See *Stride Toward Freedom*, chapter "Pilgrimage to nonviolence"

[87] Joseph Washington, *Black Religion: The Negro and Christianity in the United States* (Lanham MD: University Press of America) 8.

Would Gandhi agree with Washington's analysis that such a fusion between love and nonviolence could never occur? In the Montgomery situation, an immediate means of compelling the African American to act on behalf of justice was needed, and many espoused violence as such a means. King, however, found the method of resistance for African Americans in Gandhi's massive campaigns for civil disobedience and militant nonviolence. As noted in our earlier analysis of Gandhian spirituality, *ahimsa* is the positive practice of love. The element of love is already present in the philosophy of nonviolence as practiced by Gandhi; therefore, Gandhi would see no separation between love and nonviolence. King states,

> It was in this Gandhian emphasis on love and nonviolence that I discovered the method of social reform that I had been seeking for so many months. The intellectual and moral satisfaction that I failed to gain from the utilitarianism of Bentham and Mill, the revolutionary methods of Marx and Lenin, the social contracts theory of Hobbes, the "back to nature" optimism of Rousseau, and the superman philosophy of Nietzsche, I found in the nonviolent resistance philosophy of Gandhi. I came to feel that this was the only morally and practically sound method open to oppressed people in their struggle for freedom.[88]

Constantly, King discussed the importance of nonviolence as the method for black people to claim their freedom. In other words, the method of nonviolence had tremendous psychological importance for African Americans. Through nonviolence, African-American resistance would inform white people that the racist stereotypes as irresponsible clowns had come to an end. It was not by accident that Gandhi's influence on King enabled a whole people to see that they were children of God, Harijan. Masses of African Americans embodied the dignity of struggle, of moral conviction and self-sacrifice, which a spirituality of nonviolence elicits. King concludes that through nonviolence, "The negro was able to face his adversary, to concede to

---

[88] *Stride Toward Freedom*, 77.

him a physical advantage and to defeat him because the superior force of the oppressor had become powerless."[89]

---

[89] Martin Luther King, Jr., *Why We Can't Wait* (New York: Harper & Row, 1964) 40.

4

PEACEMAKING AS SPIRITUAL
DIRECTION TOWARD SAINTHOOD

We learn from Gandhi that the chief component of spirituality is the
most successful method and strategy to free South Africa, India, and
the United States. Michael Quirk believes that Americans tend to
romanticize Gandhi, thereby obscuring his most enduring
contributions to humanity. Quirk provides the example from when
the film *Gandhi* swept the Academy Awards in 1982:

> Here was a crowd, dressed to the nines in overpriced
> gowns and tuxedos, ready to repair speedily to various
> nightclubs for some serious debauchery as soon as the annual
> self-congratulatory rituals were to cease, waxing effusive about
> this wonderful man who would not so much as hurt a fly but
> who brought down an empire, seemingly unaware that his
> entire life stood as an indictment of the very culture of
> excess, vanity, and narcissism that Hollywood epitomizes.
> While the film was a fairly good one, the celebration missed
> the point, massively. The empire is us.[1]

---

[1] Draft copy of Michael Quirk, "Gandhi Contra Modernity," 1. Book Review of
Bhikhu Parkh, *Gandhi*, Oxford Past Masters Series (Oxford: Oxford University Press,
1997).

Most important to the discussion of this chapter is how a spirituality of nonviolence may be maintained through Christian spiritual practices that manifest authentic and integrated witness rather than the hypocrisy made manifest at the 1982 Academy Awards. At the heart of Christian spirituality, I argue, is the practice of nonviolence in which Jesus demonstrated the ultimate effect of nonviolence through resurrection. The following story provides a lucid illustration of such resurrection.

Several years ago, a Zen Master was visiting the United States from Japan. He was invited to tour a Trappist monastery in New England and was delighted by what he found there. Astonished by the life of prayer and quiet withdrawal, he said through his interpreter, "I had no idea that any Christians took silent prayer so seriously. There is much here in common with Zen."

So captivated was he that he offered to lead the entire monastery in a weeklong Zen retreat, a vigorous affair. A Zen retreat requires up to ten hours of silent meditation a day—half-hour segments of unbroken contemplation, followed by five minutes of slow walking. There are work periods and times for chanting prayers, but contemplation fills the day. And other than the spoken prayers, no talking is allowed, with the exception of a daily interview with the Zen Master in which each monk is checked on his progress with his individual *koan*.[2]

It was this sort of retreat that the Zen master offered, except that it would be adapted to particularly Christian insight. The monastery accepted his offer, and he began his retreat, joining the monks for Mass, standing with them to say the offices, encouraging them to use chairs for silent meditation. In many ways he adapted his

---

[2] Koan is a Japanese word, and koans have been used most explicitly in Buddhism; but Christianity also has its koans. Jesus' parables work as koans. A koan is a sort of puzzle, a request or a question that requires a response, but not the sort that could ever be anticipated by logical thought. One well-known koan is, "Show me the face you had before our parents were born." Another is, "What is the sound of one hand clapping?" Koans do not ask for answers; they ask for insight, for awareness.

retreat to those he was leading. He also searched the New Testament for Christian koans.

At the first interview, the monks were given their koans. When the first monk entered the room he found the Zen master sitting with two copies of the New Testament in front of him, one in English, one in Japanese. Because his English was imperfect he went from one to the other

The monk sat down in front of him and the Zen master smiled. "You know," he said in his faltering English, "I like Christianity. But," he glanced down at the books in front of him, then looked up again, "I would not like it without the resurrection."

Suddenly he leaned forward so that his face was only inches from the other: "Show me your resurrection," he said. He paused then, and smiled: "That is your koan. Show me your resurrection."

The koan is a good one. It cuts to the core of Christian belief. If, as Paul says, each Christian has already died and risen with Christ, then resurrection must be part of our lives, visible for all to see. If we have it, we should be able to show it. If we cannot show it, perhaps we never really found it. Once found, it transforms each action into sacred ritual. Each act, each deed, becomes an expression of worship of the divine energy that formed each of us and formed the world. To live the resurrection is to turn all of life into prayer and so turn all that is done, all that is said, into a long litany of praise for God.[3]

In this chapter I argue for how Christians are called to live resurrection by practicing nonviolence—especially practices of nonviolence in the Christian tradition of spiritual direction that enabled Christian disciples to show their resurrection in a manner that enables profound community. This tradition of spiritual direction became well known in the third century with the African desert father St. Antony, who sought to know God's direction without distraction and hindrance. It is from the desert tradition that a Christian learns asceticism, in which one is socialized or inculturated to see life differently. What I argue in this chapter is the recovery of such a

---

[3] This story is found in Ernest Boyer, *A Way in the World: Family Life as Spiritual Discipline* (San Francisco: Harper & Row, 1984) 82-84.

tradition to see life as essentially nonviolent. Before I begin, a further word must be said concerning how Western persons are not inculturated to practice spirituality as essentially a form of nonviolence. This is the case because Christian spirituality in the Western world lacks a relational cosmology in which one understands self in relationship to others. The Cartesian formula of "I think; therefore, I am" creates a worldview in which there is little incentive to understand the need to relate fully to the other—the greatest other being God. Because of this, there is no "reason" to be nonviolent in Western culture if the primary mode of existence is self. I seek now to make this argument through the contrast of Western and African cosmologies of the self. To set the tone of this discussion, I will first tell a story.

The context was my postulancy year in the Episcopal ordination process, 1989. I was sent off to a camp for boys and girls at Kanuga by Bishop Robert Estill, who no doubt thought I was a maverick—not following the ordination process as I should since I had just finished Princeton Theological Seminary, a Presbyterian school. I had just finished my master's degree at Yale, which counted toward my Anglican formation—somehow in my hubris, I thought people should be better treated after attending Yale than to be sent to the wilderness. I lived on the lake. And for my sake they converted a storage room into the chaplain's quarters. This was a wonderfully, kenotic, stripping environment for me, in which there were loud bullfrogs that kept me up at night. Most of all, there were snakes in the woods. Anyway, I had the reverse culture shock of returning to the mountainous woods of the South; of course, I was the only black person, it seemed, there at Kanuga.[4] But there was another minority: Robin. You see, Kanuga is an Episcopal camp, and Robin is Southern Baptist.

Robin and I communicated as minorities. She was the best counselor, achieving an award at the end of the summer. One night, there was a loud knock at my door. It was late. I knew that this was

---

[4] Kanuga Conferences Inc., has since become an international Retreat/Conference Center with a wonderful staff, extremely hospitable and multicultural.

supposed to be part of my duties as the chaplain, to be available for the little Nicodemus's who would come to me late at night, but when I opened the door, to my surprise, it was Robin, the best counselor. I immediately felt like this would be seen as a compromising position: Robin a teenage, white, female counselor; me the black male; both of us in the woods of the South. The movies of black males being lynched kept playing in my mind. I asked Robin to sit out in the lobby area as we commenced spiritual direction.

Robin was searching for her soul, for God, she said. I told her that wasn't a disorder, but a sacred situation, even if it didn't feel like it. Somehow I sensed she was on the threshold of determining her vocation, as teenagers often do. My method of spiritual direction was silently to ask God to allow my answers and questions for Robin to be vehicles of grace. I asked Robin to simply surrender to God what was already there in her life that revealed the presence of God. In those awkward moments with Robin, I realized for the first time that I had the gift of a spiritual director—especially as I somehow felt like I could get Robin to see God through her community of friends and her church. Ever since then, my goal in spiritual direction has been to help persons discover "being and becoming" in a community. I came to the conclusion that spiritual direction as a skill and vocation is ultimately about reattaching persons to community—the greatest community being God (Father, Son, and Holy Spirit). In a Western world, however, it is difficult to display "being and becoming" in Christian community when the Ku Klux Klan also call themselves a Christian community. To this problem of duplicitous discernment of community we now turn.

The Western Self vs. The African Self

Especially in this century and particularly in North American culture, individual self-determination has been exalted over the needs of the community, giving rise to "individualism" and solipsistic expressions of Christianity. For example, the question "Do you have a personal relationship with Jesus?" implies that communal relationship and salvation are inconsequential. This cultural epistemology of individualism has profoundly influenced all facets of life, including Christian spirituality. In the West, especially from the time of the Enlightcnmcnt, the self has been understood as a distinct individual, with unique value and distinct rights. Western Christians are socialized to believe that they have a right to make something of their lives, to take responsibility for their life direction, and to use their talents and gifts to the fullest. As a spiritual director, Susan Rakoczy, is helpful. Her cross-cultural experience in Ghana helped her see that such Western emphasis on individuality in spiritual direction puts supreme value on the right of self-determination, self-achievement, and self-satisfaction.[5] Such responsibility for the intentional shaping of life is good, and it flows from the Judeo-Christian understanding of the dignity and worth of each human being. What is weak in this Western dimensional worldview is the lack of bonding between the person and the community in such a way that a Western person actually believes he or she can be an individual without relationship to others.

When a Western person formed in this worldview of the importance of the person and her or his rights and responsibilities meets a more communal person (for example, an African), in the spiritual direction relationship, they meet someone whose experience of the self is distinctly different from one socialized in Western culture. In contrast to the West, the African individual does not exist apart from the community. The classic phrasing of this intrinsic relationship between the individual and the community was started by John Mbiti and carried on by Tutu. I call it an ubuntu sensibility; namely, "I am, because we are; and since we are, therefore I am."[6] The African person is part of the whole, and one's identity flows from the corporate experience, never in isolation from it since "it is the community which defines who he/she is and who he/she can

[5] Susan Rakoczy, ed., "Unity, Diversity, and Uniqueness: Foundations of Cross-Cultural Spiritual Direction," in *Common Journey, Different Paths: Spiritual Direction in Cross-Cultural* (Maryknoll: Orbis Books, 1992).

[6] John Mbiti, *African Religions and Philosophy* (London: Heinemann Educational Books, 1969) 108-109. Battle 38ff.

become."[7] The uniqueness of each person is affirmed and acknowledged, but one's own individuality and freedom "are always balanced by destiny and community."[8]

Understanding the world is also distinctly different in Western and African worldviews. It is clear, then, what misunderstandings can easily occur in spiritual direction and other helping relationships when a Western director urges Africans to assume a degree of self-consciousness and self-assertion for which their cultural experience does not appropriate. For example, key to the Western worldview is the separation of the person and the community from the world of nature. Much has been written recently about Western abuse of the environment as stemming from a perversion of the biblical mandate to "fill the earth and subdue it" (Gen. 1:28) and the need for a spirituality that will form persons and communities in care and concern for our earth. The person stands over and against creation in all its dimensions, using and abusing it for one's own ends. Domination best describes this stance in which nature is made the servant of human needs, wants, and desires. The exaltation of the uniqueness and goodness of humanity is seen in discontinuity with the goodness and value of all the other facets of creation. Humanity and the rest of creation are in a relationship of ruler to servant, rather than of interdependence, which acknowledges the truth that the earth provides humanity its basic sustenance—air, water, food, and so forth—and thus the human community is called to steward it faithfully and carefully.

The African experience is decidedly, strikingly different. In the same way that the person is vitally and organically bonded in community with others, so also is this union extended to all of creation. The African worldview shares with the Judeo-Christian tradition the understanding of God as creator of the material universe.[9] Nature, in all its dimensions, is alive with the presence of

---

[7] Benjamin Ray, *African Religions: Symbol, Ritual and Community* (Englewood Cliffs, J.J.: Prentice-Hall, 1976) 132.

[8] Ray, *African Religions,* 132.

[9] Mbiti, *African Religions and Philosophy,* 39-41.

God, and communities and their members experience God in and through creation. In contrast to the Western mode of domination, the African strives to live in harmony with nature. The various facets of creation—the sky, the sun and moon, mountains, forests and trees, rivers and water, plants and animals—all have at least implicit religious meaning and often explicit significance.

All of these elements of the African view of the world and creation thus are distinctly different in many ways from the Western perspective. The African person in the situation of spiritual direction, whether as director or directee, brings to this sacred relationship the experience of harmony with nature, a lack of domineering attitude toward creation and ecology, a sense of the invisible world alive in the visible, and a strong conviction that various spirits can communicate with the person and the community. These challenge Western perceptions of the secularity of the ecological universe, a sense of control over it, and at least a great skepticism about the existence of any kind of spirits or similar beings with power to influence human behavior. I heard a story once when reporters asked climbers how they made the difficult trek up Mount Everest. A famous Western climber replied that his troop had "conquered the mountain." It was an obstacle they had attacked and overcome. Another climber, indigenous to the area of Mount Everest, gave a different response to the question. This was a climber who had lived on and in the shadow of the mountain all his life. He said that he and the mountain had worked together to attain the peak. In short, here is the difference between Western and non-Western spirituality. One is self-centered; the other is communally-centered.

Western Christian spirituality falls short when dealing with ecological violence. What I mean is when defining a discourse of Christian nonviolence, do we teach our children that it is wrong to swat a gnat? Is it not being what God intended us to be when we eat meat? Interestingly enough, ecology means the same thing as economics—namely, the study of the household, *oikos*. "Household," in ecological jargon, means habitat or the science of the economy of animals and plants and their relationships with living organisms to their habitat. Why is Christian spirituality, especially in the United

States, so conspicuously silent about ecological issues? It seems to me that a Christian spirituality of nonviolence implies ecological maturation, a constancy of new life in flourishing relationships. New life is not a possession. It is, simply, new life—that is to say, a new world of possibilities, a new future that is to be constructed day by day. Life, after all, implies movement and growth. And perhaps this rather banal and obvious point is an indicator of what must be central for any adequate understanding of a Christian spirituality of nonviolence. Through Jesus' life, death, and resurrection, Christians learn to live life not predicated on death.

I remember watching a *Star Trek* episode in which Spock, Bones, and Captain Kirk were gathered around the bridge of the ship, reminiscing over their particular heroics. But this reminiscence was disturbing in that Captain Kirk was a bit shaken over this act of "having" to kill an alien species. Ironically, the emotionless and logical Spock was the one to console him. Spock told Captain Kirk that he need not worry so much because life, after all, depends upon death. Bones, the ship's medical doctor, who had developed a playfully antagonistic relationship with Spock, asked, "What in the hell do you mean?" Spock replied, "Well, in order for you to live, you must depend upon another's death."

Different also are Western and African understandings of religion and its relation to life. During the past several hundred years, religious belief, practice, and experience have become an option for Western persons, not a core way to organize life experience. For those who remain believers, too often religion is a separate compartment of life, with various religious duties to be "done," but with little influence on ordinary life other than the vague desire to do good and respect the rights of others. One attends church on Sunday and then gives little thought to religious commitment the rest of the week.

Organized religion in the West has seen its influence decline in many ways as this dichotomy between religion and the secular has become more pronounced. Even the rise of various fundamentalist groups has not challenged this approach since personal faith is seen as operative in a fairly narrow, restricted sphere with little social or political implication for the wider setting. The Western person brings much of this perspective to spiritual direction when the matter to be discussed is only that which is "religious." Prayer experience is important, but one's involvement with a local political party is not. Any approach or suggestion that reinforces this dichotomy in Western experience between "religion" and "life" widens the gap.

The African who becomes a Christian, Muslim, or follower of any other world religion looks for an experience of religion that also encompasses their whole life: language, thought patterns, social relationships, attitudes, values, desires, fears. It is not enough to "do religious things" regularly since their desire is for a religious worldview that will fill the world with meaning and be especially sustaining in times of fear and crisis. In the situation of spiritual direction, the African person brings her or his desire that experience of God be found in every facet of life without exception. Western directors or directees, formed in the pattern of religion as one part of life, can be disconcerted by the holistic view presented by their African brothers or sisters, but they have much to gain from it. Despite what I display as the shortcomings of Western spirituality, the distinct values of both worldviews (African and Western) can enrich each other: the Western person learning the value of community experience as formative of the person, and the African coming to a deeper awareness of her or his unique goodness and worth.

One can see through comparison of the Western and African views of self, the world, and religion that all persons are "like some others" since all are formed in the worldview of their culture. This worldview is as pervasive as the air one breathes, and it is often only through either direct cross-cultural experience or vicariously through study of other cultures that one begins to realize that the "oxygen content" of one's particular kind of cultural air is a bit different from that of their sister or brother of another culture. Sensitivity to the differences of worldviews one meets in the Christian relationship is thus a prerequisite for discernment for how the Spirit of God is nonviolent.

Nonviolence and the African Desert Tradition

The tradition of Christian spiritual direction started in the African desert. Holy people went into the desert to find God and rediscover Eden. Derwat Chitty explains in his work *The Desert a City* that the making a city of the wilderness was no mere flight, nor rejection of this earthly existence. If earthly matter were evil, why did they show such an aesthetic sense in placing their retreats and such love for all God's animal creation? Instead, Chitty argues that desert spirituality was rooted in a stark realism of faith in God and acceptance of the battle, which is not against flesh and blood, but against principalities, against powers, against the world rulers of this darkness, against the spiritual things of wickedness in the heavenly places. Violence for desert fathers and mothers was ultimately the warfare against Satan and demons that existed in the vast emptiness and desolate vacancies. The purpose of emptiness and desolation is to prepare Christian disciples for God's shalom or flourishing and to ground them in a lifestyle in which God would be most apparent. Unless God's shalom is the goal, the desert becomes a playground for masochists.

In contrast to Gnosticism in Greek and Egyptian philosophy and religion (Pythagorean, Stoic, Cynic, etc.), the African patristic figure Athanasius draws a distinctively Christian picture with Antony, whose bodily condition was not deteriorated but improved by his strange training in the ways of God's shalom. His friends marveled to see his body neither grown fat from lack of exercise, nor dried up from fasting and fighting with the demons. Physically, and in disposition of soul, he is "all balanced, as one governed by reason and standing in his natural condition."[10] Antony's perfection was reflected in his bodily condition, reflective of peace and contentment in God. A dualism that regards matter as evil has been typical of most ascetic religions and has been a besetting temptation to Christian spirituality. Antony's perfection was the attempt by Athanasius to display the teleology of the human natural condition to comprise life without decay and

---

[10] *The Life of Antony*, ch.14.

violence. The aim is to recover the Adamic condition before the fall—to find the garden of Eden again.

The word "monk" comes from the Greek *monos*, "alone"; hence, "monk" means "solitary one."[11] *The Life of Saint Antony* presents the Egyptian hermit as the founder of monasticism. His work popularized monastic ideals in the fourth-century church. The anchorite (Greek, *anchoresis*, "withdrawal") vision of holy solitaries called men and women to a separate life of prayer and contemplation, and it continued to influence the development of Christian spirituality through people like Julian of Norwich, but—at least in terms of the sheer number and influence of its adherents—monastic communities superceded the hermit's hut as places of spiritual instruction and formation.

Cenobitic (from the Greek word for "common") monasticism drew more directly upon the koinonia concepts of shared life and fellowship as a basis for monastic life. Pachomius is traditionally identified as the founder of communal monasticism with its emphasis upon shared work and shared worship under a common "rule" of conduct and practice. Benedict of Nursia authored and popularized one of the most influential of these monastic rules. St. Benedict's rule epitomized Western monasticism up through the Middle Ages, aiming for the perfection of the individual soul through the living of Christian life in community. This life was lived in the rhythmic harmony established by liturgical prayer, manual labor, and *lectio divina* (the meditative study of the Scriptures).[12] Obedience marked out the way to humility, and humility pointed the way to love; love was esteemed as the path to perfection.[13]

---

[11] James E. Goehring, "Monasticism," in *Encyclopedia of Early Christianity*, edited by Everett Ferguson (New York: Garland Publishing Col, 1990) 612-19 (hereafter: EEC).

[12] Cf. Lane, Christian Spirituality, 19-26, for a brief but useful discussion of "Benedictine Spirituality."

[13] See Benedict's twelves steps of humility in Olivia Thatcher and Edgar H. McNeal, eds., *A Source Book for Medieval History* (New York: Charles Scribner's Sons, 1905) ch. 1, of the Rule, 442-46.

Antony earnestly prayed for purity of heart in which to see God. He gradually cast out the temptations of his own thoughts, until the demons, expelled by his spiritual contentment in God, began to attack him violently from without, even as Satan in the wilderness assaulted the Lord ("and the angels waited on him," Mark 1:12). Demonic forces seek only to perpetuate a violent reality. Antony's life was the attempt to live another reality—one in which the shalom of Eden could remanifest. This desert sage trained himself to live within the temptations of life in such a way as to provide guidance and direction for others out of their own temptations. Herein, the climax is when Antony went into one of the tombs near the village, shutting himself in, to be so assaulted that his friend found him unconscious and carried him to the village church, believing him to be dead—but he woke up in the night and insisted on being taken back to the tomb. Then Antony challenged the demons to attack him again. This time, Antony vowed the demons would not defeat him with violence. Antony prayed with urgency that God would deliver him from evil, and then the quiet light of the Christ dispersed the demonic fantasies. When this warfare ceased, Antony asked God, "Where was Thou? Why didst Thou not appear from the beginning to cease my pains?" God replied, "Antony, I was here: but I was waiting to see thy contest."[14] At this point Antony broke new ground. God's reply became another epiphany to see that he was ultimately called to the desert. His old ascetic master could not go to this extreme—"for as yet there was no such custom." Antony then crossed the Nile and shut himself in for twenty years of solitude in a deserted fort, where bread was brought to him twice a year.

In this isolation and solitude, Christian spirituality is accused of quietism and irrelevance to society. This accusation becomes even more problematic as Christian spiritual direction almost becomes synonymous with psychoanalysis. Alan Jones, in his work *Soul Making*, articulates such a position as he sees the desert tradition alongside the modern tradition of psychoanalysis. For Jones, both invite a person to look deeply at reality. Desert spirituality and

---

[14] *The Life of Antony*, c. 10.

psychoanalysis bring a person to the brink of vast emptiness, which only God can fill. And both help to keep a person in the fellowship of the believers. Jones makes the qualification, however, that the desert and psychoanalysis are metaphors for a way of believing, for attentiveness, focus, receptivity, and change. The question that Jones and others have difficulty answering about the construct of desert spirituality and psychoanalysis is this: How does Christian spirituality mature persons in community to withstand and even conquer the violence of the world? In other words, how does one move from occupation with the metaphors of self to a healthy person who creates community instead of anarchy—the results of violence? In no way do I see psychoanalysis, which focuses on the functionality of an individual, capable of answering this question. Jones's focus on solitude, however, is a crucial concept of spirituality that may involve the construction of the individual within society. Henri Nouwen writes, "Solitude is the furnace of transformation. Without solitude we remain victims of our society and continue to be entangled in the illusions of the false self."[15]

In order to answer the question of how communities spiritually mature, Antony's call into the desert must first be understood through how he was enticed by the Gospel vocation to become *teleios*—"perfect." As an orphan, at the age of twenty, Antony heard in the Sunday gospel in church the words that became his life's aim: "If you wilt be perfect, go and sell all that thou hast and give to the poor, and come and follow Me."[16] In Christ's commission to Antony, the discovery of how a spirituality of solitude informs mature spirituality is made. In other words, Antony's ascetical training provided the basis for the desert to be transformed into a city. The eremitical ascetic was not called to the desert to be alone, but to build a city—a community. Such a community would only be perfect according to Jesus' commission if there were no poor or oppressed. In short, the criteria for spiritual maturity was in how Antony grew to

---

[15] Henri Nouwen, *The Way of the Heart: Desert Spirituality and Contemporary Ministry* (New York: Seabury Press, 1981) 25.

[16] *The Life of Antony*, ch.2

understand his life as a vessel used to build Christian community.[17] Following Christ's perfection necessarily leads to the harmony of all creation; therefore, the existence of the poor is an affront to the reality that Christ intends for the world. The world has deserts because it has the poor. Antony's commission was to turn the desert into a city, into a community. The desert was made a city by monks coming out from their own secular lives and into solitude so that they could facilitate the heavenly citizenship of all people.

What is the desert? On one side, the desert is represented as the natural domain of the demons, to which they have retreated after being driven from the cities by the triumph of the church and into which the heroes of the faith pursue them. Interestingly enough, Christian ascetics derived their very identity from the milieu of the desert, in which their commission to be perfect by giving their all to the poor could be achieved. Antony even compared a monk out of the desert to a fish out of water.[18] Anachoresis was the event in which individuals like Antony, sometimes whole communities, would withdraw into the deserts or swamps to escape from the intolerable burden of taxation and the political oppression to start again—to rebuild the city.

There are costs, however, in the ascetical pursuits of the desert tradition. This raises the problem of who is able to practice asceticism. And how does one discern between asceticism and masochism? Ernest Boyer is helpful when he recounts this story:

> Two years ago I sat in a crowded room at Harvard Divinity School as Dr. Sharon Parks gave a talk on what she called the spirituality of the desert. This is a way of life that takes its name from those men and women among the early Christians who interpreted the gospel as a call to a life of solitary prayer, left the comfort of family and friends, the

---

[17] One of the most important texts on the need to articulate Christian maturity comes from Bernard Haring, *Christian Maturity* (New York: Herder & Herder, 1967) 13.

[18] *Alphabetical Pophthegmata*, G. LXV, Antony 10.

security of home and village, and set out to live alone in caves or small huts in the harsh Egyptian desert. As she described this life of deep commitment, solitude, prayer, and reflection, I felt its attraction and recognized my own need for a way of life something like this.

But I also felt something else—a sense of frustration. Married and the father of three sons, I was deeply involved with the needs of my children and of the family as a whole. Was such a life possible with the commitment of a family?

The lecture ended. I sat still for a while and tried to draw my conflicting emotions together, then made my way to the front of the room.

Dr. Parks was putting away her notes. She looked up.

"Just one question," I said. "Is there childcare in the desert?"[19]

It is with Pachomius that one sees anachoresis more on the healthy basis of whole communities dispersing into the desert to build cities through his cenobitical (communal) spirituality rather than Antony's eremitical (individual) spirituality.

Pachomius was a pagan boy, conscripted at the age of twenty for Maximin's last war against Licinius. Pachomius was taken with the other recruits down the Nile, many for their last time. They were shut up for the night in the prison at Luxor in which existed a large portion of the ancient Egyptian temple. The Christians of the place came with food and drink to comfort the poor Pachomius and his comrades. Pachomius, asking what it meant to be shown such hospitality, was told that Christians were merciful to strangers and to all people. Again, Pachomius asked, "What would a Christian be?" Again, Pachomius was told, "They are those who bear the nave of Christ, the only-begotten Son of God, and do all good to all, hoping in Christ who made heaven and earth and us people." Hearing of such grace, Pachomius was fired with reverence for God and with joy. And

---

[19] Ernest Boyer, *A Way in the World: Family Life as Spiritual Discipline* (San Francisco: Harper & Row, 1984) xi.

withdrawing apart from the others in the prison, Pachomius stretched out his hands to heaven to pray for humility and community.

As Pachomius matured in his Christian faith, he developed the three stages of spiritual warfare: first, the inner conflicts with one's own thoughts; second, the stage of demonic onslaught from without; third, the recovery from the demonic onslaught in which one experiences victorious growth. In this last stage the Christian disciple experiences the wonder-working stage of perfect faith, which gradually gives place to the calm of perfect knowledge.[20] So where Antony seeks to be perfect ("I no longer fear God: I love Him."),[21] Pachomius seeks to learn and to do God's perfect will. Both, however, see perfection as maturation in the spiritual life. This insight by Antony and Pachomius illumines current culture in which politicians, religious leaders, and teachers know of our longing to remain infantile. In such a culture, the following paradox is often missed—namely, it takes a spiritually mature person to enter the kingdom of God as a little child.[22]

Matthew alone, of all the synoptic writers, uses the word *teleios*, or perfection. *Teleios* relates to the completion or the reaching of a goal. *Teleios* is the goal of the spiritual life, which reflects the breaking into history of a new style of life. Matthew invites his hearers to develop a spirituality that would set them apart from society (5:46–47). Jesus said, "In a word, you must be made perfect [*teleioi*] as your heavenly Father is perfect [*teleios*]" (Matt. 5:48). This passage does not allow us to think that we can enter some sort of

---

[20] For an interesting discussion of Pachomius, see pachomian koinonia, vol 1: *The Life of St. Pachomius and His disciples*. Cistercian studies, 45 (Kalamazoo: Cistercian Publications Inc. 1987).

[21] *Life of Antony*, ch. 32.

[22] I owe this insight to Alan Jones, *Soul Making*, in which he states three imperatives of mature believing

First to Look: a contemplative willingness to see what is there in front of us without prematurely interpreting what we see. Second, to Weep: if you look long enough and accurately, the tears will begin to flow. The fruit of honest contemplation is the "the gift of tears." And third to Live: Joy is the fruit of desert patience. The sure sign that our attentiveness has been focused and honest and the tears cleansing is joy.

once-and-for-all state of perfection, setting us apart from our society. Matthew shows that our share in the perfection of God is both possibility and process. Hebrews also says that Jesus was perfected through his submission to God's plan, becoming the power of eternal salvation to those who identify with his pattern of submission (Heb. 9:8–9). So whoever lives under this authority of God's reign is also "made perfect" in the way Jesus revealed perfection to be manifest. Becoming perfect as God is perfect is impossible on our own—it requires community.

Poverty of the Spirit and Spiritual Direction

We ask who are the poor in the Bible and church tradition. How can this guide us in our response to both material poverty and poverty of being? The Christian tradition distinguishes two kinds of poverty—material and spiritual. Each of these is further broken down into voluntary (positive) and involuntary (negative) dimensions.

Jesus' poverty of spirit is detachment for, not detachment from. Detachment needs an accompanying orientation. "My soul is restless, and it shall remain restless until it rests in You, O God," cried Augustine of Hippo[23] In his *Spiritual Exercises*, Ignatius of Loyola, the founder of the Jesuit Order, proposes that detachment should be the fundamental attitude of a Christian. He recognizes the danger of people being owned by what they own. For him, a Christian can only be committed to Christ—to the "greater glory of God" (*Ad Majorem Dei Gloriam*). The value of all things depends on whether or not they serve this end:[24] "So that, as far as we are concerned, we do not set our hearts on good health as against bad health, prosperity as against poverty, a good reputation as against a bad one, a long life as against a short one, and so on. The one thing we desire, the one thing we choose is what is more likely to achieve God's purpose."[25]

---

[23] *The Confessions of St. Augustine*, translated by F.J. Sheed (New York Sheed & Wood, 1965) 3.

[24] Ignatius of Loyola, *Spiritual Exercises* (London: Burns and Oates, 1963) 80.

[25] Ibid.

Spiritual detachment can be pervaded by a way of being willingly present for God, an orientation, a stance of our whole being, which encompasses whatever way we are knowing at a given time. This open, nakedly trusting, willing presence for God's loving truth can be lost when we "lean forward," graspingly, for individualistic interpretive knowledge; then our knowing loses its immediate openness to God and becomes more insular. We need our thoughts to grow out of and feed into our immediate givenness to God.

Since our interpretive theologizing is relative to a mystery that transcends our capacity to understand fully, we can have honest differences of interpretation with one another. When we gather together to probe this deep mystery that we sense is at work in us, we can trust that where two or three are gathered together in true willingness for God, Christ's Spirit will guide us, even if our probing leaves us at different places of understanding or uncertainty at a given time. The great advantage of a Christian spirituality of community is that individuals become a little less tempted to have the right words and answers to things with our cognitive minds, while still valuing those minds for what can come through them. Thus, God's active presence is realized to pervade both our knowing and our unknowing, and we do not have to press our knowing beyond its limits at a given time. There are, however, many who fail to know God's presence because community is lacking. The following story helps me explain:

> Clara held the cup tightly in her hands. "Since the children have gone," she said, "it just doesn't seem worth going on. It used to give me such happiness, them just being around. I never wanted anything else. To be married, to have a family.... Even when I was a little girl, I played with dolls and looked forward to when I grew up and could have real babies of my own. And now...do you know, sometimes I don't even feel I exist any more? People say, 'You're free now. The kids are off your hands. Get out, enjoy yourself!' But I don't know what this 'self' is. I've spent my life fitting in, filling the gaps, making myself into what others seemed to want. Trying to please. I know the children took advantage of

me at times. And my husband, too, especially lately. Sometimes I think he'll really leave, like he's threatened, because there is no one there to keep him home. He despises me, I can see it in his eyes. Gets furious when I can't make up my mind. But how can I? Suppose I get it wrong? It was so easy before, when I could see what was needed, and just do it."[26]

By the standards in her own society, Clara is not materially poor—but she experiences an inner emptiness, a sense of being driven, a sense that there is something more, something just beyond her grasp, that would set her striving at rest. Theologians have called this inner emptiness "ontological poverty," the poverty of being. It is profoundly personal, and yet at the same time common to all people, across space and time, part of being human. It concerns the experience of self, yet, because we belong in society, it is shaped by the broader culture.

For some people, poverty of being is felt in the limits to options. Every choice we make shuts off other choices. With every door we walk through, others close behind us. When we take a particular job or marry a particular person, we say "yes" to one possibility at the price of saying "no" to others. Sometimes we make options even though the choices are not very clear. Or what seems to be the right thing to do at a given moment becomes questionable later on. As we grow older we find that at a deeper level, this is true also. We do learn more; we come to understand new things. But we also lose some of the old certainties, find that life is much more complicated than we thought; things are not so black and white. Some of us react to this with denial; we insist on holding on to a particular view of the world; we become less tolerant and less flexible. We define ourselves against others, assert ourselves by refusing to see the world as they do. But for others of us, the response is quite different. We see that our boundaries become less clear; we can no longer state, definitively, who

---

[26] Sarah White and Romy Tiongco, *Doing Theology and Development: Meeting the challenge of Poverty* (Edinburgh: Saint Andrew Press, 1997) 78-80.

we are. We see ourselves no longer as the center of our own worlds, but simply as one part in a large whole.

Others experience poverty of being in terms of lack of control. One of the sharpest ways in which we are out of control is in our need for others. This can take people in two different ways. Some, like Clara, may try to lose themselves in relationships, be so much defined in terms of others that they no longer know who they are. But the paradox is that we need others to grow; only through others can we come to know ourselves. One of the most profound forms of torture is to leave a person in a bare room, utterly alone. There is something terrible about loneliness. Part of being human is the need for one another. We cannot simply stand alone. Nor can we enter a relationship if we have no self to share.[27] Poverty of being is a given of human living. Trying to fill our emptiness with anything beyond the community of God will always fail.

When we extend our understanding of poverty to include poverty of being, it is clear that the non-poor can also be poor. Poverty of being is experienced as an inner emptiness that craves to be filled. Human beings need some achievements in order to feel good about themselves. To feel that one is doing a good job, to have children, to have the recognition of others, to have material comfort, to have a partner to love—these are not bad things. But they impoverish us when these desires become an obsession, when other people, and even ourselves, become only means to these ends. To some extent, how we respond to poverty of being is a constant choice. But there is also a wider, structural aspect to this. Different economic and political cultures treat the poverty of being very differently. Some set brakes on it; others actively emphasize it. Where people are in the social structure is also significant. Men and women, black and white, rich and poor will experience the poverty of being in quite different ways." [28]

God's perfect will is enacted in the purpose of persons to find their ultimate wealth in God's community, which is to make us persons demonstrative of the presence of God. The process of living

---

[27] See White, et. al, *Doing Theology and Development*, 81.

[28] See White, *Doing Theology and Development*, 82.

in God's community involves a total reformation of life. God's community demands that we submit to the authority of its central purpose—the flourishing of creation. From and in that *exousia* (authority), we then work to make it present in our society, with a willingness to suffer the consequences this might entail. Jesus said, "Seek first God's kingdom," ie., God's way of holiness (Matt. 6:31–33).

God's community and the world's vested interests find their central dynamics in serious tension. God's community demands for all its disciples not just a commitment of words, but a willingness to bear a cost through behavioral and relational change. Living under the spirituality of God's community calls for conversion to peacemaking and the reversal of anarchy. Consequently, we must choose which central dynamic will become the basis for our lifestyle. Matthew affirms that we are responsible for the future we choose (25:31–46). This is the reasoning in the cosmology of the ascetical figures of both Antony and Pachomius. Spirituality can never be quietistic in this framework because there is a deep sense of the fragility of personhood. This means that desert spirituality did not accept the Western dichotomy of faith versus works in how God saves us. God's community is not simply a matter of rules and regulations. Unfortunately, God's community has often become equated with individualistic concerns; herein, ideology can be used to protect unjust social arrangements in which whole communities suffer while a few individuals prosper. Crosby gives an illustration of such unjust social arrangements in his meeting with an international vice president and chief economist for General Motors:

> When I go to meetings in New York," I said, "I often stay at one of the our Eastern Province's parishes on the lower east side of Manhattan. As I walk there from the Denancey Street subway stop, six blocks away, I get the feeling that the thousands of people in that neighborhood don't really matter to our corporate world, especially a corporation like General Motors. Is this the case?" I asked. "Well, Mike," he responded, "I hate to say it, but this is the

only way it can be. We can't be concerned about them because they are outside our market projections.[29]

When resources become an end in themselves, images of God have become slaves of idols. This is idolatry. If the word "God" is not to be debased, those who want to go on using it need to experience both emptiness and desolation, According to A.N. Whitehead, Without such experiences the word "God" becomes simply a way of talking about our highest aspirations, our likes and dislikes. Few would want to be free of either their idolatrous imaginings or their fixed opinions. Instead of idolatry, the process of turning human lives over to the power of God and coming under God's life-giving influence involves the dynamic of seeking and finding God's presence in community. The process begins with seeking and finding, and this is why Antony went into the desert. The Christian disciple becomes perfect through the discovery of what is lacking in a person's life. Such growth demands the soil of reflection and the ingredients of purity of heart.

The pursuit of a commodified self who only consumes matter creates an obstacle to God's presence in community. A commodified self can never understand a flourishing way of living that signifies acceptance of God's community. This community of God's purpose is always identified with the dignity of each person made in God's image and the need for all people to share in the goods of this earth. Failing to live in God's community, we inevitably develop a spirituality void of sacrificing anything of our individual power; therefore, the natural instinct toward the violence of self-defense gives way to proactive violence on behalf of a few—even as we continue to "go to church" and say "Lord, Lord" (Matt. 7:22). God can be made an idol of the Protestant work ethic to reinforce these individualistic ideologies that legitimize a certain social order in which God is perceived to bless certain individuals. For example, maleness was the essence of power, possession, and prestige. Maleness was the peak of perfection, understandable at certain times in the church's history. Or white

---

[29] Michael Crosby, *Spirituality of the Beatitudes: Matthew's Challenge for First World Christians* (Knoll, Mary NY: Orbis 1995) 40.

churches refused to believe that black people could contain the image of God and historically refused the Eucharist based on such beliefs.

Contemporary Christians, like those embracing the "base-communities" movement in Latin America, continue to evidence the power of the Christian concept of *koinonia*, which provides the basis of Christian spirituality.[30] Gustavo Gutiérrez, writing from a Latin American context, agrees that "the development of the community dimension of faith is a characteristic of Christian life in our day."[31] For Gutierrez, rediscovery of the "community dimension" is crucial for our times because it counteracts several important misconceptions about Christian spirituality, two of which are particularly damaging. First, "Christian spirituality has long been presented as geared to minorities. It seems to be the peculiar possession of a select and to some extent, closed group."[32] And " a second characteristic of the Spirituality in question, and one that is also being challenged today, is its individualistic bent. The spiritual journey has often been presented as a cultivation of individualistic values, as a way to personal perfection."[33] For Christian spirituality to be powerful in its own context, Gutierrez argues, these perceptions must be overcome in favor of a spirituality that has its basis in community and in solidarity with the sufferings of Christ and Christ's people. Hence, "spirituality is a community enterprise. It is the passage of a people through the solitude and dangers of the desert, as it carves out its own way in the following of Jesus Christ. This spiritual experience is the well from which we must drink. From it we draw the promise of resurrection."[34]

The good news of God's community must be proclaimed on behalf of all the nations (Matt. 24:14). It demands that we deeply experience God's presence within community so that individuals or persons might be converted continually to God's vision of creation. Of course, this presents the problem of hermeneutics: How does one discern God's vision from one person's vision? The answer for such

---

[30] Rahner, *Practice of Faith*, 167-75.
[31] Gutiérrez, *Our Own Wells*, 128.
[32] Gutiérrez, *Our Own Wells*, 13.
[33] Gutiérrez, *Our Own Wells*, 14.
[34] Gutiérrez, *Our Own Wells,* 136

discernment is this: Instead of turning God's community into the ideological legitimization of a few individuals, the activity of the spiritual life is the very sign of God's grace enacted on behalf of the world. We know when God is speaking when we begin to see and hear shalom for all of creation. Shalom signifies the reign of God breaking into the world (Matt. 12:28).

As Antony taught us, this all must be accompanied by a deeper sign: the witness of our lives committed to those in need. Personal salvation is anachronistic when applied to the desert spirituality. Salvation is never a certain reward. The community of God is not a matter of once-and-for-all membership. Jesus explained, "Mark what I say." Self-assured members of the community were warned, "Many will come from the east and the west and find a place at the banquet in the kingdom of God with Abraham, Isaac, and Jacob, while the natural heirs of the kingdom will be driven out into the dark. Wailing will be heard, there, and the grinding of teeth" (Matt. 8:11–12).

While traditional exegesis presented the "natural heirs of the kingdom" as the Jews, recent scholarship has extended this passage to include those in the church, especially church leaders, who seemed to think they were beyond criticism because of their position in the church. Christian ascetics saw that the parable of the tenants portrays a Jesus who makes it clear that the very one rejected by the structure, probably in the name of God (Matt. 21:31), would be the first to enter it (Matt. 21:42)

So the impetus for the ascetic was that salvation could not simply be known as an individual; instead, one also had to develop a communal sense to know how all the nations and creatures were being saved. What is rejected is a spirituality that stresses individualism to the exclusion of communal obedience that identifies individuals to the poor and oppressed. Equally, membership in the church does not assure a place in the community of God. Michael Crosby's *Spirituality of the Beatitudes* explains this difficult notion through community of salvation, or the "nation that will yield a rich harvest" (Matt. 21:43) as that community of all persons whose spirituality reflects their experience of God's reign (see Matt. 9:37–38; 13:4–30, 36–42). Even though baptism and circumcision signify entrance into the community, remaining a full member of the community requires more. Matthew says that all kinds of people not considered part of the community (8:11; cf. 2:1f) will come within God's community if they submit to the gospel in which all are called to flourish. Often times they will be members without realizing it (25:38, 44). Only those who live communally in goodness will be recognized by the King as those with spiritualities reflective of salvation.

Finally, this all means that the community of God is not a matter of personal religious experience. This shocks the Western ear to hear that personal experience is secondary in the spiritual life, but if one looks closely at the desert tradition, as with Antony, one sees that the primary importance of religious experience was not for the self—unless such experience leads to concern for others beyond the community. "I" must be revisioned in the image of God, the unknowable and inexhaustible God revealed to us in Jesus. To really believe we are made in God's image means a revolution in self-understanding. "I" would have to be understood in terms not only of the life, death, and resurrection of Jesus; "I" would suddenly become unknowable and inexhaustible, and so would everyone else. Alan Jones convincingly states that: "It [understanding 'I' in the image of God] would mean giving up my patterns of knowing and feeling with regard to God and the world. The implications of this for self-understanding are momentous. Just as God is 'hidden' from us, so too are we 'hidden' from ourselves and from each other."[35]

Where there is a need for a Christian spirituality of nonviolence today is in the recognition that personal experience cannot exist apart from communal experience. Our relationships with God bear this out. This means that spirituality's best definition is the grace of becoming enough of a person to experience God's community. This is why nonviolence is crucial to Christian spirituality. The purpose and perfection of God's reign are fully exemplified in Jesus' practices of nonviolence. The authority of Jesus' nonviolence establishes his identity as the saving authority of God, the person inaugurating God's salvation. Jesus is the anointed one, the one alone able to forgive sins

---

[35] Jones, *Soul Making*, 27.

because he does not inflict the violence that would match the offense. This means Jesus is also God because God alone has the power to forgive sins (Matt. 9:6; 21:23–27). In his person Jesus becomes the way in which other persons become sinless. Such personhood will continually entail a process of becoming, more and more, one who shares in the perfection of God. This sharing process of becoming more of a person is what I ultimately call God's community.

Redirecting Spiritual Direction Toward Nonviolence

I propose two contributions that the spiritual traditions of spiritual direction can make toward peacemaking: discernment and communal habit. Spirituality seeks to interpret the particular ways God seems to move directly within and among us, inviting us into deeper communion and into compassionate, creative callings. It also deals with the intentional spiritual disciplines that help us notice and freely respond to these invitations and in the process help us notice that which is not of God's community. As Antony learned in the desert, we are then able to respond appropriately to the counter invitations to God's—those that emanate from insular egos and societal forces and from the violence of evil. Christian spirituality is particularly done in the light of our communal experience as the church.

Discernment
First, let us look at what I mean by discernment. Seen as an aid to the discernment of God's presence in one's life and as a means of accountability for one's faithful response in all of life, it serves as a reality check, a preservation from the myopia of narrow, self-centered vision. It also sharpens one's awareness of solidarity with all God's people and challenges one to choices for responsible love. There is an obvious problem of discerning peaceful practice in the Western world. Reduction of conflict by means of a phony "peace" is not a Christian goal. Justice is the goal, and that may require an acceleration of conflict as a necessary stage in forcing those in power to bring about genuine change. A problem arises: What is this

accelerated conflict, and what form can it take? For example, "Would it be legitimate to describe both the physical force used by a rapist and the physical forced used by a woman trying to resist the rapist as violence?"[36] Are stones thrown by black or Palestinian youth really commensurate with buckshot and real bullets fired by police killing thousands of people? Questions continue: What, then, is a "lawful" use of force against individuals or property? On a larger scale, are wars fought by nation-states only?

How does one characterize the nation-state that the Christian community is supposed to obey (that is, oppressive, lenient, moderate, democratic)? What are the moral reasons for going to war (or engaging in systemic conflict) given by your nation-state? Are these various moral reasons compatible with the dictates of the state, and are they compatible with the church? What is the public's awareness of the effectiveness of the church in peacemaking? Soon a related question emerged concerning the responsibility of Christians regarding tyrannical rule. Rewritten from the perspective of the oppressed, theology is rediscovering the significance of traditional theological teaching on tyrannical rulers. To what extent were the oppressed permitted or obligated to resort to arms to remove the tyrant?

Many black South African Christians saw themselves with no alternatives between violence and nonviolence. They said they were simply at war, and when one is at war, one chooses tactics that work. If nonviolent tactics work, fine; if not, then nonviolent direct action is one of many strategies of warfare with no intrinsic relationship to principled pacifism. Bonhoeffer argued, "To maintain one's innocence in a setting such as that of the Third Reich, even to the point of not plotting Hitler's death, would be irresponsible action. To refuse to engage oneself in the demands of necessity, would be the

---

[36] *The Kairos Document: Challenge to the Church* (Braamfontein: The Kairos Theologians), 1985. This manifesto came from the grassroots to challenge the churches to resist apartheid. The distinction the authors have made between "State Theology," "Church Theology," and "Prophetic Theology" is a permanent contribution to theological thought.

selfish act of one who cared for his own innocence, who cared for his own guiltlessness, more than he cared for his guilty brothers."[37]

Walter Wink is helpful here as he articulates the thesis that Jesus' third way of turning the other cheek is not intended as a legal requirement to be applied woodenly in every situation, but as the impetus for discovering creative alternatives that transcend the only two that we are conditioned to perceive: submission or violence, flight or fight.[38] Julian Edward Kunnie, a black South African theologian, disagrees with Wink. In the following quotation, we learn firsthand what I am trying to articulate as to the competition between Christian narratives of who has the right to call for peace and when what we call peace may be phony for those caught up in the conflict:

> The situation extant in South Africa in recent history has functioned as a classical case in point on the subject of the debate between "violence" and "non-violence" (remember Walter Wink's arrogant assumptions about South Africa in The Third Way, an exhaustible theological feud for which Western Christendom is highly culpable. In this highly biased work, Walter Wink, the American Biblical theologian suggests that black people in South Africa explore the possibility of a "third way" in response to the violence of colonialism and capitalism in South Africa. Wink writes as an isolated white observer making his intrusion into the ethics of struggle in South Africa representative of an American imperialist intervention and reverberating with racist undertones. Black people in South Africa do not possess the luxury of engaging in this kind of "aesthetic" exploration, owing to the fact of their being exploited by Western capitalist nations such as the United States, from where Wink hails.[39]

---

[37] Cited by John de Gruchy, *Bonhoeefer and South Africa* (Grand Rapids: Erdmans, 1984) 98.

[38] Wink, 26.

[39] Julian Edward Kunnie, Bridges across the Atlantic Relating Black theologies in the United States and South Africa focussing on social analytical methodologies and utilizeing James Cone and Desmond Tutu as respective symbolic figures. 241.

In a valiant search for justice and human dignity, the United States constructed the Constitution, which is an ideal universal basis upon which all may participate in constructing a peaceful society. There are two problems with the Constitution. The first problem with the U.S. Constitution is that we really don't believe it. The second problem is that there are so many different beliefs in what it means. What this contradiction ends up meaning is that although the appeal of self-evident truths concerns equality and rights to life, liberty, and pursuit of happiness, there is still the journey to provide some cogent philosophical basis for what appears as self-evident. In the end, what appears to be self-evident may only be mutually antagonistic positions: "We are thus a society that may be in the unhappy position of being founded upon a moral contradiction."[40] The only self-evident truth about the Constitution is that it reminds us not to kill each other, that perhaps there is something innate among people that must kill; therefore, we need some moral guideline to remind us not to pursue our natural tendency, something like the U.S. Constitution.

Perhaps, in its most useful sense, Christian spirituality can come to mean a habit of discernment: that ongoing availability and sensitivity to God. This habit permeates all of life and determines choices. The problem with Christian discernment is that too many people have quoted Augustine—"Love God and do what you will"—to rationalize and excuse inappropriate behavior. Even Thomas Merton's axiom, "Whatever is demanded by truth, by justice, by mercy or by love must surely be taken to be willed by God," can lead many astray if there is no interpretive framework by which to distinguish which God to love and which justice to follow. This is why Christian spirituality must depend upon the community of the church as opposed to the individualism of Western culture. Habits of discernment can help us practice an authentic Christian spirituality. The questions involved for the habit of discernment follow: (1) Am I

---

[40] Stanley Hauerwas, *A Community of Character* (Notre Dame: University of Notre Dame Press, 1981) 216.

seeking to grow in my availability to God, my presence for God in all of life? (2) What is my sense of attentiveness to God's presence in my life? (3) And what is my belief in God's active involvement in the present moment? Discernment is the habit of viewing all of life through the eyes of faith and, in that faith stance, noticing the movements of the heart to determine which of these movements are leading to greater love and authenticity, focusing one in on God, and which of them are turning one in on oneself. Christian spirituality, in the end, is the habit of discernment rooted in the conversion of individuals to form the multitude of saints.

Communal Habit

Secondly, habit and practice of the presence of God in community are necessary to discern peace in the world (other cultures do this better than Western cultures). Spiritual direction is helpful only when we can stay as an open channel for God's presence. A change of paradigm may be in order—namely, spiritual direction may be a more dynamic process as group or community spiritual direction as the histories of individuals who were once aggregate identities merge toward what identity outside of self may look like. The community process assists individuals further than a mere spiritual director and directee in that the merging histories of individuals create more attentiveness in the discernment process. As Simone Weil states, Those who are afflicted have no other need than for those capable of giving complete attention.[41] I often wonder about those on death row, who have Christian conversions and begin to model the life of Christ, I wonder if this ability to attend to them is what in fact may have cured them, as national attention turned to them.

Spiritual direction always has been a vital part of the Christian tradition.[42] Seen as an aid to the discernment of God's presence in one's life and as a means of accountability for one's faithful response

---

[41] See Simone Weil, "Reflections on the Right use of School Studies," in *The Simone Weil Reader*, ed., George Panichas (Mt. Kiskno, NY: Moyer Bell Limited, 1977) 51.

[42] Group Spiritual direction: Shared Experience in Responsible Love (Rosemary Dougherty)

in all of life, it serves as a reality check, a preservation from the myopia of narrow, self-centered vision. It also sharpens one's awareness of solidarity with all God's people and challenges one to choices for responsible love.

The group setting is a viable means for spiritual direction. It not only is expeditious in terms of numbers to be served; at its best, group direction has the potential for the formation of a spiritual community, which may well provide a paradigm for other discerning groups. Its effectiveness, of course, is dependent upon an environment appropriate to all spiritual direction. As in one-to-one direction, each individual has begun a journey with God long before she or he comes into direction. The choice for direction is simply a way of owning God's love and the desire to respond to that love by asking others to help discover the implications of that love. An atmosphere of intentional prayer precedes and follows the group sessions, permeating the time together, as all seek an attitude of trustful openness, ready to share what is given as the fruit of prayer and reflection and ready to hear what rises in the silence and words of a small group session. Each member, then, assists in the attentiveness to the Holy Spirit, who is the true director, and prays to be freely available to God for whatever God's love might evoke. Together, we risk the discerning light of God's love, praying to be transformed into the personality of God.[43]

There are some specific guidelines for group spiritual direction:

(1) Pray for others in the group between sessions in whatever way possible.

(2) Be consistent in whatever practice seems best to reflect and honor your unique relationship with God at this time, perhaps journaling about what you perceive, sense, or want concerning your attention to God and the way God seems to be dealing with you in all facets of your life. It could be helpful to notice the following: (a) desire for God; (b) desire to desire God; (c) persons and circumstances

---

[43] *Guidelines for Group Spiritual Direction* (Rose Mary Dougherty, SSND, 1993).

that seem to attract one to God; (d) the way that one senses awareness of God; and (e) how one resists God.

(3) Before coming to the group, spend time in prayer, reflecting on the persons in the group, reflecting on the journal entry since the last meeting. Allow for the possibility that something entirely different may show itself in the actual moment of the group's sharing.

(4) Come as early for the group as possible, and be prepared to start on time. Since some people might be using the room for prayer before others arrive, please enter the room in silence.

(5) During the time of the small group sharing, simply try to be available to God in whatever way seems appropriate. Try to be considerate of others in the group by confining sharing to the allotted time, including what you share about yourself and the group's response. Look upon the group's time of sharing as a time to talk about relating well to God as God is experienced in all areas of life.

(6) Hold in reverence and confidence what is heard in the group.

(7) If you know you are going to be absent, let someone in the group know. If it is possible and you are comfortable doing so, send a note to group members, describing as well as you can what seemed to be going on between you and God during the past month. Perhaps you will be able only to talk about the way you would like people to be praying for you during the month. Hopefully this will ease your sharing at the next meeting; it may also give a focus for a time of prayer for you during the session.[44]

We are all created to be in relationship to a larger other; after all, community is our image of God. We were created to realize complementary relationships. Herein is the difference between spiritual direction and psychoanalysis, namely, that there is the consciousness of a third party in spiritual direction. In spiritual direction, the focus of two is on God as the true director, and the focus is not merely horizontal among space and time.

God's presence is shalom, and the creature longs for such presence. Because of sin, we are more apt to create gods of

---

[44] ibid

convenience than to seek the presence of the Holy God. Because of God's holiness and because of human sinfulness, it is, simultaneously, a threatening and enthralling event for a human being to stand in God's presence. Even for someone like Moses—one of the greatest prophets of God and the only one who spoke to God "face to face, as a man speaks with his friend" (Exod. 33:11)—to actually see God's face invited certain death (Exod. 33:17–23). Spiritual pilgrims who have sought God's presence in prayer, reflection, or visionary experiences have found it to be a comforting and disturbing presence. Rudolph Otto's *The Idea of the Holy* notes five salient features resident in an experience of God's mysterious presence (*mysterium tremendum*): (1) awfulness or a sense of deep awe; (2) a sense of "over-poweringness" (Majestas); (3) a sense of urgency; (4) a recognition that one has met the Wholly Other; and (5) a sense of fascination.[45]

A sense of the absence of God, such as occurs in John of the Cross's *Dark Night of the Soul*, is an equally awe-filled and overpowering experience since it can lead to a resolute detachment from worldly things that purifies the soul and allows it to wait in darkness for the piercing presence of God. Through active and passive experiences of divine absence the soul is purified by God and is transformed into godlikeness, just as wood is dried and transformed into fire by divine light: "The soul is purged and prepared for union with the divine light just as the wood is prepared for transformation into the fire...by heating and enkindling it from without the fire transforms the wood into itself and makes it as beautiful as itself."[46]

Not only is God's presence an "enkindling" and purifying presence, but it is also a nurturing and gracious presence. Hence, Julian of Norwich noted, "As truly as God is our Father, so truly is God our

---

[45] Rudolph Otto, *The Idea of the Holy*, translated by John W. Harvey (London: Oxford University Press, 1936) 12–41.

[46] Kieran Kavanaugh, O.C.D., and Otilio Rodriguez, O.C.D. eds., *The Collected Works of St. John of the Cross* (Washignton, D.C.: Institute of Carmelite Studies, 1979), "The Dark Night of the Soul," ch. 10, 350.

Mother."[47] She found the motherhood of God expressed in three foundational ways: "The first is the foundation of our nature's creation; the second is his taking of our nature, where the motherhood of grace begins; the third is the motherhood at work. And in that, by the same grace, everything is penetrated, in length, and in breadth, in height and in depth without end; and it is all one love."[48]

There is a profound sense in which all of one's life is lived out in God's presence (Latin, *coram Deo*), and this recognition becomes a powerful tool for understanding all of one's life as being consecrated unto God. The Carmelite lay brother Nicholas Herman, known as "Brother Lawrence," cultivated and practiced this sort of life, and its character has been preserved for us under the title *Practice of the Presence of God*. Without forsaking the *mysterium tremendum*, Brother Lawrence advocated a style of spirituality that developed a continual sense of being in God's presence and the practice of returning to God's presence through deliberate acts of prayer. He aspired to a habitual sense of God's presence that penetrated and invigorated all of a Christian's life. Brother Lawrence wrote: "The presence of God...if practiced faithfully works secretly in the soul and produces marvelous effects...and leads it insensibly o the simple grace, that long sight of God every where present, which is the most holy, the most solid, the easiest, the most efficacious manner of prayer."[49]

Brother Lawrence wrote over 300 years ago that "it is not necessary to be always in church to be with God, we can make a private chapel of our heart where we can retire from time to time to commune with him peacefully, humbly, lovingly."[50] Interestingly enough, Brother Lawrence, at age eighteen, joined the army during the Thirty Years' War. Frequent skirmishes were taking a heavy toll on all sides. At one point he was captured and about to be hung as a

---

[47] Edmund Colledge and James Walsh, eds., *Julian of Norwich: Showings* (New York: Paulist Press, 1978) 296.

[48] Colledge and Walsh, *Julian of Norwich: Showings* 297.

[49] Brother Lawrence of the Resurrection, *The Practice of the Presence of God*, trans. John Delaney (Garden City, NY: Doubleday, Image Books, 1977) 110.

[50] Brother Lawrence, *The Practice of the Presence of God*, 65.

spy until he managed to convince those who held him that he was simply an unlucky soldier of the other side. He was released and returned to his unit but was later wounded in Swedish raids. The wound ended his military career as he returned home haunted by memories of the carnage and brutality he had seen. He decided to withdraw from the world as a hermit, a lifestyle that lasted for only a short period.

After giving up the life of a hermit, Brother Lawrence returned to Paris and applied for admission as a lay brother at a monastery in Discalced Carmelites. He was professed two years later, in 1642, and given the name by which he would be known from then on: Brother Lawrence of the Resurrection. It is as if Brother Lawrence already knew the insight of the Zen Master's koan about showing the resurrection.

What set Brother Lawrence apart was that he saw the extraordinary within the ordinary, the sacred in the routine. Lawrence was "more united to God in his ordinary activities than when he devoted himself to religious activities which left him with a profound spiritual dryness."[51] His insights into work and prayer were recorded by Abbe Joseph de Beaufort, who kept notes of several conversations he and Brother Lawrence had together and joined these with a small collection of Brother Lawrence's letters to form a little book called *The Practice of the Presence of God*. In these conversations, set down in the shorthand manner that gives Brother Lawrence's thoughts in terse phrases, it is possible to glimpse the full realization of the sacrament of the routine, the awareness of God ever-present. For Brother Lawrence, "the time of prayer was no different from any other time, that he retired to pray when Father Prior told him to do so, but that he neither desired nor asked for this since his most absorbing work did not divert him from God."[52]

Most famously, Brother Lawrence became known for welcoming everyone with humility. Brother Lawrence teaches us that to cook is to pray. The lesson of Brother Lawrence is the realization that life has one purpose above all others—to give love to God and to those

---

[51] *The Practice of the Presence of God*, 47.
[52] *The Practice of the Presence of God*, 41.

near you and to allow yourself to be loved in turn. Brother Lawrence teaches us "that we should not weary of doing little things for the love of God who looks not at the grandeur of these actions but rather at the love with which they are performed."[53] He knew that there is nothing great about great deeds if they are done without love. Without love even those deeds that earn prestige, wealth, and power become hollow and empty. With love, the smallest, most ordinary of actions becomes sacred. But love is not something that we can will in ourselves, nor is it something we can force ourselves to have. Some love we seem to be born into, as with the love of a child for her parents. Other love seems to take us by surprise, as with the romantic love that comes, as the expression has it, when we "fall in love." But neither of these loves, powerful as they can be, is enough to transform the totality of life in the way that makes every act into sacred ritual. For such as this, love must be mined in a way that opens it into an expression of that eternal love we have so long called by the name of God.

It is not always easy to accept a love so freely given. We assume that it cannot be truly meant for us. This, too, is something Brother Lawrence knew:

> I regard myself as the most wretched of all men, stinking and covered with sores, and as one who has committed all sorts of crimes against his King. Overcome by remorse, I confess all my wickedness to Him, ask His pardon and abandon myself entirely to Him to do with as He wills. But this king, filled with goodness and mercy, far from chastising me, lovingly embraces me, makes me eat at His table, serves me with His own hands, gives me the keys of His treasures and treats me as His favorite. He talks with me and is delighted with me in a thousand and one ways.[54]

Too often, we see ourselves as despicable. Behind the façade, the manners, the laughter, the stylish clothes we use to convince

---

[53] *The Practice of the Presence of God*, 50.
[54] *The Practice of the Presence of God*, 69

ourselves and others to the contrary, this is how we really feel. It is not in God's eyes that we appear this way, but in our own secret self-scrutiny. In God's eyes we are marvelous and wonderful. We delight God, as Brother Lawrence says, in a thousand and one ways. To accept God's love is to accept ourselves as lovable—lovable not for what we have done, not for what we say, not for how we act, but lovable deep down, for who we are. It takes time to convince ourselves of this. And it is for this reason that, for Brother Lawrence, living in the presence of the Lord requires practice. It takes practice for us to allow ourselves to see the beauty of who we are. We need help with this practice, and Brother Lawrence makes several suggestions. I have modified them and divided them into four points: (1) reflect before beginning each task; (2) repeat a short prayer as you work; (3) reflect after you finish each task; (4) work at stability in your daily tasks. We cannot effect our own salvation. These exercises are merely ways in which we come to feel the love that is already there. We do not somehow force God's love by praying; we only help ourselves to recognize the love that has always been held out to us all along. To find this awareness of the presence of God in each moment of your life is to discover the secret of the sacred within the ordinary, which is the heart of the sacrament of the routine. It is, as I said, to know moments of great and unexpected joy. Brother Lawrence in fact confesses that it "sometimes causes me interior, and often exterior happiness and joy so great that in order to moderate them and prevent their outward manifestation, I am obliged to resort to behavior that seems more foolishness than piety."[55]

For many people, faith means nothing more than a set of beliefs to which they may either agree or disagree. To have faith is much like having an opinion, the only exception being that where other opinions might concern politics or sports, this is an opinion on whether or not God exists. Living the presence of God, though, faith is transformed from an opinion to a relationship. God is not a belief to which you give your assent. God becomes a reality that you know

---

[55] *The Practice of the Presence of God*, 68,69.

intimately, meet every day, one whose strength becomes your strength, whose love, your love.

God is always present to us. The greatest thing we can do in life is to teach ourselves to be always present to God. The small, routine tasks that fill every day spent in the care of others may seem to be a barrier to this, but they need not. They may be turned into one of the finest of spiritual disciplines, a special sacrament of the routine through which what to others appears the most ordinary and mundane of tasks is revealed to be a sacred act, an act of prayer. Prayer is nothing more or less than this, being present to God. And so this is a spirituality that makes all of life into prayer, a prayer of love, a prayer of help for others, a prayer of courage. It is a prayer that spans a lifetime, a prayer of great beauty.

While prayer is one of the main avenues into God's presence, it is by no means the only one. The community of faith—reaching all the way back to Passover (Exod. 12) with its liturgy and sacred reenactment—has entered God's presence through Word and sacrament. The Lord's Supper is one of the means whereby the mysterious presence of God is made tangible and accessible to the worshiping community. Catherine of Genoa experienced a transforming sense of God's presence as she prepared for her Lenten participation in the Mass; on 23 March 1473, she felt herself overwhelmed by a sense of the love of Christ and her own utter unworthiness. From May 1474 until her death in 1510 Catherine practiced daily communion as a way of experiencing the presence of God. Spiritual pilgrims as diverse as Bernard of Clairvaux and Thomas à Kempis experienced a tangible sense of the presence of God through meditation upon Holy Scripture. The inner voice and outer Word merged as à Kempis described "how Christ speaks inwardly to the soul": "'I will hear what the Lord God speaks within me.' Blessed is the soul that hears the Lord speaking within it, and receives comfort from His Word. Blessed are the ears that hear the still, small voice of God, and disregard the whispers of the world."[56]

---

[56] Thomas a'Kempis, *The Imitation of Christ*, translated by Leo Sherley-Price (New York: Penguin Books, 1952) 91.

5

PEACEMAKING:

RE-ENVISIONING WESTERN CHRISTIAN SPIRITUALITY THROUGH NONVIOLENCE

In this book, I have assumed all along that a rift has developed between personal spirituality and communal spirituality, making impossible any coherent account of a Christian spirituality of community and nonviolence. Christian spirituality is least effective when it comes to the topic of violence because such spirituality carries the Western tendency to separate our bodies, souls, and minds into neat compartments. Then we can rationalize pathological tendencies as belonging to one of these compartments and proceed to adhere to quietistic spiritualities in which ultimate existence is individual existence. But the thesis of this book is to counter this understanding of what Western Christian spirituality often means by asserting that spiritual formation does not so much admire goodness, as participate fully in the mystery of goodness—namely, God.

In summary, we have looked at the problem of defining Christian spirituality in the North American context. I have tried to expose the reader to the Western relative position of spirituality defined through individualism and how that often compromises our integrity in our practice of God's presence in the world. It is vital that we own up to our Christian faith if we are going to negotiate the next millennium. If we say we are a Christian community, and yet condone abusive nation-state behavior against poorer nations, then we have compromised our habits of discernment given to us by our Triune God. I say this is important for the next millennium because our world is growing more interconnected and the nice divisions we used to believe in are slowly fading. For example, we are seeing a new form of war. This form of war is no longer between two countries, but now against ideologies: A war on terrorism. Now, "the enemy" has taken up a religious war against Christian identities as synonymous with the dominant power. We see this in occurring in Northern Africa and the Middle East. What I hope we can practice within Christian spirituality are proactive solutions in a violent and capricious world.

In the West, especially from the time of the Enlightenment, the self has been understood as a distinct individual, with unique value and distinct rights. Persons have the right to make something of their lives, to take responsibility for their life direction, to use their talents and gifts to the full. Such emphasis puts supreme value on the right of self-determination, self-achievement, self-satisfaction. Christian spirituality is not just an academic exercise or a nice hobby to do when you have time. It is an active commitment to live one's faith, critically and questioningly, lovingly and hopefully. Latin American theologians have described this process of Christian spirituality as the pastoral cycle, in constant revolution from experience to analysis to reflection to action and on again.

Such personal responsibility for the shaping of one's life is a good and flows from the Judeo-Christian understanding of the dignity and worth of each human being. What is weak in this dimensional worldview is the bonding of the person with the community. Especially in this century and particularly in North American culture, individual self-determination has been exalted over the needs of the community, giving rise to "individualism" which found its most skewed expression in the "Me Generation"—my needs above all else. This cultural value has profoundly influenced all facets of life, including politics, economics, and religion. In the "Me Generation," a split occurs between public and private spirituality. For example, theology instructor Gerd Luedemann, who taught at Vanderbilt Divinity School, no longer believes in Christianity, yet he still is a theology instructor.

An article in the *Tennessean* states that Luedemann suspects a lot of churchgoers share his split personality of believing one thing in private and professing something else in public. Now, Luedemann says he is finally coming out of the closet with his disbelief. Luedemann states, "People know Christianity is not true, but they won't address it publicly. It's the skeleton in the closet. But I want to get the discussion going. That can only happen if you don't mind being stigmatized."[1] The article describes Luedemann as a fifty-two-year-old friendly man with a twinkle in his eye even as he declares traditional Christian belief is no longer possible. He insists liberal Christianity is dishonest when it does not admit its skepticism about the faith's miraculous claims. He thinks anybody who wants to be a serious Christian ought to take up fundamentalism. His hunch is that many other churchgoers feel what he feels but don't admit it—a deep disconnection between the miraculous world of Sunday morning Bible teaching and the daily world of rational laws of nature and social change. Luedemann said people owe it to their integrity to seek truth and risk abandoning cherished beliefs. "Why are we educating people?" he asked. "Is it just a hobby? Are we interested in truth? It's cynical to say that society can't tell the truth to itself. We live only once. We have to have the courage to seek the knowledge of who we are."[2]

In Scripture, I learn many things, but one lesson stands out: Do not attempt to possess things, for things cannot really be possessed. Only, make sure you are not possessed by them, lest your God change. Jesus shows us that in some degree we are constantly choosing our identity through heavenly worth or through material worth. If we choose the former, that is, heavenly worth, we develop a human character that is incapable of seeing human nature as other than it really is—of infinite worth. If we only choose the latter, material

---

[1] The *Tennessean* August 29, 1998.
[2] The *Tennessean*, August 29, 1998.

worth, we develop a human character that is incapable of seeing human nature as other than its highest form of rationality. So, for many scholars, like Luedemann, caught in an enlightenment cosmology, the highest form of humanity we can aspire to is a rational anima. Jesus teaches us that if we live in heavenly value then we live in the reality that no earthly object can satisfy us; therefore, no human being should exist as an object but as a subject. For you see, any creature or thing set up as our final end, inevitably blocks our vision of the true God. And since an idol is not God, no matter how sincerely it is treated as God, it is bound to fail. Even good motives for idolatry cannot remove the objective fact that the idol is an unreality. As Augustine thought, "Food in dreams is exactly like real food, yet what we eat in our dreams does not nourish: for we are dreaming."[3]

Problematic of Peacemaking Spirituality

Why is "spirituality" more popular than the institutional church? A response to Maggie Ross' "Pillars of Flame," written ten years ago (1988). Jesus' sermon teaches us that we, who call ourselves the church, are able to proceed, not because we share a common rationality, but because we find ourselves to be people who care about something[4]. The most important task for us is to derive a cohesive methodology by which we may think theologically about nonviolence without reducing the Christian church to another manipulative form of an ideological movement.

To guard against manipulative ideology, Christians must learn to see themselves defined *in medias res*, in the middle of things, in the middle of an adventure. We are a connected people dependent upon the Christian narrative to inform us as to who we are. Therefore, our sermons are vital as we continue our enacted story. If we do not see

---

[3].Augustine, *Confessions*, 3.6.
[4] See Stanley Hauerwas, *The Peaceable Kingdom* (South Bend: University of Notre Dame Press, 1983) 18.

and hear ourselves defined through our Christian story, then we naturally fall into sophistic games in which ethics is seen as "acts" abstracted from contingencies of history, the moral self cannot help but appear as an unconnected series of actions lacking continuity and unity." In other words, our sermons will continue to be caricatures of Monty Python movies in which the expression of our story can only be a comedy. If we do not take seriously the integrity between the proclamation of our narrative and our lifestyle, then the church delves into the demonic in which we confuse the ways of God with the power of death. In other words, we can easily fall victim to the worldview that our lives are our own and that we live because of the accidents of nature and that we must maximize our existence before we simply return to primordial matter.

What we proclaim as a church is a much different narrative—that even when we do return to nature as dust, that Jesus has somehow effected the resurrection not just of our souls but of our bodies. That somehow, when we die, we become like inanimate seeds, bodies that planted in the earth, and even though we could not imagine the massive tree resulting from an inanimate tree, so too, can we barely imagine the life that result from our return to the dust. In fact, Jesus proclaims in the Sermon on the Mount that we are to be happy, even in the face of powers of death. However, only Jesus truly models beatitude or happiness; we often fall short and are exposed as modeling manipulative attitudes.

Peacefulness: What the Church Is

The church must be a community of moral discourse. It is through such a unique community that individuals are able to run a marathon of character development toward the ultimate good, namely, God. It is from Scripture, and human reason shaped from the tradition of the church that we are continually nurtured to survive in this way in the world. For we are well acquainted with God's story of being with us, and this community called church must sustain a theological ethic drawn from ongoing implications of its commitment across generations as it necessarily faces new challenges and situations. It is from this dynamic church that we can begin to understand that a Christian character formed from this church has no stake in the absolute preservation of life as an end in itself.

My view of the church is that we are ontologically the methodology of peacemaking in the world. In other words, we are in the image of God who is able to be diverse and one at the same time, community and individual at the same time. We are the living model of creating a community or environment that allows conflict without that conflict destroying community. We do not hide from the truth, but embrace it in all of its complexities because we know the truth will set us free. This means that we know we will struggle internally with societal symptoms such as whether or not to accept fully black people, those who were once slaves, or gay and lesbian people, who just got off the list of medical associations for being physically disordered. From our inception as the church, we know that we have never been a community without internal conflict, but we know that who we are in Christ makes us the kind of people who are to embrace the tensions of the world and release these tensions through prayers and right action.

All of this means for me that the church makes theologies of just war appear inconsistent because the church is to be distinctive from finite worldviews of the world by modeling an atmosphere of reconciliation of disparate identities. Tutu, addressing the Mother's Union, displays such disparate identity when he states, "You can't carry a baby for nine months in order for it to become cannon fodder for AD47s and R1 rifles."[5]

So, I assume we as the church are different from the world. I assume clear distinctions between the church and world as Tutu demonstrates through his view of a church school:

> What makes a church school distinctive? It can't be that
> you perform well on the sports field. We would certainly want
> you to do that—but that is done also by schools that are not

---

[5] Tutu, "Mass Action—for a Better Sense of Values," NCW News, January 1993.

church schools. It can't be that you do well in your public
exams. We certainly want you to [be] full of distinctions —
but that is something that happens in nonchurch schools.
Ultimately, it is not merely excellence in sports and in
scholastic spheres. The thing that will be distinctive is that
the school has a certain atmosphere, a certain tone, where the
most coveted attributes are possessed by people who are
compassionate and caring, who are concerned about others,
who want to serve others especially those less privileged than
oneself, to be protective of those weaker than oneself, to
stand up for the rights of the oppressed, of the weak of the
outcast, of the voiceless, and will be marked by excellence in
the desire to serve Christ by serving Him in the least of
these.[6]

Christian tradition, especially through interpretations of the
Bible, has depicted God as ordaining war and sanctioning it for the use
of establishing order. More easily to display in the Old Testament,
interpretations of just war has been construed in the New Testament
through Jesus throwing the money-changers out of the Temple and
the passage of Romans 13 in which the early Christian community
was exhorted to honor civil authority. Through this tradition,
hermeneutical questions arose.

The church not only is a plausible and impossible story, but we all
must keep training take seriously Jesus' way of being in the world,
Jesus' way of success. We train in contemplation; more particularly,
we contemplate what life is in the Spirit. From contemplation and
prayer we can begin to understand that a Christian character formed
from this church has no stake in the absolute preservation of life as
an end in itself, and unlike Jack Kevorkian, we can have the vision
from a well trained character to see the strong tendency for doctors
to assume that care is synonymous with cure. Thus medicine defines
sickness as that which can be cured or controlled. As a result, the
dying become the ones doctors, our secular priests, cannot help. As

[6]Tutu, Handwritten Address, "Installation of Michael Bands as Chaplain—Bp,"
February 15, 1987.

soon as it becomes clear that the doctor can no longer cure, it then means retreat from the sufferer, the patient. In such a situation, a doctor like Kevorkian, who can no longer care medically for the patient, sees that person as already dead.

We have been listening to and trained by a different narrative in which God dies, and from this possibility and beyond to the resurrection, we learn the awful lesson as a church that caring is not to be identified with curing, but with the kind of character that faces death squarely by believing in the resurrection and the life.

Jesus' church is not totalitarian ("I must do this kind of work in the church because my mother always did it, or I must serve on this committee so that someone on it can see that I am working in the church, or I must go to Sunday school because my dad will spank me), but rather Jesus describes to us the habits and virtues of a community that embodies the peace that Christ has now made possible. Happiness, or beatitude, is to be made a reality by us, who call ourselves the church, committed to the process necessary for reconciliation to one another. The process of reconciliation and forgiveness is the engine that drives the many parts of the Sermon. Only a people who have learned to ask for forgiveness—that is, a people who know the hard task is not to forgive but to be forgiven—are capable of being the kind of community of saints that can support one another in the demanding task of forgiving the enemy. I guess, herein is the greatest lesson for us this morning: When the Beatitudes are divorced from the context of the church (from you and me), they cannot help but appear as impossible laws to be applied to and by individuals, but that is against what the Beatitudes intend. Instead, Jesus teaches us that individuals divorced from the community of the Beatitudes are incapable of living the life the Beatitudes depict. The Beatitudes only make sense in the understanding that a new community has been brought into existence that makes a new way of life possible. That community is us, the church. Yet we live in a world of such conflicts that we cannot negotiate a world such as this unless we are trained with virtues sufficient to sustain us in that endeavor.

As Christians we learn that in the most profound sense, one cannot teach spirituality. This is true in the same sense of the irony that many of us fail to pray the way we really do pray. In other words, much of what is required in the spiritual life cannot be produced on demand; rather, what is required in the spiritual life is often the cultivating stillness by which we can see what is already happening to us. Ironically, this cultivating stillness is not quietism, the state of complete paralysis, but it requires certain practices, intentions and disciplines by which we go further into the life of God. As a professor of Christian spirituality, the most prudent thing I can do as a teacher is help equip you with interpretive skills by which to see the particular ways God moves directly within and among us, inviting us into deeper communion, and into compassionate, creative callings. The way that I do this is by exposing you to some of these practices, intentions and disciplines by which we go farther into the life of God.

Saintmaking

Saintmaking is the process of healing the gross double standards in the Christian life. We say and preach one thing, but de facto we do the other and are being formed to do the other. Often we justify doing the other even though we say and preach the condemnation of what we justify. We say and preach sexual purity, while we are all but sexually pure. We say and preach nonviolence and still believe in just war. We say and preach self-sacrifice, while we at the same time privilege most things around the good of the self. We say and preach in Christ there is not Jew or Greek, slave or free, male or female, while our primary identities remain in race, socio-economic class and gender. From where do these double standards come? The answer seems to lie in the process of becoming a saint.

Sainthood connotes a way of talking which seems to suggest that the Religious life is "higher" or more perfect than the life of involvement in the world, and this would be challenged by Protestant moralists. But it is a mistake to talk of higher and lower, and it is a misunderstanding of the expression "counsels of perfection." In moral theology, counsels are exhortations that are helpful toward the attaining of the good life, but are not binding, as precepts are. The "counsels of perfection," also called the "evangelical counsels," which arc the exhortations to poverty, chastity, and obedience.

Christian spirituality demands that persons formed in Christ involve themselves in the life of the world. Especially in an age of affluence and of the overprizing of comfort and wealth, this same spirituality equally demands that some should hear the evangelical counsels and witness to the realities of prayer, aspiration, and true holiness. This is far from being escape or withdrawal, but it demands nonattachment and self-renunciation.[7]

Our double standards either cause a shifting worldview, or our double standards are the results of a shifting world view. Our cosmology of "going to church" is a new one. Now, we go to church on Sundays with the intent of leaving it. Christians originally saw themselves as the church, albeit imperfect and wanting; nevertheless, they were the church from whom they could not leave. As Peter said so well to Jesus, "Where else can we go? You have the words of Eternal Life." Our character does not match Peter's character, which was formed in the relentless irruptions of Jesus' presence. Instead, our world is different on Sundays from the rest of the week. Jesus is one way in certain space and time and different in another. The god we preach on Sunday bares scant resemblance to the god we often adore on Monday mornings and Friday nights. Our dualistic cosmology of God is so neat and pedantic that we easily separate and relegate God's space and time to an hour on Sunday in a certain building with similar people of socio-economic class.

In this current cosmology in which God is neatly wrapped in Sunday mornings, I have a difficult time articulating the spiritual processes underway which are making us into saints. What I particularly worry about is how Christians may recover the ascetical tradition of sainthood and virtue making without the unnecessary trappings of becoming a medieval nun or monk. The medieval cosmology of saintmaking was not necessarily any better than ours.

---

[7] John Macquarrie, *The Westminster Dictionary of Christian Ethics*, 132.

The terms "monk" and "nun" come from the Greek word *monos*, meaning alone, which originally defined the Christian ascetic who was separate or holy in relation to the common life of the world. In other words, they too saw a double standard and thought that the only way to overcome the dichotomous split was separation from the world. So the church developed in opposition to the world so that a Christian person did not have to be hypocritical. In the medieval world there were degrees in which you practiced Christian integrity. You could be alone (monk or nun) in monastic community (cenobitic monasticism), you could be even more distinct as an individual Christian as an anchorite (from *anachoreo*, to withdraw) or hermit (from *eremos*, dweller in the desert).

Traditionally with Christians who fled to the desert from the persecution of Decius, monasticism became the form of intense Christian piety. The East still has much more appreciation for the heroism of the hermit. But Basil of Caesarea, along with Pachomius, preferred the common life as the normal sphere for the exercise of Christian virtues.[8]

"Virtue" is the translation of the Greek *arete*, which simply means any kind of excellence. So a knife's *arete* would be its sharpness, that of a horse its speed, and that of an athlete her skill. These examples of virtue suggest that it was also thought to enhance power either by building on potential or by creating habits. Thus, as a moral category the virtues are dispositions that form passions and/or create habits. As Aristotle suggested, virtues are a "kind of second nature" that dispose us not only to do the right thing rightly but also to gain pleasure from what we do (see *Aristotelian Ethics*).

The question arises for Western Christians: who then is the virtuous Christian, the excellent Christian in our world of *sola gracia*? The usual subliminal responses point to characters like Mother Teresa who serves as the example of Christian sainthood. If you ask the general public in the United States who is more virtuous (excellent) like Jesus, and then asked them to choose between Mother Teresa or

---

[8] See Stanley Hauerwas's definition of virtue in *Dictionary of Christian Ethics*, 648ff.

Pat Robertson, there is usually an implicit agreement. I had this conversation with Tony Campolo in one of my field education colloquies (I was the only MDiv student among Tony's other MBA students who were all being trained to start cottage industries in developing countries or in underdeveloped urban areas). Campolo said that the American public, even the 700 Club members, would choose Mother Teresa as the most excellent Christian to the naked American eye.

A story is told of one American who made a pilgrimage to Mother Teresa's Mother House in Calcutta, India. He had seen her legendary figure during early morning mass in the chapel of her convent of Lower Circular Road. It was a vast room also used as study room and dormitory by the hundreds of young Indian woman of her novitiate—the room's only decoration was a crucifix on the wall with the inscription "I Thirst."

Campolo's insight about Mother Teresa's acknowledged more excellent way of Christianity takes us further into a problematic of Western Christianity. Campolo went on to say to me that a folk religion resides in much of American Christianity in which a person may have one standard of excellence modeled by Pat Robertson and the other standard modeled by Mother Teresa. I brought up in our colloquy that this "folk religion" causes the severe problem of making Mother Teresa into the prototype Christian because the 700 Club members who accept to levels of virtue can then relegate Mother Teresa's virtue to some celestial realm that they in their habits and disciplines never train for. In other words, Mother Teresa becomes the 700 Club's surrogate Mother in whom they claim as the ultimate realistic Christian without having to practice and grow in the formation of what made Mother Teresa this kind of excellent Christian

Am I just picking on the 700 Club? No. Mainline Protestantism is just as much to blame in making the Mother Teresa's of the world the great surrogate mother of sainthood. Inherit in our image of Mother Teresa is an unrealizable virtue or the fulfillment of moral and spiritual growth simply by having faith and grace (the typical Protestant outlook). In other words, Protestants have no means of assessing who in fact is a saint because we all are saints. No one is more spiritual than another. The judgment of many liberal Christians on the Christianity of the 700 Club or other televangelists is usually: "We all know this is a bunch of crap." Implicit in this judgment is the problem of discerning what is a more excellent form of Christian spirituality. As we conclude our discussion of a Christian spirituality of nonviolence, let us look at this problem of judging spiritual and moral growth in more detail with Greg Jones and Stanley Hauerwas's appropriation of Christian virtue.

There is the return to the virtues, in particular that any coherent account of moral judgment requires as its central focus an understanding of how a person's character affects and shapes the judgment that is made. For Greg Jones, the most coherent account of moral judgment is one grounded in, and lived in relation to the mystery of the Triune God. How the virtues are acquired and character formed reveals that theological claims about such matters as God, the world, and life and each make a decisive difference for how the activity of moral judgment is construed.[9] Greg Jones' work here helps me in arguing for a spirituality of nonviolence in that he believes that people learn to describe their actions and lives in one way rather than another, and that people learn to acquire and exercise the virtues ingredient in making wise judgments. Such learning occurs in and through the social contexts of particular communities, especially connected to particular theological (or anti-theological or a-theological views).[10] It is interesting therefore that Jones states, "it is important to attend to the ways a person is inducted into, and formed in, such a tradition."[11] For Jones, A Christian person is inducted into and formed in the mystery of the Triune God, who is central to the most coherent and truthful account of moral judgment and the moral life that can be offered.

Living in the mystery of the Triune God carries with it the understanding of "personhood," a definition of character that has the

---

[9] Jones, *Transformed Judgment,* 2.

[10] Jones, *Transformed Judgment,* 2.

[11] Jones, *Transformed Judgment,* 3.

struggle to live in relation to others. "On this view," states Jones, "becoming a person involves the struggle of learning to live in relation to others—paradigmatically the other who is the Triune God."[12] For Jones, because the production of personhood requires learning to be in relation, it is important to specify how friendships and practices are central contexts in which such learning takes place and is related to others. Jones argues in particular that the primary friendship a person ought to have is with the Triune God who has befriended humanity in Jesus. Such friendship calls forth a life of transformational discipleship, which is learned in and through the friendships and practices of Christian communities. Jones makes as his central claim the interesting point that, from the standpoint of the Christian tradition, the moral life requires not only formation but transformation in moral judgment.[13] Practices like baptism, Eucharist, forgiveness-reconciliation, and interpretation of Scripture enable transformation of friendship with the Triune God.[14]

Jones' position helps make my point for a spirituality of nonviolence in which persons learn personhood through a particular communal lens. The problematic arises when oppressed communities practice the mystery of the Triune God. Inevitably, black scholars revert to strategies of self-love, self-respect, self-regard as the proper quest for black identity. Cornel West states, "The difficult and delicate quest for black identity is integral to any talk about racial equality. Yet it is not solely a political or economic matter. The quest for black identity involves self-respect and self regard, realms inseparable from yet not identical to political power and economic status. The flagrant self-loathing among black middle-class professionals bears witness to this painful process. Unfortunately, black conservatives focus on the issue of self-respect as if it is the one key that opens all doors to black progress. . . The issues of black

---

[12] Jones, *Transformed Judgment*, 3.
[13] Jones, *Transformed Judgment*, 73-120.
[14] Jones, *Transformed Judgment*, 120-158.

identity—both black self-love and self-contempt—sit alongside black poverty as realities to confront and transform."[15]

My argument for the necessity of the nonviolent lifestyle of the Christian has practical implications which I now specifically show through how a Christian person negotiates a violent world. This concluding chapter attempts a rescue of current forms of Western Christian spirituality by naming how personal spirituality entails the arduous journey of becoming a saint. This chapter involves the reader in the observation that the process of becoming a saint includes the transformation into nonviolence. My assumption is that saint making is not a natural process, but a supernatural one. What is deemed "society" does not naturally make saints. Society produces "professionals," who Howard Thurman states, fall into peril.[16] I conclude, that the goal of the spiritual life is not a Christian professional but the saint who, through the communal practices of the church, helps others make the connections between love of self and love of neighbor.

The church understands, however, that there is no natural connection between love of self and love of neighbor. In fact, Christians understand that obedience is required for individuals to love one's neighbor. Jesus explains, "I will be with you only a little while longer. You will look for me and as I told the Jews, where I go you cannot come; now I say to you, I give you a new commandment: Love one another, As I have loved you, so you also should love one another" (John 13:33–34). I argue in this concluding chapter that Christian spirituality is always about peace making as these connections between self and other bond tighter together.

---

[15] Cornel West, *Debating affirmative Action: Race, Gender, Ethnicity, and the Politics of Inclusion*, ed., Nicolaus Mills (New York: Delta Books) 86-87.

[16] Fluker, *A Strange Freedom*, 231

Suffering and Sainthood

To become a saint requires the ability not only to survive suffering but to move beyond to a state of flourishing. Thurman is helpful in articulating a Christian spirituality of sainthood by articulating his own view of the flourishing life which he calls the grand fulfillment. Thurman states, "To seek to know how he may enter into such a grand fulfillment is the essence of all wisdom and the meaning of all human striving. Of course, he may be mistaken. But to be mistaken in such a grand and illumined undertaking is to go down to his grave with a shout."[17] Thurman's theodicy is basically answered in how "The startling discovery is made that if there were no suffering there would be no freedom."[18] Thurman continues that "The ultimate logic of suffering, of course, lies in the fact of death. The particular quality of death is to be found in what it says about the future."[19] In order to understand suffering, one must see the context of death, as Thurman believes, "Death is seen as being an experience within Life, not happening to Life." [20] Thurman's theodicy is best seen in his following observation:

> If the answer to his suffering is to face it and challenge it to do its worst because he knows that when it has exhausted itself it has only touched the outer walls of his dwelling place, this can only come to pass because he has found something big enough to contain all violences and violations—he has found that his life is rooted in a God who cares for him and cultivates his spirit, whose purpose is to bring to heel all the untutored, recalcitrant expressions of life.[21]

Thurman "recognizes that death, through its part in defining duration, does establish a form or aspect of life, and in so doing gives life a meaning and a purpose. It provides a measuring rod for values to

---

[17] Fluker, *A Strange Freedom*, 54.
[18] Fluker, *A Strange Freedom*, 50.
[19] Fluker, *A Strange Freedom*, 50.
[20] Fluker, *A Strange Freedom*, 51.
[21] Fluker, *A Strange Freedom*, 53.

be worked out within a particular time interval."[22] Such an interval could be described as the process of becoming a saint who continues to confirm life in the midst of a violent world. Thurman concludes that "I believe that such confirmation of life in us is the work of the Holy Spirit of God."[23]

To become a saint is to participate in the process of embodying the presence of God in the world. To participate in this mystery requires exstatic individuals who understand that God is not embodied in the caprice of individualism. Thurman states of the saint, "Always his God must be more than his thought about God, more than his private needs, demands, or requirements." [24] to embody the presence of God through the Holy Spirit, enables the suffer to overcome the meaningless of death.

"Must I finally be overcome and destroyed by [suffering]? The answer is to be found in the testimony of the human spirit. It is not to be found in the books or the philosophies."[25] The answer can only be embodied. "The man who suffers must say yea or nay,"[26] must be the kind of person who answers this question in how they have negotiated a violent world.

Thurman describes a man who appears to be saintlike, "yet there came a time when, in his encounter with personal suffering, he seemed stripped of every resource. His life became increasingly barren."[27] This movement from suffering to flourishing requires the initial stage of purgation in which one engages the ultimate question of existence on account of coming in contact with one's mortality. Thurman observes, "that suffering is given; it is part of the life contract that every living thing signs at the entrance."[28] Even though a person signs a contract to live and suffer, It is important to understand the meaning of suffering. Thurman states,

---

[22] Fluker, *A Strange Freedom*, 51.
[23] Fluker, *A Strange Freedom*, 53.
[24] Fluker, *A Strange Freedom*, 52.
[25] Fluker, *A Strange Freedom*, 53.
[26] Fluker, *A Strange Freedom*, 53.
[27] Fluker, *A Strange Freedom*, 47.
[28] Fluker, *A Strange Freedom*, 50.

"But if the person comes to grips with his suffering by bringing to bear upon it all the powers of his mind and spirit, he moves at once into a vast but solitary arena. It is here that he faces the authentic adversary. He looks into the depth of the abyss of life and raises the ultimate question about the meaning of existence. He comes face to face with whatever is his conception of ultimate authority, his God."[29]

Survival in the dark night of the soul depends not so much on the ability of the individual to negotiate a way out; instead, there is the increasing awareness to depend on the other. In a strange way, suffering creates community as the wounded huddle close to one another in order to survive the next onslaught. Thurman states:

The first thing his reflection brings to mind is that there is a fellowship of suffering as well as a community of sufferers. It is true that suffering tends to isolate the individual, to create a wall even within the privacy that imprisons him, to overwhelm him with self-preoccupation. It makes his spirit miserable in the literal sense of that word. Initially, it stops all outward flow of life and makes a virtue of the necessity for turning inward. Indeed, one of the ground rules of man's struggle with pain is the focusing of the ergies **(spelling??)** of life at a single point. All of him that can be summoned is marshaled. This is true whether he is dealing with sheer physical pain or the more complex aspects of other dimensions of suffering. The pain gives his mind something else to think about and requires what approximates total attention."[30]

The community is important as individual sufferers seek resources outside of their individuality. Thurman continues, "As already suggested for some all resources seem to be cut off completely and the withering of the spirit keeps pace with the disintegration of the body...."[31] A search for external resources is crucial as the individual sufferer learns that pain is its own end. Thurman is helpful as he concludes, "Thus suffering may times seem an end itself for

---

[29] Fluker, *A Strange Freedom*, 45

[30] Fluker, *A Strange Freedom*, 44-45.

[31] Fluker, *A Strange Freedom*, 46.

generating energy in the spirit, as indeed it does. If the pain is great enough to lay siege to life and threaten it with destruction, a demand is made upon all one's resources. . . It is important to hold in mind that this is the way of life—when life is attacked, it tends to rally all its forces to the defense." [32]

In many ways, Thurman sheds light on the importance of community through African practices in which an individual lacks the ability to survive death on one's own. This is why the community must continue to pray for the dead that they may keep moving beyond this life. Such African practices are interestingly similar to some of the European mystics mentioned in the book. For example, Thurman's affinity for Simone Weil is obvious in his writing.[33] Where African Christian Spirituality is helpful in articulating a spirituality capable of containing suffering is the African penchant for God the Creator. Thurman states:

> I cannot escape the necessity of concluding that the answer to suffering is to be found in experiencing in one's being the meaning of death. To state it categorically, it is to have one's innermost self or persona assured that the finality of death, which is the logic of all suffering, is itself contained in a more comprehensive finality of God Himself. Such a God is conceived as the creator of Life and the living substance, the Creator of existence itself and of all the time-and-space manifestations thereof.[34]

Christian spirituality is especially suited to provide communities resources from which they may be able to move from suffering as its own end. Deep in the Christian faith is the understanding that suffering can be redemptive. Thurman states:

> despite the personal character of suffering, the sufferer can work his way through to community....Sometimes he discovers through the ministry of his own burden a larger

---

[32] Fluker, *A Strange Freedom*, 46.

[33] Fluker, *A Strange Freedom*, 46-47.

[34] Fluker, *A Strange Freedom*, 53.

comprehension of his fellows, of whose presence he becomes aware in his darkness. They are companions along the way. The significance of this cannot be ignored or passed over. It is one of the consolations offered by the Christian religion in the centrality of the position given to the cross and to the suffering of Jesus Christ.[35]

Through the life of Christ the meaning is given to the world that there are innocent who suffer. The innocent who suffer, "Their presence in the world is a stabilizing factor, a precious ingredient maintaining the delicate balance that prevents humanity from plunging into the abyss. It is not surprising that in all the religions of mankind there is ever at work the movement to have the word made flesh, without being of the flesh."[36]

When I was at Princeton seminary in 1988, I was given a summer grant to go to India. From May through August I lived in India; half of my time in Bombay, observing a Christian Social Work Agency, and the other half of my time traveling throughout India. Needless to say, this was a life changing experience in which one of the highlights was meeting and praying with Mother Teresa.

At the end of a long journey from Madras to Calcutta by train, I found myself exhausted. My window of time in Calcutta was short, and I knew despite my exhaustion, I needed to go to the Mother House of the Missionaries of Charity to see when they met for morning prayer. I couldn't find the place and my exhaustion exacerbated my frustration.

I decided to head to the seminary that I would be staying at the night. As a weary traveler at sunset, I meandered through streets of Calcutta, horrified that human beings ran through the streets like horses. Competing with Mercedes Benz and beat of Fords, these human horses were pulling a higher class or caste of people through the narrow streets.

---

[35] Fluker, *A Strange Freedom*, 47.
[36] Fluker, *A Strange Freedom*, 49.

I finally arrived at the seminary of the Church of North India. What I heard at dinner did not lesson my fatigue: If I wanted to meet Mother Teresa, the only time would be tomorrow morning at 6:00 am at Morning Prayer. "You're lucky she's here," the Dean of the Seminary told me over dinner.

Early that morning, We set out from the seminary to attend Morning Prayer. I was with one other Indian seminarian I befriended at Breakfast. He said that he would go too, because he had never met Mother Teresa. We arrived and entered the gates of the Mother House. We assumed that morning prayer would be in the building that looked like their chapel and headed towards it. There was a narrow stair case we had to climb, but when we got to the top, we read the sign on the door: Eucharist for Catholics Only. My feelings were hurt but we continued in.

The chapel was an upper room of sorts, with Roman Catholic Sisters of Charity kneeling on the floor, praying fervently. They looked like an bobbing ocean at high tide, with their white and blue habits in ebb and flow. I was honest with myself, I wasn't coming to pray. And I especially felt justified in my lack of piety since I was told I couldn't take the Eucharist. I looked for the destination of my journey, Mother Teresa; she was on the right side, praying, inconspicuously amidst the blue tide of Sisters. With my Indian friend, I pretended to pray in the back of the chapel, but was more eager to watch Mother Teresa. We were not alone in the back of the chapel, there were other Western pilgrims seeking out this holy person, knowing that we could only find her if we came to pray.

After the service, I clumsily asked Mother Teresa what the most important thing is in spirituality. That was the way I asked it. The atmosphere did not allow me show off my theological language and there was no one around I could impress with my spiritual prowess because after all, I standing in front of Mother Teresa. What is the most important thing in spirituality? You could guess her response: prayer.

A reporter once asked Mother Teresa how she prays, she responded, "We begin our day by seeing Christ in the consecrated bread, and throughout the day we continue to see Him in the torn bodies of our poor. We pray, that is, through our work, performing it with Jesus, for Jesus, and upon Jesus.... The poor are our prayer. They carry God in them."[37] Continuing her interview, Mother Teresa states, "The most important thing is silence. Souls of prayer are souls of deep silence. We cannot place ourselves directly in God's presence without imposing upon ourselves interior and exterior silence. That is why we must accustom ourselves to stillness of the soul, of the eyes, of the tongue...God is the friend of silence. We need to find God, but we cannot find Him in noise, in excitement. See how nature, the trees, the flowers, the grass grow in deep silence.[38] The more we receive in our silent prayer, the more we can give in our active life.[39]

As I now look back on my experience of meeting Mother Teresa, I am no longer ashamed of my zeal or my puppy like affection of seeing someone who was like a rock star to me. I am not ashamed because I realize that by looking at a life such as Mother Teresa's I was in fact praying. She was showing me God in the world.

Mother Teresa's answer to my clumsily question was not so much in her words as in her life. What is the most important thing in spirituality? Her answer was her life, her curved spine from years of picking up people heavier than herself off the streets. This was the real answer to my question. And from her life I learn three other things.

First, Community. She shows me that prayer is more a communal activity than an individual activity. Prayer is the work of the church. Prayer must be communal because we cannot keep it up on our own. Inevitably, we fall exhausted into doubt.

Second, Discipline. Her life shows me that when praying for the world, you must keep at it because you will be tempted to stop, to doubt whether what you are doing is meaningful. Through daily prayer she showed me how to overcome inevitable conflict and temptation. Through discipline you prepare to withstand the challenges of life.

---

[37]Mother Teresa, *The Love of Christ: Spiritual Counsels* (San Francisco: Harper & Row, 1982) 8.

[38]Mother Teresa, *The Love of Christ*, 8.

[39]Mother Teresa, *The Love of Christ,* 8-9.

And Third, I learn from Mother Teresa a God who interacts with the world secretly, unobtrusively, subtlety or in a way we seldom notice until we rewind and recount our experiences together. But such a God requires complete devotion. There is a Hindu story of young man who testifies to this fact as he left home and traveled a great distance in search of a spiritual master whom he at last found sitting in prayer beside a river.

> He begged the man to take him as his disciple.
> 'Why should I?' the teacher asked.
> 'I want to find God,' the other answered
> Slowly the master rose to his feet and looked the young man over. 'And how badly do you want to find God?" he asked.

The other hesitated, not sure how best to answer. But before he could come up with words that seemed appropriate, the master grabbed his shoulder and dragged hi down the bank and into the river where he held him under the water. Seconds passed, then a minute, then another minute. The young man struggled and kicked, but still the teacher held him down until at last he drew him coughing and gasping out of the water.

'While you were under the water, what was it you wanted?' the teacher asked, when he saw that the other was at last able to speak again.

> 'Air,' the young man said, still panting, 'just air.'
> 'And how badly did you want it?'
> 'All. . . it was all I wanted in the world. With my whole soul I longed only for air.'
> 'Good,' said the teacher. 'When there comes a time when you long for God in the same way that you have just now longed for air, come back to me and you will become my disciple.'[40]

---

[40] Bouyer, A Way in the World, 28.

Mother Teresa taught me that Holiness aligns motive to action
in such a way that the holy person affects the world for the good
although the world may not fully feel or understand the initial
operation. Jesus states in the Gospel of Matthew, "When you do some
act of charity, do not announce it with a flourish of trumpets, as the
hypocrites do in synagogue and in the streets to win admiration from
men" (Matt. 6:2). And "Your good deeds must be secret, and your
heavenly Father who sees what is done in secret will reward you"
(Matt. 6:4). Perhaps, now we can better understand today's Gospel of
Mark 1:40 (NRSV) A leper came to him begging him, and kneeling he
said to him, "If you choose, you can make me clean." 41 Moved with
pity, Jesus stretched out his hand and touched him, and said to him, "I
do choose. Be made clean!" 42 Immediately the leprosy left him, and
he was made clean. 43 After sternly warning him he sent him away at
once, 44 saying to him, "See that you say nothing to anyone; but go,
show yourself to the priest, and offer for your cleansing what Moses
commanded, as a testimony to them." 45 But he went out and began
to proclaim it freely, and to spread the word, so that Jesus could no
longer go into a town openly, but stayed out in the country; and
people came to him from every quarter.

People who flock to the life of a saint like Mother Teresa, are
often desperate and can be quickly overwhelming. This is why we
must resist the urge to say the poor will always be with us; there is
nothing I can really do to change this reality. But there is something
we can all do. We can keep looking at saints like Mother Teresa and
discover how secret holiness affects both the world and the Church.
The following example of a Catholic priest's work among a leper
colony illustrates what happens when we keep looking at holy lives as
our own examples of how to live.

There the leper stood, straight up, in his arms a small
basket of cabbage. In his arms, because on his hands not a
single finger was left. He said to the Father of the lepers....I
have lost my fingers and my hands, but I have kept my
courage. I wanted to be someone, someone who works and
sings, as you have said to us. So I learned to help myself with

my hands—and without hands. A hundred times the tool fell to the ground. A hundred times I got down on my knees to pick it up. I have just brought in my first vegetables. I give them to you, because it is you who taught me that I was not an unwanted.[41]

Many say, I'm not Mother Teresa, I'm not a priest who works with Lepers, I'm a simple person, average, no saint. If some of you believe this, my response to you is don't say that as if that gets you off the hook, as if only a few are called to the holy life. All of us are called to be holy. In our second lesson, Paul states in 1Cor 9:24 (NRSV) "Do you not know that in a race the runners all compete, but only one receives the prize? Run in such a way that you may win it. 25 Athletes exercise self-control in all things; they do it to receive a perishable wreath, but we an imperishable one. 26 So I do not run aimlessly, nor do I box as though beating the air; 27 but I punish my body and enslave it, so that after proclaiming to others I myself should not be disqualified."

Many are still not convinced that extraordinary persons like Mother Teresa really matter to their normal lives. A professor in seminary once told me he would rather have a Christian Bill Gates than a Mother Teresa because Bill Gates could better affect the economic system to alleviate poverty. I disagreed with his notion on the grounds that people need more lives Mother Teresa to inspire conversion and transformation so that the Bill Gates of the World know what to do with their money. Vision of God is given in ordinariness, in the breaking of bread and in people who never get well known for their acts of mercy.

Our spirituality is not so much a practice for a later opportunity in which it will be "serious" when people find out about how good we are, but our spirituality manifested in secret practices of kindness are already quite serious. In other words, the final act of salvation history reveals that following Christ depends on our being concerned about

---

[41]Haring, *In Pursuit of Holiness*, (Liguori, Missouri: Liguori Publications, 1982) 34.

the needs of our neighbor (Mt. 25:31ff.) Okay, some of you may say, if I can't be Mother Teresa . . . a Christian Bill Gates, or Catholic Priest working with Lepers, how can I can be faithful with the life I've got. The following prayer by Mother Teresa may provide a good beginning:

> Lord, give me this vision of faith, that my work will never become monotonous. I will find joy in indulging the moods and gratifying the desires of all the poor who suffer.[42]

To confess Christ in our baptismal profession of the mystery of the Trinity, demands that we resolutely struggle against ourselves. We must suffer and die so that Christ may live in us. One cannot expect to become a saint without paying this price, and the price is "much renunciation, much temptation, much struggle and persecution, and all sorts of sacrifices. One cannot love God except at the cost of oneself."[43]

Perhaps, the disparity between the goal of Christian spirituality and its descriptive display is due to what such a lifestyle would look like in our ordinary lives. I posit that such a lifestyle looks impossible because this lifestyle means becoming dead to sin and alive to God in Christ (Romans 6:1–19). Pauline and Johannine writings provides the pseudo-Dionysian language of unitive and transformative dimensions in the Christian life (1Jn 4:13ff and Rom. 8:1–15). Pertaining more to the thesis of this book, Paul points to the impossibility of the Christian lifestyle in that we are to die to sin. The impossibility is broken only in light of the Christian's relationships with God and neighbor. For Paul, death to sin is only possible through the ongoing relationship to the life, death, and resurrection of Jesus. The New Testament describes how such relationships occur through discipleship to Jesus (Mt. 4:18Ff). To follow Christ means to proceed steadily and incrementally in the life of Spirit. As one follows, so does one grow more deeply spiritually and is recreated more in the image of God.

---

[42]Mother Teresa, *The Love of Christ: Spiritual Counsels* (San Francisco: Harper & Row, 1982) 7.

[43]Mother Teresa, *The Love of Christ,* 21.

Such discipleship then takes on a life of pilgrimage to God. Such pilgrimage resembles an impossible lifestyle in which lambs are amidst wolves, and traveling without purse and food in order to trust God in the journey ("Looking to Jesus the pioneer and perfector of our faith" (Heb. 12:2), who has left us an example that you should follow in his steps" (1 Pet. 2:21).

In the end we are called to be saints through practices of nonviolence.

Modern Christians do not feel very comfortable calling themselves "saints. The word conjures up pictures of heroes and heroines of the faith, as depicted by sacred art, with their halos well intact. But the popular conception of the term saints will not bear close comparison with the Christian teaching. In the Hebrew bible, "holy" (Zodesh) described persons, places, and things that had been separated from normal use, and were set apart or consecrated unto god. The NT uses "saints" (from Lat. sanctus) to translate various words for "holy" (Grk. Hagios). It describes Christians as people who are consecrated unto God, progressing Christ and being sanctified by the Holy spirit; "saints" describes the church and her members from the standpoint of their position (in Christ) and from the standpoint of their potential of being sanctified or made holy by God's grace.[44]

The "communion" in the term communio sanctorum means "fellowship" or "sharing" (Grk. Koinonia).[45] The fellowship or communion that characterizes the Christian church is created by "sharing" in Christ and His benefits. It means "sharing" in God's grace (Phil 1:7), the gospel (1 Cor 9:23), the Holy Spirit (Phil 2:1), and the Eucharistic body and blood of Jesus Christ (1 Cor 10:16–17). Eucharistic fellowship with Christ unites the many individual members of the church ("though we are many") in "the cup of blessing," and forms them into "one body" (1 Cor 10:16–17). The Johannine narrative focuses our attention on the transforming and reconciling power that the "flesh and blood" of Christ have for the individual

---

[44] S. Rankin, "Saints, Holy," in *TWBB*, 214-16.
[45] F. Hauck, "Koinonia," in *TDNT*, Vol. III, 804ff.

Christian. For example, Jesus said, "...he who eats my flesh and drinks my blood has eternal life, and I will raise him up at the last day....He who eats my flesh and drinks my blood abides in me, and I in him" (Jn 6:53–56). Jesus remind us that the individuality and uniqueness of the "many members" are also to be affirmed and safeguarded. Because of the depth of this "fellowship" in Christ, Christians are said to share in the glory that is to be revealed (1 Pet 5:1), and to be "partakers" ("sharers") of the Divine nature (2 Pet 1:4).

The sharing in and with Christ undergirds and empowers fellowship among Christians. As Gustavo Gutierrez noted, "the breaking of the bread is at once the point of departure and the point of arrival of true Christian community."[46] Koinonia, in this sense, describes the abiding in the company and friendship of Christians (2 Cor 6:14); it is a fellowship based upon a sharing in the life and knowledge of God through the gospel (1 Jn 1:2–3). The Eucharist, perhaps more than any other single event, epitomizes the fellowship with Christ that creates koinonia among Christians (1 Cor 10: 16–17). Hence the earliest Christians ". . . devoted themselves tot he apostle's teaching and fellowship, tot he breaking of bread [Eucharist], and the prayers" (Acts 2:42). So deeply interwoven were the concepts of "coming together as a church" (1 Cor 11:17) and "coming together to eat" the Lord's supper (1 Cor 11:33), that the word that stands for "to come together" (Grk. Synaxis) quickly became a shorthand expression for the gathering of Christians for the Lord's supper and worship.[47] St. Ignatius of Antioch used it (d. 117), for example, when he urged Ephesians to "try to gather together more frequently to celebrate God's Eucharist, and to praise him."[48] The Didache, (an anonymous Christian instructional treatise of the late first- or early second-century) used synaxis to describe the reconciling practices of "every Lord's Day": "On every Lord's Day—his special day—come together and break bread and give

---

[46] Gustavo Gutiérrez, *We Drink from Our Own Wells: The Spiritual Journey of a People* (Maryknoll, NY: Orbis Books, 1984) 134.

[47] Geoffrey Wainwright, *Doxology: The Praise of God in Worship, Doctrine, and Life* (New York: Oxford University Press, 1980) 142.

[48] Richardson, ed., *Early Christian Fathers*, 91.

thanks, first confessing your sins so that your sacrifice may be pure."[49]

The Christian has "fellowship" with Christ in His sufferings (Phil 3:10), and "partnership" in the work of Christ in the world (Phil 1:5). So significant was this fellowship (koinonia) among the early Christians that they shared their material possessions (Acts 2:44). They sold their goods and pooled their resources so that they might be able to support each other (Acts 2:45) and give tot he less fortunate (Rom 15:26). St. Paul's benediction tot he church at Rome, which invoked God's blessing upon them in "steadfastness and encouragement," anticipated that through the manifestation of those blessings they would be "in accord with Christ Jesus," and in living "in such harmony with one another. . . that together you may with one voice glorify the God and father of our Lord Jesus Christ" (Rom 15: 5–6). So saying, the apostle indicated that union with Christ, lived harmony among Christians, and the fellowship of Christian worship are inextricably wound together.[50]

Christian fellowship and community have long been considered essential tot he development of Christian Spirituality. This recognition began in the pattern of the church established in the Day of Pentecost (Acts 2:42–45), as well as in the churches of the Pauline missions, and it continued in the ancient church of the first three centuries. Self-denial and the contemplative life have long been elements of spirituality; in the monastic withdrawal from society early Christians pursued holiness upon avenues that had been traveled by both Jews and Greeks before them. But the growth and wide-spread popularity that monasticism enjoyed in the fourth century and thereafter also reflected something of the changing character of the church.

The counter cultural character of the early church—the oppressed and persecuted church of the martyrs—made the church's identity as being "in" but not "of" the world as obvious as it had been

---

[49] Richardson, ed., *Early Christian Fathers*, 91,

[50] Cf. F. X. Lawlor, "Communion of Saints," in NCE, IV:41-43; G.W.H. Lampe, "Communion," in IDB, I:664-66.

sinful. The NT church, on these terms, was described as the "assembly" or "summoned" Christians, a community of persons (Gk. Ekklesia). The church became first tolerated (313 AD) and then supported by the Roman government (324) under Emperor Constantine the Great, and the by the end of his reign (337) the Romans had become Christians—at least in a nominal way.

The marriage of the church and state, which in Constantine's mind would preserve and enhance both, significantly altered both church and state. It became increasingly difficult for the church to stand apart from popular culture in the Christianized Roman Empire, and as the church grew through the infusion of nominal Christians her task and identity began to undergo significant changes. As the church became more enmeshed in politics it became difficult to maintain her prophetic stance over against the state; as the church was blessed financially and in numerical strength it became increasingly difficult to maintain the koinonia that was so much a part of the oppressed fellowship.[51] The church of the houses and catacombs was become the church of great cathedrals and imperial endowments, and a few among the saints began to believe that in her acquisition of wealth, property, and popularity the church was losing the path that led to perfection. Christians began to pursue holiness outside the functions of the local congregation, and the monk gradually replaced the martyr as the person who most epitomized the Christian life of radical discipleship.

Christian monasticism initially took shape through the counter cultural reaction of solitary individuals who withdrew from the world in pursuit of holiness. The monks sought to live lives of self-denial and utter obedience to God and in this way they marked out both the means and goals of Christian Spirituality. Abba Germanus, one of the Desert fathers, described the means and the goal of the ascetic life in this fashion:

---

[51] Cf. H. Richard Niebuhr, *Christ and Culture* (New York: Harper & Row, 1951) for the standard discussion of "this enduring problem" and various models that approach resolutions of it.

Everything we do, our every objective, must be undertaken for the sake of...purity of heart. This is why we take on loneliness, fasting, vigils, work, nakedness. For this we must practice the reading of he Scripture, together will all the other virtuous activities, and we do so to trap and to hold our hearts free of the harm of every dangerous passion and in order to rise step by step to the high point of love.[52]

---

[52] Colm Lubheid, trans., *John Cassian: Conferences* (New York: Paulist Press, 1985) "Conference One," 41.

GLOSSARY

Adharma: immorality, unrighteousness

Ahimsa: non-injury, nonviolence, suffering love

Aparigraha: non-possession, non-possessiveness

Ashram: a Hindu monastic environment or hermitage, place of contemplation

Atman: soul, the spirit of God in humanity

Avatar: incarnation of God

Bhagavat: A Hindu classic

Bhagavan: Holy person

Bhajans: Hindu hymns

Bhakta: Devotee or Disciple

Bhakti: Devotion to God as way of salvation

Charkha: Spinning Wheel

Dharma: Duty, Law, Righteousness

Duragraha: Holding on to falsehood, evil, violence

Harijan: People of Hari or people of God, Children of God

Hartal: A Strike

Hind: A variant of the name India

Jiva: life, soul

Mantra: a prayer,

Moksha: Heaven

Prakriti: Nature

Prayashchitta: Penance for sin

Purana: Sacred History

Sadagraha: a variant of Satyagraha

Sadhana: practice, asceticism, striving, achievement

Sanatana, (ni): universal,

Sarvodaya: the welfare of all

Sat: Truth, Being

Satya: Truthfulness

Satyagraha: holding on to truth, suffering for justice

Savarnas: the people of castes

Shudhi: Purfication

Swaraj: Indigenous Government, Noncolonial rule

Varnashrama: social order on the basis of division of labor

Yajna : Sacrifice, selfless action

BIBLIOGRAPHY

Printed Sources

Anderson, J. "Cognitive Styles and Multicultural Populations."
   Journal of Teacher Educators, 1988: 39 (1): 2–9
Bonhoeffer, Dietrich *The Cost of Discipleship* (New York: Macmillan)
   1961.
Bouyer, Louis, *Orthodox Spirituality and Protestant and Anglican
   Spirituality*. London: Burns & Oates, 1969.
Boyer, Ernest. *A Way in the World: Family Life as Spiritual
   Discipline*. San Francisco: Harper & Row, 1984,
Carter, R.T. "Cultural Value differences between African Americans
   and White Americans." *Journal of College student Development*,
   1990: 31 (1) 71–79
Chatterjee, Margaret, *Gandhi's Religious Thought*. South Bend:
   University of Notre Dame Press, 1983.
Cooper, G. "Black Language and Holistic Cognitive style." *Western
   Journal of Black Studies*, 1981, 5:201–207
Friere, P. *Pedagogy of the Oppressed*. New York, Seabury Press,
   1970.
Gandhi, M.K. *Satyagraha in South Africa*. Triplicane, Madras: S.
   Ganesane, 1928.
Giligan, C. "Remapping the Moral Domain: New Images of Self and
   Relationship." In C. Giligan, J.V. Ward, and J.M. Taylor (eds.),
   *Mapping the Moral Domain: A Contribution of Women's
   Thinking to Psychological Theory and Education*, Center for the

Study of Gender, Education and Human Development, no. 2. Cambridge: Harvard University Press, 1988.

Gollnick, D.M., and Chinn, P.C. *Multicultural Education in a Pluralistic Society.* New York: Merrill, 1990.

Green, MF (ed) *Minorities on Campus: A Handbook for Enhancing Diversity.* Washington, D.C.: American Council on Education, 1989.

Greer, Rowan ed. *Origen.* New York: Paulist, 1979.

Hale-Benson, J.E. *Black Children: Their Roots, Culture, and Styles,* (Rev. ed) Baltimore: Johns Hopkins University Press, 1986.

Hauerwas, Stanley and L. Gregory Jones, eds., *Why Narrative? Readings in Narrative Theology.* Grand Rapids: Eerdmans, 1989.

Holmes, Urban T. *Spirituality for Ministry.* San Francisco: Harper & Row, 1982.

Jackson, B.W. "Black Identity Development." In L. Golubschick and B. Persky (eds) *Urban Social and Educational Issues.* Dubuque, Iowa: Kendall/Hunt, 1976.

Jesudasan, Ignatius. *Gandhian Theology of Liberation.* Anand, India: Gujarat Sahitya Prakash, 1987. (An abridged edition of this book was published by Orbis Books, Maryknoll, New York, 1984 and 1986.

Jones, Greg. *Embodying Forgiveness.* Grand Rapids: Eerdmans, 1999.

Kochman, T. *Black and White Styles in Conflict.* Chicago: University of Chicago Press, 1981.

Kolb, D.A. "Learning Styles and Disciplinary Differences." In A.W. Chikering and Associates eds) *The Modern American College Responding tot he New Realities of Diverse Students and a Changing Society.* San Francisco: Jossey-Bass, 1981.

Kolb, D.A. *Experiential Learning: Experience as the Source of Learning and Development.* Engle-wood Cliffs, NJ Prentice Hall, 1984.

Jones, Cheslyn, Geoffrey Wainwright, and Edward Yarnold, *The Study of Spirituality.* New York: Oxford University Press, 1986.

Lesser, G. "Cultural Differences in Learning and Thinking Styles," In S. Messck (ed.), *Individuality in Learning.* San Francisco: HarperCollins.

Lossky, Vladimir, *Mystical Theology of the Eastern Church.* Crestwood, N.Y.: St. Vladimir's Press, 1976.

_____, *Orthodox Theology*. Crestwood, N.Y.: St. Vladimir's Press, 1989.

MacGregor, J. "Collaborative learning: Shared Inquiry as a Process of Reform." In M.D. Svinicki (ed) *The Changing Face of College Teaching*. New Directions for Teaching and Learning, no 42. San Francisco: Jossey-Bass, 1990.

Mathis, Rick. *Prayer-Centered Healing: Finding the God who Heals*. Liguori,MO: Liguori Publications, 2000.

Nouwen, Henri. *The Way of the Heart: Desert Spirituality and Contemporary Ministry*. New York: Seabury Press, 1981

Ouspensky, Leonid and Lossky, Vladimir. *The Meaning of Icons*. Crestwood, NY: St. Vladimir's Press, 1989.

Mueller Nelson, Gertrude, *To Dance with God: Family, Ritual and Community Celebration*. New York: Paulist Press, 1986.

Palmer, Parker. *The Courage to Teach*. San Francisco: Jossey-Bass Publishers, 1998.

Ramirz, M., and Price-Williams, D. R. "Cognitive Style of Three Ethnic Groups in the US," *Journal of Cross-Cultural Psychology* 1974:5(2): 212–209.

Rice, Edward. *The Man in the Sycamore Tree*. Garden City, NY: Doubleday, Image Books, 1972

Richard of St. Victor, *The Mystical Ark* (trans. Grover A. Zinn), I, 4.

Sheldrake, Philip *Spirituality & History: Questions of Interpretation and Method*. New York: Crossroad, 1992.

Tomlin, E. W. F. *Simone Weil*. New Haven, Yale University Press, 1954.

von Balthasar, Hans Urs, "Nine Theses in Christian Ethics" in *Readings in Moral Theology No. 2.*, eds. Charles E. Curran and Richard McCormick. New York: Paulist Press, 1980, 190–207.

Wainwright, Geoffrey, *Doxology: A Systematic Theology*. New York: Oxford University Press, 1980.

Wangerin Walter, "The Door Interview," *The Wittenburg Door*, 1989.

_____. *A Miniature Cathedral*. Harper & Row: San Francisco, 1987.

Weil, Simone. *Gravity and Grace*. New York: Putnam Press, 1952.

Wolpert, Stanley. *Gandhi's Passion: The Life and Legacy of Mahatma Gandhi*. New York: Oxford University Press, 2001.

Helpful Websites Relating to Nonviolence

World Council of Churches Decade to Overcome Violence
www.ecumenismnow.org

Families Against Mandatory Minimus
www.famm.org/index2.htm

Human Rights Watch
www.hrw.org

US Department of Justice
www.ojp.usdog.gov

Amnesty International
www.amnesty.org

Federal Bureau of Prisons
www.bop.gov

The M.K. Gandhi Institute for Nonviolence
www.gandhiinstitute.org

INDEX